D0466736

BEST SEAT
IN THE
HOUSE

ROBERT
FULFORD

BEST SEAT
IN THE
HOUSE

*Memoirs
of a
Lucky
Man*

COLLINS
TORONTO

First published 1988
by Collins Publishers
100 Lesmill Road, Don Mills, Ontario

© 1988 by Robert Fulford

All rights reserved. No part of this publication may be reproduced, stored in a retrieval system, or transmitted in any form or by any means, electronic, mechanical, photocopying, recording or otherwise without prior written permission of the publishers.

CANADIAN CATALOGUING IN PUBLICATION DATA
Fulford, Robert, 1932-
  Best seat in the house

1st ed.
Includes index.
ISBN 0-00-215438-2

1. Fulford, Robert, 1932-   . 2. Editors — Canada —
Biography.   3. Journalists — Canada — Biography.
4. Critics — Canada — Biography.   5. Canada —
Intellectual life — 20th century.   6. Arts — Canada —
History — 20th century.   I. Title.

PN4913.F84A3   1988   070.4'1'0924   C88-094974-0

Printed and bound in Canada
by T.H. Best Printing Company Limited

For Geraldine

CONTENTS

ONE

Teentime

"EVERY CHILD of an alcoholic," says the American poet Robert Bly, "receives the knowledge that the bottle is more important to the parent than he or she is." This knowledge, though never discussed by anyone, was embedded in my childhood. My father — Ab to his friends, A.E. Fulford when his name appeared as a byline — was an intelligent, affectionate man, but the six of us who lived with him had to share his intelligence and his affection with alcohol, a rival of great charm and power. Often, we took second place. Why this should have been so, I never learned: it was the great mystery of my childhood. He did not speak seriously of his feelings about anything; if life disappointed him, as I'm sure it did, he didn't mention it. He and I were never out of touch with each other, but we were never quite in touch, either.

Liquor severely limited my father's life, but it also helped him become a newspaperman. He was born in Ottawa in 1905, the son of a printer and the youngest in a large family. He left school in early adolescence and went to work as a copy boy, first at a newspaper and then in the Ottawa office of the Canadian Press, the co-operative agency through which the newspapers of Canada exchange news. In the early 1920s, his boss on the night shift at CP was Tim Shea, an editor in his twenties. Shea was an alcoholic; often, as the evening wore on, he badly needed help with the job of editing news stories and passing them on to the head office in Toronto. He came to rely on his copy boy, who showed an uncommon aptitude for words and never needed to be told anything twice. The more Shea drank, the more my father was called on to do, and the more he learned. Eventually their superiors came to know who was doing the work, and my father was made a junior editor.

He became what addiction specialists call a functioning alcoholic: heavily dependent on liquor yet able to do his work, often exceptionally well. In 1934, by now an occasional reporter as well as an editor, he was sent to Callander, Ontario, to write some of the first versions of the great national news story of the era, the birth and childhood of the Dionne quintuplets. He wrote about them so often that when he met the prime minister in the late 1930s Mackenzie King said, "Ah, the Quint man." In 1939 he followed George VI and the queen on their tour across Canada and wrote hourly reports of their progress; it was the only time he ever saw much of the country. But his real skill was editing, and over the years he developed into a virtuoso of the pencil. As a rewrite man — like most newspapermen of his day he typed two-fingered, at astonishing speed — he could quickly turn long and incoherent cables from correspondents into crisp news stories. He was also a demanding but sympathetic teacher; a dozen newspapermen who learned their craft on the CP desk have told me that he was their mentor.

He married Frances Gertrude Blount, the daughter of an Ottawa bookseller and the grand-daughter of a newspaper editor. They had four children, Joan Anne (born 1926), Diane (1928), Robert (1932), and Wayne (1933); the household numbered seven, because my mother's mother always lived with us. The year I was born the Canadian Press brought my father to the head office and we moved to Toronto. We settled in the Beach district, at the southeast corner of the city, and lived there in a series of duplex apartments and houses for all of my childhood and youth. My mother still lives in the Beach, and I stayed there until I was married for the first time, at the age of twenty-four.

Fashion long ago transformed the plain streets of my childhood. For the last fifteen years ad executives, architects, and TV producers have been frantically bidding up the prices of what once seemed dumpy little houses. When I go back there now, driving past ambitious restaurants and pretentious antique stores, I have to struggle to remember the Beach as it was in the 1930s. Then it was more village than city, a self-contained world where just about everyone came from British or Irish stock and most people agreed that the Empire would last forever. A half-hour streetcar ride connected us to the core of Toronto and those who had jobs went there every day; otherwise, Beach people kept to themselves. We had everything we needed — schools, churches, stores, movie houses, even a little library. Above all we had the beach itself, a mile-long strip of sand on Lake Ontario, and more parkland than a child could ever explore — I think I was ten years old before I understood that not everyone in the world could walk a block or so from home and find a huge park. The Beach was the perfect place to spend a childhood, though less than wonderful as a background for adolescence.

Like everywhere else, the Beach was poor in the 1930s, but poor in a polite way. Everyone seemed to have at least a little money, and unemployment was considered at worst a temporary condition; my guess is that those who were persistently unemployed quietly moved away. Many of us were precariously clinging to the shabbiest bottom rung of the middle class, and some were letting go, but that didn't seem obvious. I can't even remember the word "Depression" being used in conversation — perhaps, like the Middle Ages, it was something you could name only when it was over. I can't remember anyone complaining of hunger, and my mother made certain that, one way or another, all of us had warm clothes. My father's salary was meagre, and twice during the Depression it was cut by 10 per cent; but our situation was fortunate compared to the misery elsewhere. We didn't much miss the benefits of affluence that middle-class people now take for granted — summer cottages, cars, vacations in distant places — because most of our friends couldn't afford them either.

We hardly even noticed that our apartment was cramped. Around 1970 I learned that a friend of mine was living in the lower duplex at 22 Wineva Avenue, where my family had spent the years 1932 to 1938. With my wife and children I dropped in on her one Sunday afternoon and toured, three decades after leaving it, my first home. The room that my brother and I once shared now seemed appropriate for use as a cupboard. The whole apartment was just about right for my friend, her thirteen-year-old son, and their dog. Yet seven of us were crammed in there for a half a dozen years, and it seemed — perhaps childhood homes usually do — the natural order of things.

Today the Beach is solid New Democrat country, heavily politicized, but during my childhood people in the Beach talked little about politics and cared less. We sent one Conservative nonentity to Ottawa at every federal election and another to the Ontario legislature at every provincial election. Neither of them was heard of again until they showed up to solicit votes a few years later. All I remember about the federal MP is that he owned a fertilizer company and that in the early 1940s, as his contribution to the war effort, he had his gardener spell out "VICTORY TO THE UNITED NATIONS" in flowers on the hill beside his driveway; all I remember about the provincial MPP is that he held his seat longer than any other member, without becoming known for anything else.

So far as I'm aware, people in the Beach never complained about their representatives' failure to accomplish anything remarkable. In fact, if one of our men had become a cabinet minister, or otherwise distinguished himself, we might have been alarmed. He would have been getting above himself, and we in the Beach tried not to do that. We were unambitious — for ourselves, our district, our city, and our country. We were perfect colonials, in the sense that our own local situation had little reality for us. We knew that what the British did was important (at school we sang "There'll Always Be an England" on every conceivable occasion) and we knew that what the Americans did was important (everyone had an opinion about Franklin Roosevelt) but we saw nothing of importance in the actions of Canadians and we never dreamt that our own corner of the Empire could do anything worth noting. We asked nothing of our politicians because we couldn't imagine that we deserved better than we had. My father sometimes voted for the CCF, the predecessor to the NDP, but without any show of passion and without any hope for the party's success. He didn't even mind when, for a couple of days during the provincial election of 1945, I was paid by the Conservatives to distribute anti-CCF leaflets ("CCF — Cancels Canada's Freedom").

He did mind, though, when I announced that I expected to march in one of the annual parades of the Orange Lodge. During my first year in high school I was in the bugle band, and the bandmaster (otherwise the school janitor) told us that in July we would be going to the town of Orillia to march with the Orangemen. In all innocence, I reported this news to my father. "You will like hell!" he said. I was taken aback. I knew that my father had been brought up a Roman Catholic and had left the church after marrying my mother, a Protestant. Vaguely I knew that this was why none of us went to church or Sunday school. Being unable to decide on an appropriate denomination, my parents had simply abandoned religion, and so far as I know never missed it. What I didn't understand, because it had never come up, was that the Orange Lodge was viciously anti-Catholic and that my father had retained his dislike for Orangemen long after losing his affection for the Church.

"What's wrong with marching with the Orangemen?"

"If you don't know the answer," my father said, stubbing out his cigarette angrily, "I'm not going to tell you."

That remark was sufficiently uncharacteristic to make me fearful, so I withdrew from the conversation and found the answer elsewhere. In the end I grew tired of trying to play the bugle and left the band before the parade. But I remember the incident as the closest that my father and I ever came to a discussion of religion.

THERE WAS something special, Malvernites liked to say, about Malvern Collegiate Institute. It had to do with school spirit. The principal when I arrived there, Lorne H. Clarke, liked to lecture us on school spirit. His favorite anecdote concerned former Malvern students who had become prisoners of war in Germany. Some of them had their Malvern football sweaters when they were captured, the sweaters had worn out, and the prisoners had written to the school for replacements. Our principal loved to dwell on this scene — Malvern boys, behind barbed wire in Stalag something-or-other, parading about in their tattered Red and Black sweaters with the big M. Now *that,* he liked to say, was school spirit. As he told the story, loyalty to Malvern and loyalty to the Allied cause in the Second World War (which at this point was only months in the past) seemed to carry approximately the same moral weight.

My only private meeting with him was unpleasant. During my first few months at Malvern, when I was thirteen, a secretary summoned me to his office. On his desk lay a copy of the songbook my class had used during music instruction in the previous period. In my copy I had written, in large block letters, SHE WAS ONLY THE FARMER'S DAUGHTER BUT ALL THE HORSE MANURE. The music teacher, an unamusing man with a Groucho Marx moustache, had seen me writing and ratted on me.

Clarke looked up. "Did you write in this book?"

"Yes sir."

"Your sister went to this school?"

"Two of them, sir."

"Yes, well, the sister I know is a fine girl. Would you like her — or *any* nice girl — to see what you have written here?"

"No, sir." *Oh, God, when can I get away from this ridiculous old bore?*

"Well, you must replace the book and…"

I didn't know it at the time, but Malvern in those years was developing a certain notoriety among the educators of Ontario. Each spring, when Grade 13 students across the province wrote the same examinations and were graded by strangers, Malvern's results were calamitous. The Ontario average was 77 percent, the Toronto average 86, the Malvern average 68. Apparently Clarke had made it abnormally easy at Malvern to pass through the lower levels and had ended up with more students writing Grade 13 exams and therefore more failures. He was a pioneer — his system would be universal a generation later — but the board of education refused to see it that way and took the view that Clarke was running a mediocre school (that was true too, of course). In March, 1947, the board relieved him of his post and assigned him to teach mathematics at another school.

This happened while I was facing up to the possibility of my first failure, in Grade 10, so the newspaper stories explaining that it was easy to get to Grade 13 at Malvern threw an especially unpleasant light on my own achievement. Clarke's firing, however, was a welcome diversion. Our student council came to his defence and threatened a strike, then agreed not to strike if the board would re-open the case and explain its decision. When the board did reconsider, and Clarke was still fired, a more radical student leadership took over: the social democrats having failed, we in effect turned to the Bolsheviks. Our Lenin was a football hero named Stan Boyd, who conducted a strike vote and then led us out of the school.

Was ever a strike more popular with the strikers? I remember a nearly hysterical meeting at a football field during a snowstorm, Stan shouting through a bullhorn about truth, justice, and democracy. At a rally in a church basement, a sympathetic parent — many parents were on our side — urged us on by reading a quote from *Macbeth:* "Lay on, Macduff, And Damn'd be him that first cries 'Hold, enough.'" We cheered.

Though the strike lasted only a few days and never had any hope of restoring Clarke to his job, it was the highlight of our school year. The newspaper accounts agreed that we struck out of love for our principal, but the newspaper accounts were wrong (a circumstance that surprised me more at that time than it would today). In fact, I didn't like Clarke at all and didn't know anyone who did. We struck for the joy of striking, and because it was much less boring than going to class. Every since, I have viewed the activities of student politicians with suspicion.

The strike left behind another odd memory. When pressed, the board of education produced a statement giving four reasons why Clarke was fired. The first was the Grade 13 average, the second had to do with reports of truancy at Malvern, and the fourth referred to dissatisfaction among Clarke's staff. The third reason is the one that, in 1988, expresses in all its horror the attitudes of respectable WASP Canada in the 1940s. It read: "3. Citizens in the neighbourhood of the school have frequently complained about students from the collegiate scattering food and papers on the streets and lawns at noon hour, and otherwise misbehaving themselves. This matter has been drawn to Mr. Clarke's attention on different occasions." Signed by several of the leading citizens of the day, that passage perfectly illustrated the meanness and fatuity — and of course the neurotic obsession with cleanliness — that dominated the public life of Toronto in my youth. Clarke's successor, our former football coach, did not greatly improve academic standards, but he did devote serious attention to the question of littering. And when he retired we could say of him what we say of all true Torontonians: he left the world a neater place than he found it.

When we were not on strike, we at Malvern made desultory attempts at understanding mathematics and chemistry, learned the more boring facts about Canadian history, and listened in sullen silence while our English teachers taught us that literature was something of only marginal importance and in any case was exclusively the work of dead Englishmen. The English courses offered either thunderingly obvious plays and novels (*Julius Caesar*, *Great Expectations*) or works of such slim merit that their appearance on the provincial curriculum surprised even our teachers. I remember our sense of outrage when we discovered that the set play for Grade 11 — the work we would read aloud in class at agonizing speed and study in painful detail — was *The Admirable Crichton*, a lightweight turn-of-the-century comedy about the English class system by James M. Barrie. Even in 1948, even at Malvern, we knew better.

None of our teachers, so far as I recall, ever worried about the meaning of education. While they might have found it difficult to say why we should study any specific fact or idea, they had no doubt about the overall purpose of schooling: it was to help us get ahead in the world. But what did getting ahead mean, exactly? My guidance teacher knew. He was an amiable man who cheerfully embraced the materialism of the society we would all soon be entering. He told our class that after long study he had concluded that the best possible career was in sales. Salesmen, he said, made more money than anyone else, and with less effort. At Malvern that seemed a reasonable idea. Later, when my marks grew dismal, he suggested that if I wanted to be a journalist I should transfer to a technical school, take a printing course, and then try to get promoted to editorial work. My great-grandfather, Edward Clissold, had done just that in the nineteenth century, moving from a printshop job on Horace Greeley's New York *Tribune* (where, family legend has it, he was the only typesetter who could read Greeley's handwriting) to the editorship, eventually, of the *Advertiser* in London, Ontario. By the time my guidance teacher suggested that route to me, almost no one in the world had followed it in forty years. At Malvern we didn't make a fetish of being up-to-date.

My richest educational experience at Malvern, as it turned out, was the typing course. I switched my option to typing after failing Latin, and by persistence somehow overcame my wretched lack of co-ordination. By the time I left Malvern I was among the best typists in my class, and ever since I've been the fastest typist wherever I've worked — though seldom the neatest. Typing students also took a short course in business machines, which was given by a man with an unusual — for Malvern, a radical — approach to society. One day, while instructing us in the use of adding machines, he said we might also like to know something about economics. He informed us that the purpose of economic activity was to support society so that society could support the arts. The arts, in turn, made life worth living, thus justifying all the attention we gave to the economy. This was the only interesting idea I ever heard from a teacher at Malvern.

IN 1948 I WAS sixteen years old, an incompetent student and a junior journalist of severely limited accomplishment. Little chunks of my writing had begun to appear anonymously on the sports pages of the three Toronto newspapers and I had occasionally babbled on this or that radio show, usually about music or sports. Now, for no sensible reason, I decided I was ready to be the host and producer of a radio program. It would be a show for "teenagers," a demographic group recently invented by the advertising business. Teenagers were of course different from adolescents, whom they replaced in the popular imagination: while adolescents might sometimes be sad and defeated, teenagers were always happy and confident. They were not at all like me, but they would be my listeners.

This brilliant idea was unfortunately a bit late: most of the radio stations in Toronto already had disc jockeys eagerly pursuing the new audience. Only one, CHUM, lacked a teenage program, so I decided to go to its offices and present myself. At that time, for a reason best understood by the broadcasting regulators in Ottawa, CHUM was licensed to operate only in the daylight hours. When the sun went down, as it did at an embarrassingly early hour on winter afternoons, a melancholy announcer would intone, "We end our broadcasting day…" and the transmitter was shut off. CHUM grew rich in the rock boom of the 1960s, but on the day in 1948 when I knocked on the door it appeared to be supported mainly by patent-medicine commercials and the meagre sums that evangelists paid to have their sermons broadcast. It was pathetic, clearly the place for me. Then as now, I was both brash and frightened — brash enough to think I should be on the air but not nearly confident enough to imagine that I was any good. Perhaps, in the humble circumstances and near secrecy provided by CHUM, my talents would be acceptable.

CHUM's dowdy one-storey building was only a block or so from the former girls' school on Jarvis Street that housed (as it still does) the real core of radio, the Canadian Broadcasting Corporation. Some of the great events of my life were waiting for me at the CBC, but in 1948 I wisely assumed that the corporation would have no interest in me. At CHUM, however, I was given a surprisingly warm welcome. When I gave my name to the receptionist she showed me quickly into the station manager's office. He listened attentively to my views about a program for teenagers and then said gravely that he was turning me over to the program director.

Showing me out, he asked, as if it were an afterthought, "Are you related to Dick Fulford?"

"Uh, my father says all the Fulfords in Canada are related."

"Well, you're a wild breed."

This curious remark hung in the air. Down the hall, the program director also listened attentively, and to my delight we were soon talking about when my show might start. Three weeks later I learned that Dick Fulford, one of the rich Fulfords from Brockville, Ontario, was the owner of the station. He was no relative of mine (my people are the poor Fulfords), and I never met him, but by the time the people at CHUM discovered that they were not humoring some idiot nephew of their owner, "CHUM Teentime" was ready to go on the air for half an hour on Saturday afternoons.

I was paid ten dollars a week when I was paid, which wasn't every week. No matter. Along with four or five other students, I flung myself enthusiastically into the production of the program. The result was not quite the triumph we had hoped it would be. It was heard mainly by the close friends and relatives of those involved — and not by all of them, at least after the first show. In a few months "CHUM Teentime" left the air, its passing unnoticed.

Four decades later, it's hard to explain why I did it. Certainly it wasn't easy — talking on the radio made me nervous, as it still sometimes does, and for years afterward my stomach tightened reflexively whenever I heard the opening bars of "Raincheck," the Duke Ellington record we used as a theme. The subject matter of the program — teenage dances, school sports — held little interest for me, and a career in commercial radio was never among my dreams. Then what was I doing?

Perhaps I was stumbling toward my destiny. Elspeth Cameron, who writes biographies, says that she always searches for a moment in the young life of her subject when for good or ill he begins to turn into himself. "CHUM Teentime," absurd as it seems in retrospect, was such a moment. In a way, it contained the form of my life before the content existed: at sixteen I was already an editor and a writer, though with no idea what to edit or write. There, as so often in later life, I worked with friends I recruited, directing them and helping them with their work while practicing my own craft. The material of the program was silly, but the activity was satisfying in itself. We were making *something*, awful as it was. The taste of the program, so far as it had any, was my own — the theme record expressed what would turn out to be my lifelong interest in Ellington. And there was something else that makes it look like a characteristic moment: a piece of luck. Over the years I've often marvelled at my good fortune at being in the right place at the right time, and I've developed a superstitious respect for the luck of the draw. At CHUM, the luck of having the same name as the station owner gave me an odd little edge that I didn't even know about.

None of this was clear to me then. I would have said that I was hanging around CHUM in order to get "experience," which everyone agreed was a good thing to have. I might also have admitted, a bit shamefacedly, that I was enchanted by the atmosphere of CHUM and found the men who worked there raffishly attractive. Most of them had little to offer the world except pleasant voices and overblown ambitions, but there was something exciting about their easy assumption that they belonged to the great world of professionals. They lived on one of the bleaker fringes of show business, and most of them had no notable future — though one announcer, Larry Mann, became an actor and eventually a marginal sort of TV star, the portly businessman in the Bell telephone commercials of the 1980s. Most of them didn't care about the insipid records they played on their programs, and cared even less about the news they read — they simply ripped it off a teletype machine and spoke it into the microphone without even glancing at it first; the bulletins were as fresh to them as to the listeners.

What they did care about was their careers, and in a corner of my mind I can still hear them happily lying about the high-paying network commercial assignments they were plotting to get and about their intimate friendships with this or that star — Stan Kenton, Johnny Ray, or even Frankie Laine. I stood at the edge of their circle, warming myself on their egos, and though they didn't really include me in their conversations they were nice enough not to exclude me either. They cherished a view of themselves as cynical and experienced, beyond surprise — they were the first men I ever knew (though by no means the last) who took articulate pleasure in their own corruption. They were guys who knew the score. One disc jockey had a fan club of his own, which he paid a high-school student to manage. He had heard they did it that way in Hollywood. A senior announcer, who briefly cast himself as my mentor, looked up from the turntable one day and gave me, as slowly and carefully as if he were explaining scripture to a Sunday School class, his considered view of radio. "The trouble with kids in this business," he said, "is that they don't know what it's all about. They think it's all about glamour. That's crap. It's about *money*." He later became a used-car salesman.

But there was a more painful reason why I was attracted to CHUM, or to any other journalistic enterprise that came my way. I was trying desperately to be someone other than the boy I clearly was. I was a failure not only as a student but also — this was more depressing — as a teenager. I couldn't begin to live the ideal of bright, social, athletic youth. Sports, for instance, were impossibly difficult, an occasion for humiliation rather than joy. In childhood, when it didn't matter, I loved pick-up games of hockey, soccer, and touch football, and like most Canadian males I still remember the reassuring weight of a hockey stick and the wonderful bone-weariness at twilight when we played far too late on the hockey cushion in the park, defying our mothers and the park keeper alike, until reluctantly we went home because it was too dark to see the puck. Games were magic to me then, they were consolation as well as excitement. But in high school my physical awkwardness became painfully obvious. I couldn't begin to compete with the natural athletes among my contemporaries — such as our school quarterback, Don Getty, who later helped Edmonton win the Grey Cup and later still became the premier of Alberta. I couldn't even imagine myself on the same field with such splendid creatures, and I regarded them with awe and a certain resentment. Girls, too, were a part of any proper teenaged boy's life, but I found them unapproachable and incomprehensible. What did you *say* to them? Much later I was relieved to discover that someone who couldn't talk to girls could nevertheless, in the fullness of time, hold splendid conversations with women. It turned out that they had to grow up, too.

Other boys, similarly defeated by sports and girls, happily spent their energy on their studies. This was the obvious course for me, as the most bookish member of my class, but I found academic work just as difficult and embarrassing as the rest of my life. What was manageable to my friends — solving geometry problems, memorizing French verbs — was painful and abhorrent to me. In public school I was good enough to skip a grade, but high school was too much for me. I scraped through Grade Nine and then failed Grade Ten. That year I took Latin because my father (who had none) assured me it would help my English; in June my mark was 12 out of 100, which may have reflected generosity on the teacher's part. I repeated Grade Ten, falling a year behind my contemporaries and then charged into Grade Eleven, determined to make everything right and at last become a scholar. Briefly, something like that seemed to happen. For a time algebra was exciting, and the other courses bearable; in June all my marks were better than pass. The next year, however, I was in trouble again. In the spring I failed some crucial Grade Twelve subjects — French and chemistry were particular disasters — and dropped out of school. My father was bitterly unhappy, my mother only slightly less so, but they had to agree that there was little point in continuing.

That was thirty-eight years ago. Writing this, I look out on the quadrangle of University College on the University of Toronto campus, where for one academic year I hold an unlikely title, Barker Fairley Distinguished Visitor in Canadian Culture. Occasionally a thought strays through my mind: of all the hundreds of students and teachers who use this building, I may be the only one who failed to complete high school. Sometimes I still puzzle over how such a thing could have happened. My parents were puzzled at the time, and so were my teachers — one history teacher, a Mr. Sage, told our class I was the best student he had ever had but that I had never written a good exam paper. There were solemn meetings with teachers, encouragement and threats from my father, help from my mother with memory work. At one point a retired schoolteacher tutored me for a few hours a week in French. There was shouting and there were tears. None of it worked. In class I was restless, impatient, and absent-minded. At home, pretending to confront my textbooks, I always found a way to be distracted.

I can dimly remember trying to convince myself that failure was the result of superior intelligence: with brilliant insight I had seen through the emptiness of the school curriculum and the shallow lives of ordinary teenagers. Even I didn't believe that. The curriculum was indeed empty — astonishingly so, in retrospect — and the lives of the boys and girls around me were certainly shallow. But there were other students who understood our environment at least as well as I did and still managed it to their advantage. No, the source of my misery was elsewhere. Later it became clear to me that there are people for whom school simply never acquires meaning. What is obvious to even below-average students — for instance, that some piece of homework must be done, even if it seems boring or unpleasant — never impresses itself on such people in a permanent, internalized way. They must acquire their education elsewhere if they are to acquire it at all, and must endure their school years as best they can, taking comfort in whatever diversions come to hand.

The melancholy truth is that I spent my adolescence trying to escape from it. I couldn't wait for the end of what Susan Sontag has called "that long prison sentence, my childhood," and playing at journalism was my principal diversion. The reason I showed up at the CHUM studios in 1948 was the same reason I spent as much time as I could hanging around the sports departments of the newspapers. I was the most dedicated member of the Toronto Secondary Schools Athletic Association Cub Reporters' Club, an organization of incipient journalists who covered school sports for the papers and the radio stations. For a time I made a pest of myself at another radio station, CKEY, until the news editor graciously allowed me to write some items for broadcast, at no fee. Ingeniously and perversely, I put my energy into everything except what was expected of me. I was trying to vault out of adolescence, into something that resembled manhood. I was trying to ignore my youth, in the hope that it would go away.

PEOPLE WHO KNOW about my lack of athletic talent, and also know that I can seldom be persuaded to watch even five minutes of a hockey game on television, tend to greet with slack-jawed wonder the news that my first job in the newspaper business was writing sports. Friends of mine have wondered aloud what sports editor in his right mind would ever hire someone like me.

The truth is that I never quite applied for the job and was never quite chosen for it: I *snuck* into the newspaper business, by the only back door I could pry open. As I saw it, the trick was to get myself inside before anyone knew I was on the doorstep. Somehow I managed to pull it off.

My campaign began almost by accident one summer, when my father asked a friend of his, the news editor of *The Globe and Mail*, to take me on as a summer replacement copy boy.

When I arrived at the *Globe* office, and was shown around the building by one of the old hands, I had the warming sensation that I was arriving at my new home. The energy and purpose in the office stirred me, and I began working about five times as hard as I ever had in school. In a few weeks I was the best copy boy on the staff and the fastest copy boy anyone could remember. When sent on an errand, I ran — I ran like a bat out of hell, hell being Malvern Collegiate.

Soon I knew the whole *Globe* building intimately, from the presses on the ground floor to the accounting department at the top of the building and even the penthouse squash court built for his private use by the publisher. I studied every detail of newspaper production, from the arrival of news over the wire to the finished papers running off the press. Occasionally I sat in the telegraph room where news stories came over the wire in Morse code, pounded out by operators in small-town railway stations across the country. Indulgent compositors sometimes let me handle the type (a serious breach of International Typographic Union rules in those days) and one night the press room boss let me push the large, black button that started the presses and set the whole building gently vibrating.

In those days it was often said that a newspaper was one of the few places where a man could work under precisely the same conditions his grandfather had known. In fact, we were still only one invention past Gutenberg. We were living in the age of Ottmar Mergenthaler, the German watchmaker who in the 1880s had perfected an effective form of linotype and made Gutenberg-style hand-setting of type obsolete. Often, on my message-carrying rounds, I would stop to watch the operation of his masterpiece, a huge apparatus that dwarfed the man who sat before it and gently stroked its big, flat keys. To one side was a pot where a torpedo-shaped piece of lead was slowly turning into the hot metal that would be cast into type. Above the operator's head the gears chunked away, sending the characters running smoothly down their brass channels to the assembler that would organize them in neat rows and produce sharp-edged lines of type. I'd watch the compositors put the type together in pages on "the stone" — a huge steel table — and then, having locked up a page, transport it by the "turtle," a heavy steel dolly, to the machine that would begin the process of turning it into curved plates to be fitted on the press.

All the knowledge that was generously spread before me by the printers that summer is now obsolete, but acquiring it gave me a sense of confidence. It was the first time in my life when I truly understood how things around me worked, and also the last. Certainly I have never since felt so close to an industrial process, or so much a part of the beautiful logic of production.

During the school year the *Globe* used me as a part-time copy boy on Friday and Sunday nights. Every Friday afternoon I fretted through my last two classes, anxious for the moment when I could show up at the *Globe*, rip some crucial bulletin off the teletype machine, drop it in the telegraph editor's tray, and imagine that I was in the newspaper business. By then the *Globe* had come to represent in my mind everything that was exciting and promising; school, on the other hand, was everything dead and frustrating. The men in the *Globe* news room were alive in some special way, connected to the great events of the moment. The city editor, Doug MacFarlane, was from central casting — a big, tough, cynical guy who snarled his commands to reporters literally from the corner of his mouth. Alex Barris, a wise-cracking New Yorker, brought his knowledge of jazz and American liberal politics to the reporting staff and did me the enormous favour of taking my views seriously — or at least pretending to. George Bain, a handsome young war hero who was covering Queen's Park and turning into the best political columnist of his generation, was so poised and aloof that I could barely work up the courage to speak to him.

Even the political stance of the paper was satisfying, because it played into my youthfully cynical views of how opinion was formed. The publisher, George McCullagh, was a right-wing admirer of George Drew, the Ontario premier who became the Tories' federal leader. In the news columns and editorials of the *Globe*, Drew was pictured as a hero of Napoleonic stature, his every fatuity treated as a brilliant inspiration. In the privacy of the news room, he was regarded as a pompous fraud, if not a fascist. In the 1949 federal election McCullagh, not quite certain that Drew would win, took matters into his own hands — he bought time on some radio stations and explained why the citizens should vote for Drew and the Tories. When they returned Louis St. Laurent and the Liberals instead, my idols in the news room were not unhappy. They rather liked their publisher, and enjoyed his pose as a playboy millionaire, but they were not anxious to see him turn into the political force he dreamt of becoming.

This was my first glimpse of what I later came to know as the routine politics of journalism — owners who think one way, journalists who reflexively think the other. Some might have found the cynicism of the *Globe* reporters and editors deadening; for me, at seventeen, it was intoxicating. I watched these men, sometimes eavesdropped on their conversations, studied what they wrote and what they said — I did everything but look over their shoulders while they banged out their stories on clattering manual typewriters. Passionately I yearned to join them. I imagined that if I could be a journalist life would forever afterward be intensely interesting.

The sports department would be my first stop. It was hardly more than a suburb of journalism, but it was the one place where I could hope to find accommodation. For a couple of years I had contributed sports items from my school. Now I began to write occasionally about other schools, and soon I was transferred to the sports department, as the lowliest employee above copy boy — I was a part-time cub reporter and rewrite man, but still had to run messages and fetch coffee. Sitting on the sports rewrite desk, headphones to my ears, I took down reports of hockey games in distant corners of Ontario, turning the notes that local reporters read to me into paragraphs that could be published. I worked even harder than I had as a copy boy.

A few years later, at the age of twenty-one, I read *The Sun Also Rises* in a Paris hotel room and noted Jake Barnes' view that "in the newspaper business…it is an important part of the ethics that you should never seem to be working." Perhaps, in the years since, I have occasionally managed to feign inactivity; but in my first couple of jobs I didn't fool anyone. I was desperate. My typewriter was all that stood between me and high school, and I banged away at it urgently.

And, sure enough, when I decided to leave high school the *Globe* sports editor, Jim Vipond, took me on full-time. I was already sitting at a desk in his department; making me a member of the permanent staff required only a brief memo to the business office. I now found myself, at eighteen, an editorial employee of *The Globe and Mail*. Admittedly, I had to cover school football and all the other obscure sports that everyone else was too important to write about — lacrosse, table tennis, sailing, even lawn bowling. But if writing is defined minimally, as the preparation of acceptable sentences and paragraphs for publication, then I was learning to write just about as fast as I could type. Some Sunday nights, sitting on the sports rewrite desk from 5 p.m. to 2:30 a.m. without a break, I turned out more than four thousand words for the Monday paper.

This impressed even my father, who was now something of a coach to me. My mother had earlier been a more powerful literary influence: it was she who first instructed me in storytelling by patiently telling me, over and over again, the stories I wanted to hear; and it was she who became my careful first listener when finally I started learning to tell stories of my own. But once I began receiving bylines in the *Globe*, I also began getting critiques from my father. I would bring my copy of the paper home at 3:30 or so in the morning, he would read it on his way to work a few hours later, and when I arrived at the *Globe* in the afternoon my mail box would contain a note from him, expertly criticizing the language I'd used that day. My father might have found it hard to deal with me as a son, but now I had become something distantly resembling a newspaperman. *That* he could understand, and he was able to play the traditional elder's role of passing on tribal wisdom. For my part, I now had a way of not only attracting his attention but also pleasing him.

He was anxious that I not write like a typical sports writer. Once, instead of using a simple word like "defeated" or "beat," I wrote that one team "prevailed over" another. That drew a note solemnly pointing out that by international agreement sports writers were prohibited from using the word "prevailed"; the Havana Treaty of 1938, my father claimed, had turned it over to weather forecasters for their exclusive use, in phrases such as "prevailing winds." The last note I had from him — shortly before his second heart attack killed him in 1957 — advised me to stop using the word "very" so often, on the grounds that it exposes a faulty vocabulary and a weak style. To this day I think of him, lovingly, whenever I strike "very" from my own or someone else's copy.

In a journal I briefly kept in the 1950s I outlined a novel about a musician who played with both the Toronto Symphony and a jazz group. "He doesn't have much sympathy for his father, who is a studio musician exclusively and seems more interested in his work as a union official and his garden than in playing anything adventurous — yet he somehow communicates to his son his feeling for craft." Nothing in the journal indicates that, at the time, I understood the meaning of this passage.

THE PEOPLE in the sports department at the *Globe* — now my full-time colleagues and my part-time journalism teachers — were even more skeptical of the *Globe* management than were the political reporters. One major reason was Maple

Leaf Gardens. In those years the Toronto Maple Leafs were not only a good hockey team, they were a national institution of mythic power; but in our office they were the source of journalistic pathology. Under the orders of our sports editor and our managing editor, we treated the Leafs with a mixture of adulation and pusillanimity that I have not seen equalled anywhere since, even in the federal Liberal Party under Trudeau. I can't remember whether our publisher at that time served on the board of the Gardens, but it didn't matter — we couldn't have lavished more respect on the Leafs if the *Globe* had been the team's public relations department. We even took seriously the legendary owner of the team, Conn Smythe, a nasty little martinet whose permanent air of self-congratulation suggested that he believed no one in history had ever before founded a hockey team or built a rink.

We in the office (and the eighteen-year-old rookie above all) obeyed orders but muttered resentfully in the background. All the time I was there no one spoke of the Leafs; we spoke of "the heroes," and always with an edge — "Did the new lead on the heroes come in yet?" This view of the Leafs spilled over into our attitude toward other teams: we liked to think that we saw through them. Some sports writers, perhaps when on the road, might identify with the team they were covering and even hope for its success, but no one admitted such sentiments around the office. I don't think I ever met a sports writer whose instincts as a fan had survived his years in the press box.

In a way the most cynical of all our writers was Bobbie Rosenfeld, which may have had something to do with the fact that she was the only genuine athlete among us — and almost the only first-class athlete I ever knew in the sports writing business. She was in her mid-forties then, but she seemed ancient to me, and pathetic. As a writer she was more tolerated than admired, and people didn't talk much about the daily column she wrote on women's sports. I picked up her personal history in bits and pieces. In the 1920s she had

been a magnificent athlete, a kind of Gretzky or Howe: everything she tried, she did better than anyone else. At basketball, softball, tennis, or running, she was clearly the best in
southern Ontario, then clearly the best in Canada, and finally
among the best in the world. In 1928, at the Olympics in
Amsterdam, she won a gold medal in the sprint relay and a
silver medal for herself in the 100 metres. At the time there
were few ways for a woman to turn this kind of talent into a
career (it was hard enough for men) and in any case she
began to suffer from arthritis some years before her life as
an athlete ran its normal course. By the time I knew her she
walked with obvious difficulty. She had given up trying to
work as a coach, she had never really learned much about
reporting, and now she regarded the whole business of ath-
letics with rueful suspicion. The stars our sports pages celebrated every morning — Canadian hockey players, American
baseball players — were no more impressive to her than
accountants. When she spoke of her own sports career she
always moved the conversation around to the physical ail-
ments of athletes. I believe she thought that her arthritis
was the result of prolonged physical exertion. Writing amused
her, but only a little. Hearst's New York *Journal-American* was
delivered to her every day, and once she pointed out a Hearst
columnist to me — "I steal my best aphorisms from him," she
said. When she went back to work, I looked up *aphorism* in
the dictionary.

Bobbie was the first lesbian I knew as such, and every day
her moment of greatest happiness — happiness I could see
her almost physically trying to hide, for reasons it took me
years to understand — coincided with her companion's arrival
at our office to pick her up after work. Once this lady mentioned that she and Bobbie were looking for a new apartment
and needed two bedrooms — one for Bobbie's trophies. In
1950 a poll of sports writers across the country named Bobbie
the Canadian women's athlete of the half century. That

pleased her, though it merely confirmed the obvious; there really wasn't anyone else in her class. Bobbie would have laughed at the idea — a rough, grinding, bitter laugh — but her melancholy life became a part of my education, and a part I wouldn't like to have missed.

Nor would I want to have missed my most direct encounter with journalistic corruption. The phrase "conflict of interest" was not widely used at the time, but even had it been available it would have been pitifully inadequate to describe the byzantine interconnections of sports writers and their subjects. In those days it was widely assumed that many sports writers took bribes, and I saw nothing to persuade me otherwise. We young sports writers, still wondering about the rules of our new trade, sometimes discussed the subject, and took the view that bribes (never called that) were justified because newspapermen were desperately underpaid. In any case, our employers required us to write, unbribed, the kind of adulatory garbage that bribes were intended to encourage.

So sports writers and copy editors routinely accepted small fees to write press releases for promoters; they were then in a position to recognize the quality of these releases and escort them into print. For a couple of months, when I was nineteen, I wrote the press releases for a stock car racing promoter, a creep who dreamed aloud about a great national chain of race tracks. Direct bribery was more rare, and tended to be limited to the established sports writers. I was bribed, in a clear and unequivocal way, only once. One December, after I'd been a sports writer for a couple of years, the press agent for Maple Leaf Gardens told me to stop by the cashier's wicket and pick up a message left there for me. When I gave my name the cashier handed me an envelope containing $100 in crisp new bills. My Christmas bonus. It was an acknowledgement, obviously, of the fact that at age twenty I was turning into the sort of chap the Gardens liked to keep happy. I took the money, because, I told myself, it might be my last chance to know what it was like to be bribed (it wasn't all that nice). I wish I could add that I immediately gave it to the Salvation Army.

In those years the *Globe* sent me to cover water skiing at the Canadian National Exhibition, canoe races in Ottawa, rowing in St. Catharines, lacrosse in the suburbs of Toronto. While writing about sports I learned at least a bit about the world. At the Royal Canadian Yacht Club on Toronto Island I sat copying out boat-race results while a club secretary in the next office explained to someone over the phone how difficult it was to keep Jews out of the RCYC and how he was accomplishing this (in his unequivocal view) heroic task. I wrote an article in which a coach explained why smoking cigarettes was bad for athletes and the sports editor actually said, "I'd better double-check this with the advertising department." The story didn't run, and no one thought the incident unusual.

I covered a caber-tossing competition at the local Highland games and wrote an article explaining the "cultural connotations" of that event, to the great amusement of the desk man who sensibly crossed out about half my adjectives. My approach to caber-tossing indicated that I was probably in the wrong place, doing the wrong sort of work. There were other signs. In my third turn around the seasonal sports cycle, I noticed that some of my colleagues wrote the same witty phrases about certain events that they had written the year before about roughly the same events. That was ominous, and the feelings I was developing about sports were even more depressing. I still loved working the rewrite desk and the copy desk, and being called on to edit or rewrite the work of much older men greatly nourished my ego. But on the days when I was scheduled to attend a sports event, I did not bound eagerly out of bed.

One autumn afternoon in 1952, covering a football game, I fell into conversation with the photographer who had accompanied me. I remarked that it was a good game — no doubt I would describe it the next day as tense, action-packed, and thrilling — and he said he supposed it was but that he would much rather be at a movie. I found myself agreeing. In fact, I thought, the worst movie in town, no, the worst movie ever made would be more interesting than what I was looking at. That was the moment when I faced the dreadful truth. I was a sports writer who didn't like to watch people play games.

Clearly, I needed a new subject, or subjects. What I didn't understand at the time was that the choice of those subjects, and the intensity of my approach to them, would be profoundly influenced by the best friend I made in childhood.

TWO

*T*he genius
who lived
next door

ONE DAY in my class at Williamson Road Public School the little boy in front of me turned around and said his name was Glenn Gould. We discovered that we were about to become neighbours: the house my family had just rented, 34 Southwood Drive, was next door to his. Soon we were visiting each other, and I immediately learned that Glenn was not an ordinary nine-year-old. The word "prodigy" was banned from the Gould household — prodigies were children of freakish talent, exploited by their parents and ruined by over-exposure; Mozart, in Gould family mythology, was a cautionary example. Even so, a prodigy was what Glenn was. His parents had discovered some years earlier that he had perfect pitch, and soon he had begun to pick out tunes on the piano. By the time I met him he was spending long hours at the piano every day and working with the best teachers the Royal Conservatory of Music could provide.

Glenn's parents were interested in music — Florence Grieg Gould, a relative of the composer Edvard Grieg, was a part-time singing teacher; Bert Gould, a furrier and amateur violinist, took a passionate interest in running the Kiwanis Music Festival — but the arrival of a great musician in their family was as astonishing to them as it would have been to people who knew nothing at all of music. In his lessons Glenn leapt forward at a speed no one at the Conservatory had seen before, and he demonstrated a passion for the instrument that his parents found hard to manage. Florence Gould made strict rules about how much time Glenn could play each day; at one point it was four hours, not a minute more. In childhood Glenn was never seriously ill — the worst symptom I ever noticed was unusually pale skin — but she worried constantly about his health, perhaps planting the seeds of the hypochondria that coloured his adult life. She was especially concerned about his posture. "Sit *up*, Glenn, sit up straight, *please*," she would say, again and again, as he slouched on the chesterfield. Years later, watching him perform in a position that seemed outlandish to every-one in the world but him, I wondered how much this was a way of finding his best approach to the keyboard and how much it was an odd form of rebellion.

The Goulds were willing to recognize, almost from the beginning, that their only child would be an exceptional artist, but they were unable to live comfortably with the fact that he was unusual in every other way as well. Florence Gould was a woman of propriety; when she spoke it was from a tranquil world of rules and order, a world from which conflict and tension had somehow been erased. She hated conflict, and she hated anything extreme or eccentric. Against impossible odds, she longed to see her son have a "normal" childhood, with the right amount of fresh air and exercise and the right sort of friends. In retrospect it's occurred to me that my friendship with Glenn perhaps owed something to Mrs. Gould's view that I was appropriately normal.

In my memory, she is always admonishing Glenn about something, calling him to account for a transgression of her rules. It could hardly have been otherwise, since they looked at the universe in entirely different ways. Put plainly, he was a born intellectual and she was not. He saw no reason to accept conventional opinion, however well established, and she knew nothing but conventional opinion.

Once the Goulds took me into the country north of Toronto to see the autumn colours. Glenn and I were in the back of the car, his parents in the front, Bert not talking much but Florence saying over and over again that this or that view of the woods was "lovely — *so* lovely." She used the word so often that it began to grate on me. I wasn't all that delighted with our tour anyway. Show me a hundred many-hued trees and I'll be impressed. Show me ten thousand and I forget the point.

Perhaps Glenn knew I was bored. In any case, he started a separate conversation in the back seat. He began to talk of opera singers, and in particular Enrico Caruso. In Glenn's opinion Caruso was a fraud, "a *terrible* singer."

Mrs. Gould heard that. She turned almost to face him.

"Glenn," she said, "you shouldn't say things like that."

"Why not?"

"Well, he was a great singer — and you don't know anything about it. You've only heard those few records he made, scratchy records. You can't judge him on those."

Glenn said that he had heard more than enough to make up his mind. Mrs. Gould said that Glenn was exasperating. We all fell silent.

The Goulds, from their Kiwanis Festival perspective, saw music as uplifting and educational, roughly on the level of saying grace at supper and attending the United Church. Once, after an extremely difficult concert of atonal music, I heard Mrs. Gould say that it should be put on for children in the schools. "It's so *educational*," she said. Clearly, she hadn't liked it, but felt it would be good for someone. Thirty or so years later, trying to explain his rigorous attitude to music, Glenn described himself as "the last Puritan." Perhaps he had absorbed more from his parents than he knew.

When we were about twelve, Glenn and his parents took me to their cottage near Orillia — the same cottage Glenn used as a home till the end of his life. Staying with them for a few days, I caught a glimpse of how intense family relationships could be. In my own home, affection and its opposite were diffused among seven people, but there were just three Goulds and the lines of love and tension were tightly drawn. Glenn was the classic only child, closely scrutinized and at the same time pampered and over-indulged. He explained to me that at the cottage he would sleep with his mother one night and his father would sleep with her the next, this arrangement having been worked out some years before.

Theirs was a Christian home in which swearing of any kind was a grave effrontery — "Bad language is used only by those who are too ignorant to know proper language," Bert Gould instructed me — and the Sabbath was meant to be kept with care. Although Glenn was swiftly rejecting his parents' musical opinions, he embraced their United Church morality. Alone among all my male contemporaries, he never told dirty jokes, never speculated about the sexuality of girls, and never said "fuck." Moreover, he was disturbed when other boys, such as my brother Wayne and I, used offensive language. He would ask us to stop and even threaten us ("You can't come to my cottage") if we failed to obey.

At the cottage one Saturday afternoon Glenn and his father and I went out fishing. Or, rather, Bert Gould fished and Glenn watched with disapproval while I tried to work out an appropriate attitude. Glenn had already developed an aversion to fishing as well as hunting, and he was not reluctant to remind his father of it. As the afternoon wore on, I discovered that I liked fishing, and when I said so Mr. Gould and I jokingly made common cause against Glenn. As fishermen, we decided, we would form a club and exclude him — it would be called the Devil's Eye Warbler Club, after a lure in Mr. Gould's tackle box. Glenn listened impatiently, barely pretending to be amused.

I think Bert took a couple of fish that afternoon, but not the next day. That was Sunday, and the code agreed upon by the Goulds banned Sunday fishing. Florence Gould insisted on it. Even so, the three of us were out on the lake again, just for a boat ride. At one point Bert dropped a line in the water, as if trolling. Glenn demanded to know what he was doing. Bert explained that he was just untangling his line, not fishing at all, really. Glenn looked coldly into the distance. I found it disturbing to see a twelve-year-old policing his father on behalf of his mother, but later I realized it was more complicated than that: Glenn's dislike of seeing anything killed — above all, by someone in his own family — was so intense that he was ready to use anything, including the Sunday prohibition, to prevent it. Many years later, as an adult, he told a friend that the accomplishment in his life that made him proudest was finally persuading his father to give up fishing.

For an altogether different reason, Glenn avoided the games all the rest of us played. So far as I know, he never touched a football or a baseball, and if you threw one to him — out of ignorance, or to tease him — he would silently step back and let it fall to the ground. He knew what his long, graceful hands were for, and it wasn't baseball. He understood that this in itself made him a strange kid, and sometimes in conversation he playfully magnified his aversion to balls of all kinds, even to the word itself. (The subject of balls as testicles did not come up, nor can I imagine it doing so in the Gould household.) If forced to mention some kind of ball he would call it "a censored." Once we sat together on his piano bench, learning a required piece of memory work for school by singing it to a tune Glenn had composed. The poem, which is now otherwise lost to me, contained the words "and stately led the ball." Glenn and I sang it, "and stately led the censored."

From the beginning, no one in Toronto doubted Glenn's genius — he wasn't the sort of artist who lacks appreciation in his home town. Right up to the conductor of the symphony, musical Toronto understood the size of the talent that God or good fortune had placed in its midst. Glenn never lacked opportunities to perform, but as a child he accepted only a few of them. His parents were afraid of straining his health, and income was never an issue — Bert Gould's prosperity as a furrier made it possible for him to spend about $3,000 a year on Glenn's musical education, in 1940s money. (That was roughly the sum that supported our entire family of seven, next door.) From the age of eleven until adulthood Glenn had as his piano teacher Alberto Guerrero, an avuncular Chilean who been a concert pianist in Latin America. Simultaneously, Glenn studied organ, and made his debut at the giant pipe organ in Eaton Auditorium while I sat beside him on the bench, turning the pages. It was an astounding performance: a little boy who can make a pipe organ work properly is already something of a phenomenon, but a little boy who can do it with "astonishing technique" and "interpretive intuition" (as the Toronto *Evening Telegram* said of Glenn) is a miracle. That concert was in 1945, the year we both turned thirteen and entered high school.

At Malvern, Glenn was clearly an oddity, but he was not despised for it. His prodigious and mysterious talent made him immune (or so I recall) to the cruelty that adolescents routinely visit on the exceptional among them. When he walked home from school, waving his arms as he conducted an invisible symphony orchestra and humming the parts ("pa-puh, duh-*pa*"), the other students just assumed he was acting the way geniuses were supposed to act. The news of Glenn's talent leaked through the community — from the Conservatory (where he won the highest teaching certificate

at a record age) and through the newspapers. His fellow
students came to accept it as a given that he would be a
world-famous virtuoso, even though few of us understood
what that meant or could even name one of the great pianists
of the day. Glenn played beautifully, we all knew, because
sometimes he gave concerts at the school; but we lacked the
ability to say whether he was one of the best ten young
pianists in the world, or one of the best ten thousand.

Among us, though, there was one would-be pianist who
could at least glimpse the outlines of Glenn's mountainous
talent. She was a brilliant student who had raced through
her grade exams and won every competition she entered.
She may have been, briefly, the best pianist her age in Toronto;
certainly she was the best in our district. Then, one horrible
year, through the Kiwanis competitions and perhaps through
other means, she came to understand that there was a boy,
four or five years younger, who was not just a litle better
than she but many, many times better — *and that he lived on
her street.* She was like Christopher Marlowe suddenly discovering that Shakespeare had moved into the neighbourhood. My understanding is that for a few years Glenn became
her obsession, and that it was not difficult to get her to
explain how limited his talent really was. Happily, she survived
this trauma and became a distinguished professor of literature.

At that moment, no doubt, there were wonderful adoles-
cent pianists in Lethbridge or Des Moines or Vienna, and
perhaps there was even one at a high school a couple of
miles from ours. What seems odd to me now is that we had
the young pianist in the world and somehow knew it, or
thought we did. Did all those other schools also arrive at the
collective (in their cases incorrect) opinion that their pianists
would conquer the world? I doubt it. I rather think there
was something in Glenn's confidence, an easy assumption of
greatness: he seemed to know, from early adolescence onward,
that the great musicians of Europe and American were his
peers, even though they hadn't yet heard of him.

At Malvern I was doing my best to spread the fame of my neighbour. On April 3, 1946, our mimeographed class paper, the *9-D Bugle*, carried a leading article written by the editor, me, under the heading "Personages":

"Glenn Gould started his musical education at the age of three and when he was four his parents discovered he had perfect pitch. He has since then won several medals and five scholarships in the musical world. Last year he earned his A.T.C.M., probably the youngest holder of this degree in Canada.

"He started studying the organ three years ago and on December 12, 1945, he played at Eaton's Auditorium for the Casavant Society. His latest triumph was the Kiwanis Festival where he was called by one of the adjudicators 'a wonder child.' Glenn has had many pets, including two dogs, two rabbits, four goldfish (named Bach, Beethoven, Haydn and Chopin), a budgie (Mozart) and, of all things, a skunk. He is a confirmed bachelor at 13 and thinks popular music is terrible."

That was the first piece I ever wrote about Glenn and — except for some publicity releases we concocted together — the last I wrote until he died. But in 1946 I published one more comment on him, also a reference to his views on popular music. As class scribe I was assigned to write a line about each of my classmates in the school yearbook. I described Glenn as "The Ten Hottest Fingers in Malvern," a phrase I didn't think of again until I encountered a copy of *The Malvern Muse*, opened to that page, at an exhibition of Gould memorabilia in Paris in 1986. It was the slogan of some popular pianist of the 1940s, and I adapted it because "hot" was precisely what Glenn's playing was not. By then we were occasionally arguing, in a friendly way (and with great diffidence on my part), about music. I was becoming the jazz fan I have been ever since, and Glenn was patiently explaining to me that jazz was — putting the best possible face on it — a minor and transitory offshoot of the romantic movement.

And since Glenn had no time for romantic music, then or later, he seldom agreed to listen to a Duke Ellington record with me; when he did, he let me know that it was an act of tolerance on his part.

We were operating on different levels, to put it mildly, and we were also heading toward entirely different views of music. I was beginning, dimly, to understand music as an almost physical form of expression, charged with sexuality; among many other things, music was an excitement of the senses. In Glenn's mind, music was becoming refined and bodiless, almost entirely separated from the physical. Sometimes he spoke of music as if it existed in some distant and abstract sphere, beyond physicality — he seemed to resent the necessity, in music, of fingers and wood and mouths and catgut, the limiting facts of the always flawed physical world. His decision to stop giving concerts grew naturally from this view — a public appearance inevitably included imperfections, whereas a recording could eliminate them entirely. Even more important, recordings could eliminate much of the appeal of public personalities. Glenn hated the idea of the old-fashioned, charismatic virtuoso of the keyboard. He thought "personality" interfered with the reality of the music — though he became, partly through his many eccentricities, the most celebrated instrumental personality of his time.

Were his eccentricities part of an intentionally self-created myth, or did they proceed inevitably from his neuroses? I never knew for certain, and I don't think Glenn did, either. He could act oddly, laugh good-heartedly at the oddness of his behaviour, and then act oddly again. When he was a teenager, and a young man, he had a curious habit of speaking with a German accent when he was discussing a German composer or a German book. The year he discovered Nietzsche's *Also Sprach Zarathustra*, the accent grew almost impenetrably thick. If you kidded him about it he would stop, and a few minutes later start again, all the while admitting that it was a funny way to talk. Was he satirizing himself or was he trying to work himself into a German mood?

In the late 1950s my wife and I, in New York for a few days, visited Glenn in the apartment hotel where he was staying while he made a record. He claimed to be distressed because room service did not stock, and could not obtain, something called Poland water. By that time tap water was out of the question for Glenn — he knew it was teeming with killer microbes — but so were most forms of bottled water. Poland water it had to be, and he wasn't giving in to any suggestion that he drink something else. He was twenty-five years old and sounding like an octogenarian crank whose tastes had been formed in the last century. And yet all the time, as he went through this absurd conversational dance, his eyes were sparkling and he was laughing at himself. He was beginning to explore eccentricity as a mode of life.

Arnold Schoenberg, the creator of the twelve-tone scale, was one of the composers whose work Glenn sometimes discussed in a German accent. In the early 1950s Glenn could explain to you that Schoenberg was the great composer of the twentieth century. (If you wanted to know who was most certainly *not* the great composer of the twentieth century, Glenn could give you that name, too: Stravinsky.) In his own and in Glenn's view, Schoenberg was not a musical revolutionary, as most critics said, but a composer who had continued and extended the tradition in the only way possible in our time.

It was Schoenberg who inspired Glenn and me to go into business together, as impresarios. Glenn decided that, since Schoenberg's music was almost entirely ignored in Canada, we should arrange that it be played. In 1952, the year we turned twenty — I was on the *Globe*, still a sports writer, and he was coming to the end of his life as a student and emerging as a professional — we formed a company, New Music Associates. (We briefly used the name Esoteric Attractions, but wisely abandoned it.) We duly filed papers under the Ontario Partnership Registration Act and took a business account at the Queen and Lee branch of what was then the Dominion Bank. In the next two years we arranged three concerts — a Schoenberg Memorial Concert in 1952 (he had recently died), then a performance of music by Schoenberg and his two great followers, Berg and Webern, and finally an all-Bach concert, at which Glenn played the Goldberg Variations in public for the first time. Glenn of course arranged for the singers and musicians, among them Victor Feldbrill, Barbara Franklin, and Morry Kernerman, and decided on the programs.

The first two concerts made no concession to public taste, though the Schoenberg evening included an explanatory lecture written by Glenn in the opaque style later familiar to readers of his liner notes; it was read to the audience by Frank Herbert, a CBC announcer who confessed to me afterward that he understood almost none of it. The program for the second concert carried a note under the listing for a Webern quartet: "Because this work is, on first hearing, difficult, it will be played twice." Whether that made it any clearer, I can't remember. In any case, Glenn and the rest of us took pride in the fact that at the first two concerts everything played was being given its Canadian debut. My own contribution to discussion of the musical content was, appropriately, minimal.

"But Glenn, if we are *New* Music Associates, why are we doing a Bach concert?"

"Bach is ever new."

I arranged to rent the auditorium (the Royal Conservatory's little concert hall on University Avenue cost $31.50 a night), print the tickets, send out the publicity, and line up a couple of friends to act as ushers. I also wrote the checks to the performers, all of them meagre — Feldbrill, for conducting one chamber piece, received forty dollars. Glenn and I took no fees. I have a receipt showing that, for Maureen Forrester's Toronto debut at our Bach concert, on October 16, 1954, I

paid her agent what seems to have been our highest fee —
fifty dollars.

Our first two concerts were well attended and well reviewed,
but the success of the Bach evening was severely limited by
the worst natural disaster in the modern history of Toronto.
As Maureen wrote in her autobiography, *Out of Character:*
"It was a brilliant concert, but it was the day after Hurricane
Hazel and, with all the devastation, only fifteen people showed
up." My records indicate that, despite the torrential rains,
there were eighty-six paid admissions (the hall held about
three hundred); I can still hear the applause echoing through
the mostly empty building. One of those applauding was Sir
Ernest MacMillan, the conductor of the Toronto Symphony,
who was already familiar with Glenn's work but had not
heard Forrester before. She was twenty-four that year, and
still known mainly in Montreal. After that night, as she recalls
in her book, Sir Ernest "opened up Toronto to me."

On that occasion we lost money, though not much of it.
The gross investment (musicians, hall, programs, tickets) was
$240.86, so our loss was that figure minus whatever two-
dollar (general admittance) or one-dollar (student) tickets
we sold. But while the Bach concert was no great financial
blow, it was the end of New Music Associates. Not long after,
Glenn played the Goldberg Variations at the New York concert that launched his international reputation. He never
again needed to organize a concert to have the music of his
choice heard; soon almost anyone involved in classical music
was anxious to do his bidding.

In 1957, after performing in Berlin, he came to visit my
wife and me at our apartment. He carried a translation of a
German review which called him the best pianist who had
played in Berlin since Busoni. I asked him when Busoni died
and Glenn, smirking happily, admitted that he had immediately looked up the date: "Nineteen twenty-four," he said.
Even German musical culture had embraced him. He was

still only twenty-five years old, and to a large extent he had already fulfilled the promise of his childhood.

Once I greatly annoyed Glenn, and once he moderately annoyed me, and occasionally it's occurred to me that one or both of these annoyances helped bring our friendship to an end. In the 1950s Glenn privately lavished on people close to him the full force of the eloquence that made him, by the late 1960s, the most articulate of all modern musicians. It was not uncommon to visit Glenn, or answer a phone call from him, and find oneself the sole auditor of a detailed, thoughtful, and highly imaginative lecture. Once, as I sat with him in his parents' living room on an afternoon in the early 1950s, he set out to explain to me how a certain Bach piano piece should be performed. He played the record of it by a leading Bach interpreter (perhaps Rosalyn Tureck), he played his own unreleased private record of it, and then he explained why his interpretation was the correct one. I, in my ignorance, imagined that I understood him — and I was impressed, as on many other occasions, by his vaulting confidence.

Unfortunately, a year or two later I made the mistake of telling the story to a magazine writer who was preparing a profile of Glenn. He was offended when it appeared in print, and rightly so: he wasn't ready to reveal the size of his ego in public, and he saw it as a betrayal when his close friend did so. When he spoke to me about it I explained that I felt the anecdote reflected credit on him reather than the opposite, and I apologized for my indiscretion; but a certain coolness entered our relationship. We remained in touch, though, and over the next few years I saw him in New York and Montreal as well as in Toronto. But he began to seem relatively distant. His anecdotes about epic battles with Leonard Bernstein or the difficulty of getting a piano mover in Moscow were as funny as anything I'd heard from him in our school days, but the fact that they were now delivered by an international celebrity somehow made them less rather than more appealing to me.

In 1968 it was my turn to be annoyed. At my suggestion he wrote a music review for *Saturday Night*, where I had just become editor. It was perhaps the silliest piece of his career, a paean to a Moog synthesizer album, and — for what reason I can't imagine — he delivered it as a talk over CBC radio before it appeared in print. This may have been carelessness, it may have been ignorance of the ordinary rules, or it may have been a signal that he didn't really want to write for *Saturday Night*. I was too upset to find out which explanation was correct.

IN MY EXPERIENCE friendship begins in the exchange of laughter, and dwindles when easy laughter becomes impossible. At some point in my friendship with Glenn, laughter died, friendship disappeared, and nothing remained but formality tinged with nostalgia. I think I knew something like this had happened one day when I spoke with him briefly at the Benvenuto Hotel. I was there to meet another journalist, but in the lobby I encountered a hideously pretentious society lady I knew slightly. As we waited for our luncheon appointments she told me that hers was with Glenn Gould. She spoke the name reverently, and then began chattering proudly about how well she knew him and how carefully she and her eminent husband had followed his career since they had first seen him play in short pants with the Toronto Symphony. She spoke so quickly that I couldn't get in a word about my own relationship with him, and it became one of those awkward situations where a fact, having failed to appear at the appropriate moment, can't easily be inserted later.

Suddenly Glenn was standing beside us, holding one of the floppy hats that he wore in all weather, and she was graciously introducing us. Glenn stopped her with a little gesture. "Bob is my oldest friend," he said. We smiled at each other as she stared open-mouthed at the two of us, this scruffy magazine editor and the greatest pianist of the age. We went to our separate tables, but something in Glenn's smile, something regretful, stayed with me. "Friendship with Glenn," a mutual acquaintance of ours told me a year or so after his death, "was the hardest thing I ever accomplished." Like me, he regarded Glenn as generous and loveable but hard to keep up with; unlike me, he persistently made the effort. Glenn communicated mainly by telephone, at any hour of the day or night, and he expected his friends to be available when he needed them — he literally did not understand why they might not be. He could phone at three o'clock in the morning, inquire "Have you got a minute?", and then chat for half an hour. The conflicting demands of wives, husbands, children, and day jobs seldom entered his mind and certainly wouldn't have seemed to him reasons for passing up an interesting conversation. As the years sent us in different directions, I grew less willing to deal with Glenn on these terms: the energy that might have sustained our friendship went into my own work and my family. As a result, at the time of his death in 1982 we were no more than memories to each other.

But, at least on my side, happy memories, heightened by intense gratitude. Music, Glenn's music in particular, was the real beginning of my life as a thinking adult. Listening to him play, and listening to him talk passionately about music, rearranged my perceptions and informed me of a larger world than Malvern Collegiate knew. Ever since, music has been central in my life — my best teacher, my touchstone, my most treasured glimpse of whatever eternal truth lies beyond logic and beyond what we ordinarily call knowledge.

What makes this so odd is that I am distinctly unmusical. When I sing — that is, when I cannot be prevented from singing — my daughters wince and birds fall dead from the sky. Four unfortunate children have learned from me how *not* to sing dozens of folk songs. When I listen to music, as I constantly do, I must — given my aural equipment — hear far less than people who have ordinary musical talent. Searching for a simile, I've compared my situation to that of someone with limited taste buds who can't really tell the difference between very good water and pretty good water — and yet knows that water is nevertheless essential to being alive.

"The purpose of art," Glenn wrote once, "is...the gradual life-long construction of a state of wonder and serenity..." I can barely imagine living in a state of serenity — certainly I've never managed it — but my sense of wonder remains exuberantly healthy because it was nourished long ago by the genius whom fate placed in the house next door to me.

THREE

Newspaper Days

GLENN'S INTELLIGENCE reached far beyond music. In Grade Ten geometry he mastered the textbook by the end of October, while the rest of us were just getting started, and I can still remember him explaining the Republican national convention of 1948 to my brother and me on our front verandah — he was following it by radio in his breaks from piano practice. There was only one time, in fact, when I was able to explain a complicated process to *him*. Several times he said that he couldn't imagine the system that made it possible to recreate a newspaper in a different form every day. So I sat him down one afternoon around 1950, spread a copy of the *Globe* on his kitchen table, and went through the production process ("and then the pages go to stereo") in elaborate detail. He listened carefully and, as always, asked polite and intelligent questions. He wasn't only fascinated by newspapers, of course; he was also interested in what I was doing with my life. And in the early 1950s he was wondering aloud, though in the nicest possible way, what I was doing in the sports department. After a while, as I've said, I wondered about it too, and when I decided to make a change I discovered that it was far less difficult to escape than I had imagined. One day in 1952, after steeling myself for hours, I went to the news editor's office at *The Globe and Mail* and asked him if he could possibly move me to a job on the general reporting staff — the *real* staff, as I thought of it. He said he didn't see why not, and a few weeks later I was handed over to the city editor. My working life changed abruptly on that day. I moved suddenly from a world of games to a world in which people sometimes killed each other.

Like most ex-reporters, I look back on my newspaper days as the time when I began, haltingly, to discover the world beyond my family, my friends, and my private pleasures. Then as now, a general reporter on a paper like the *Globe* lived an unpredictable life. One afternoon would be devoted mainly to concocting a few publishable paragraphs, sounding at least slightly like news, from a luncheon speech covered at the Canadian Club in the Royal York Hotel. (I heard so many boring speeches there in my youth that I still can't enter the building without a Pavlovian feeling that my skull is filling up with glue.) The next day might find me in a courtroom, sitting for hours within a few feet of a man and woman who had together killed an infant because he cried too much and resisted toilet training.

Late one afternoon in May, 1953, as I was typing up the stories I had spent the day gathering in the courts, the assistant city editor — Dic Doyle, later the editor of the paper and now a senator — came over to my desk and said that Sarnia had just been hit by a tornado and I was to drive there with two other reporters. The city we found when we arrived, late in the evening, still sits in my memory — electricity had failed so that there was no light, only the flame of the refinery against the sky. Downtown, we abandoned the car some blocks before we reached the hospital because the silent, dark streets were filled with uprooted trees. At City

Hall we found the aldermen meeting by the light of oil lamps at 11 p.m. I heard the acting mayor literally read the Riot Act to provide police powers for use against looting. I was up all that night and most of the next, living on an adrenaline rush. The late edition of the next day's paper carried my byline on the front page.

Like most young reporters, I found ways to harden myself when sent to someone's home to ask for a photo of a child who had just been killed in an accident. Strangely, no such family ever sent me away empty-handed; all of them seemed anxious to co-operate, as if the appearance of their child's face in the next day's paper would make this event less terrible or less random. Several times a sad young mother said to me something like, "I always told her, 'Don't cross the street without looking.'" When I became a parent — and anxious about my own children — those words echoed in my memory.

In my reporting days, though, it was for myself and my nascent professional reputation that I feared. If your nature contains even a few errant drops of paranoia, competitive reporting will bring them to the surface. In the 1950s I was frequently the youngest reporter assigned to whatever I was covering, and often the most ignorant. My insecurity ran wild. My nightmare was that the reporters from the other papers — amiable fellows, on the surface — would contrive to hide from me the central facts of the story and I would go to press with a report that was embarrassingly wrong. I can't recall anything like that happening, but often I was so intimidated by the opposition from the other papers — older, beefy, heavy-drinking guys who looked on junior reporters with casual contempt — that I sometimes trembled when writing my stories or phoning them in to the rewrite desk.

What made all this worse was that the *Globe* was the poorest of the Toronto papers, or claimed to be, so that on an important story a *Globe* reporter might be outmanned three to one by the *Telegram* and six to one by the *Star*. Those two evening papers, fighting a long circulation war that the *Star* finally won, were regarded in the *Globe* news room as pathetic sensation-mongers, anachronistic survivors of the age before reporters turned into journalists. The piety of my own feelings about the *Star* — with which, later, I was to be associated for nearly three decades — was expressed in a nightmare I had when I was about twenty-one. I awoke at dawn, covered in sweat, because in my dream I had foolishly quit the *Globe* and joined the *Star* — and now I could never come back again. For earnest young chaps like me, the *Star* of the early 1950s looked like one of the outer rings of hell. It was a paper that stopped at nothing to promote the causes — mostly Liberal causes — of its owners, and routinely treated reporters as clerks whose scribblings could be rewritten to suit whatever purpose seemed appropriate to the editors. In those days it was assumed that a *Star* reporter couldn't be blamed for anything that appeared in the paper, even if his byline was on it.

As for the *Telegram*, it was even worse — partly because it operated on a meaner, more penny-pinching scale and therefore lacked the grandeur of the *Star*'s corruption, but also because it seemed to have nothing that could be called a social conscience. Much later, the publisher, John Bassett, realized what was missing and apparently directed that the right sort of social conscience be designed by an ad agency. For months, slogans such as "The Telegram Cares" appeared on billboards all over Toronto. At the time this seemed laughable, and it certainly didn't save the paper, but Bassett — in this as in many other ways — was a pioneer. Today it's not at all uncommon for some gigantic corporation to express the absurd idea that somewhere in its heart — a heart purely abstract, made of marks on paper or electronic impulses in a computer — there are feelings resembling those of human beings. A measure of our civilization's decline is that we do not laugh at this sort of thing anymore, but glumly accept it as part of the intellectual background noise of everyday life.

But while we *Globe* reporters in the 1950s liked to look down on the silliness of the *Star* and the *Tely*, it was no fun to be beaten by them. And we often were beaten, not only because they outmanned us but because they took local news seriously and we, for the most part, did not. Being up against them was both comic and terrifying. Once, when there was a strike of truck drivers in the Hamilton area, I happened to be spending three weeks there as holiday replacement for our regular Hamilton reporter — or bureau chief, as the *Globe* liked to say. When a newspaper calls someone a "bureau chief" it usually means he's not chief of anything except a secretary and perhaps a translator. In this case the bureau chief didn't have even a secretary; my only staff, when I arrived to handle this assignment, my first out-of-town posting, was a middle-aged part-time photographer of dubious ability but firm opinions. He belonged to a Pentecostal sect, and he seemed anxious to express his harsh view of promiscuous youth and save younger colleagues from the sins of the flesh (in my case, he needn't have worried). We usually met only briefly, when he was taking a head-and-shoulders picture to illustrate some interview I'd written, but on one occasion we spent a long, lonely evening together, and in memory it seems typical of my reporting days on the *Globe*.

There were rumours of violence on the truckers' picket lines, and one night my photographer and I set out to discover the truth. We travelled in his car, an asthmatic Morris Minor that had probably not reached 60 mph in its best years and now seemed barely able to keep going at all. Meanwhile, the *Star* and the *Tely* had been alerted to the story and had each sent to Hamilton several reporter-photographer teams. Once in a while, as the Pentecostalist and I tootled down the slow lane toward what we hoped would be the action, we were passed — *whoosh* — by a gigantic Buick or Olds with a *Star* or *Tely* man at the wheel. One of the *Tely* men was Val Sears, who seemed just as amused by the idea of striking truckers as he was to be, a few years later, by the federal politicians he watched from his position as the living legend of the Ottawa press gallery.

At the first two places my photographer and I went, there were no picket lines — just darkened truck depots, apparently shut down for the night. We pressed on. From time to time I got out of the car at a phone booth, called the Ontario Provincial Police, and inquired where, if anywhere, trouble might be found. The desk officers provided a few suggestions, but either they were mistaken or we got there too late. That night, we not only didn't see any violence, we didn't see any picket lines — *and we didn't see any truckers*. The next day the *Star* and the *Tely* had stories about threatened violence that appeared to me more imaginary than otherwise, but at least their reporters — unless they were total liars — had found some truckers and actually spoken to them. I never did even that. By eleven o'clock it was obvious that we weren't going to get anything that would be worth putting in the paper. I phoned my editors with this sad news and they told me to go home to bed. If they were annoyed with me, they didn't let me know about it.

I found many of the editors kind and helpful, but in the years before the American Newspaper Guild finally organized the *Globe*, management paid the reporters poorly and used them callously. Sometimes our shifts were arranged — not maliciously, but unthinkingly — so that a reporter didn't have time to sleep. One night I finished work at 2:30 a.m. on the rewrite desk and then had to go home, go to bed, get up again and be downtown by 8 a.m. to cover the Santa Claus parade. On weekends there was something called "overnight police," which meant you were responsible for anything that might come up at the police station from Saturday morning until Sunday afternoon. Those who enjoyed intimate friendships with police sergeants could handle this chore from home, but someone comparatively new to the business had

to show up at headquarters and sit in the press room, trying
to work out the meaning, if any, of the squawks that could
be heard over the police radio.

Sometimes I shared the press room with the young Sinclair
Stevens, who was working his way through law school with
part-time reporting for the *Star*; all I can remember of him
is his fierce hatred of Eleanor Roosevelt and his habit of
climbing onto his desk and sleeping through most of Saturday
night. "If something happens you'll wake me, right?" Something rarely did. On at least one occasion the other reporter
in the room was Peter Gzowski, a University of Toronto
student and part-time *Tely* reporter. He had a book by John
Milton with him, and I — assuming he was reading it by
choice — asked if he liked it. "Hell, no," he said, "I'm a Joe
College. It's on the course." And so, encountering for the
first time one of the best journalists of my generation, I also
caught a glimpse of one of his paradoxical qualities. Then as
now, Gzowski rather liked to be thought less intelligent than
he really was and perhaps already dreamt of being considered
just one of the guys.

IN THOSE DAYS the *Globe* was more an anthology than a
newspaper — it was building its reputation for seriousness
on the talents of journalists who never in their lives entered
the *Globe* building and in some cases didn't even know we
published their writing. In the *Globe* you could read, carefully chosen, the best stories from the New York *Times*, the
London *Observer*, Reuters, the Associated Press, the Canadian Press, maybe Agence France Presse. We had a direct
line to the New York *Times* office and an editor who sat in
their newsroom, selecting material for us; he kept the line
running hard all afternoon and most of the evening. For
years we were allowed to put the credit "Special to The New
York Times and The Globe and Mail" on the *Times* articles,

a shameless piece of fiction. Finally the *Times* told us to knock it off and call the stories what they were — *Times* stories we bought in syndication.

This material, our own coverage of Ottawa, the sports pages, and a few columnists made the *Globe* readable; nobody much cared how well we covered murders and natural disasters. Certainly the editors seldom gave signs of undue concern. The first city editor I served as a reporter was a man of such consummate amiability that it was impossible to annoy or even ruffle him. He moved slowly when he moved at all, and often he was so late in handing assignments to reporters that by the time we arrived at the scene of a news story everyone else had departed. One winter day he sent me hurrying by cab to a fire at a huge factory in the west end of Toronto. When I arrived the smoke and flames were long gone and the building was beautifully encased in thick rolls of grey ice, like the palace of the Queen of Winter in a ballet; the firemen were trying to re-roll their ice-stiffened hoses and get them back on the rigs. They informed me that the *Star* and *Tely* reporters had been there some time before, and that even the deputy fire chief — the man who could tell me how the fire might have started and what the damage might be — was now also back at his office, thawing himself out. I returned to the *Globe* and rounded up the details by phone.

Once, in a bar, one of the best *Telegram* reporters, Dick O'Hagan — he later served both Lester Pearson and Pierre Trudeau as press secretary — remarked that *Tely* people regarded the *Globe* as an essentially amateur outfit. I could see his point. Certainly we seldom knew what to do about a murder, and on the coverage of lake swims — in 1954 Toronto people became unaccountably hysterical when a young woman named Marilyn Bell proved she could swim right across Lake Ontario — we showed no enterprise at all. We thought the evening papers made fools of themselves on stories like the Bell swim, which was true; but we did nothing that was comparably audacious.

The *Globe* educated me not only in reporting but in the subjects I was assigned to write about. The months I worked at City Hall were particularly educational, and ever since I've urged anyone who wants to understand public life to begin with a year or so spent hanging around municipal government. Among the aldermen and the city clerks, politics has the sharp tang of reality: policies that seem abstract and theoretical in Ottawa are given flesh and blood at City Hall. A developer's $100-million project, and the unfortunate neighbourhood standing in its way, may depend on a vote by some simpleton who understands neither the project nor the district and who in any case was elected by a community so apathetic that most citizens don't bother to vote.

William Kilbourn, who served as an alderman at City Hall some years after I was there, called local elections "name-recognition contests," and that's what they still often are. A total incompetent, with no public record, could become well-known to the voters (those who actually deigned to enter the polling booth) simply by putting his name on the ballot year after year, until the incumbents ahead of him resigned or died. Famous by then, he would more or less inherit a seat on council, and — barring criminal malfeasance — keep it until retirement. Toronto is by certain measures an excellent city today, but those who have dealt with municipal politics on intimate terms understand that this is by accident as much as design.

Still, the system of electing the cretinous to public office proved a great advantage to me. In my day politicians came to their jobs so extravagantly ignorant of the workings of municipal government that even the simplest procedures had to be explained to them, over and over, by the city solicitors. And as this happened a journalist could pick up a good deal of knowledge. When I got to City Hall I didn't even know what "enabling legislation" meant, and I couldn't imagine such a thing as a "legal non-conforming use." By the time I left I could give you a ten-minute lecture on either of them.

At City Hall there was nothing like the easygoing corruption of the sports beat, though once I was given a special price on a TV set by an alderman who was also an appliance dealer (poor man, he spent most of his time at City Hall campaigning unsuccessfully to make garburetors legal — not for the sake of his business, he said, but to ease the lives of Toronto housewives). The reporters, however, were as cynical about city politicians as sports writers had been about athletes and promoters. In the generation just ahead of ours there was one beloved *Globe* reporter, Dick Sheridan, who lavished infinite Christian charity on the local politicians; he was so devoted to their welfare that sometimes, during a debate, he would send a note to a politician who had made a mistake, advising him to reverse himself before the debate ended. Usually, the man would gratefully comply.

Dick explained this to me as part of his job, but the reporters of my generation saw things differently. Our motto was: no tolerance for fools. We spent as much time as we could writing down the inanities of the aldermen and putting them in print. There was one *Tely* reporter, Ray Hill, whose special talent was for creating an imaginary controversy and getting politicians to make foolish comments on it. If things were dull and an account appeared on the wire about a rabid dog biting a child in some city within a hundred miles of Toronto, Ray would go into a little trance, smile, and utter the word "epidemic." In a moment he'd be cruising the City Hall corridors, looking for politicians he could question. They, of course, were desperate to see their names in print — particularly if another name-recognition contest was coming up — and would say anything. Soon Ray would be typing out a piece about politicians viewing with alarm the possibility of a rabies epidemic, demanding a report by the health department, speculating that it might be necessary to take precautionary methods in the schools, etc. An hour later this story would be printed on the front page of the *Tely*, and five minutes after that the *Star* man would receive a phone call from an angry editor demanding to know why the *Star* had missed the rabies epidemic threatening Toronto. A day later, all would be forgotten.

It was Ray who explained to me a peculiar City Hall institution, The Truce. Sometimes, say at two o'clock on a Friday afternoon, the reporters in the press room would collectively declare a truce and simply shut down coverage of City Hall for the rest of the day. Some would head for their cottages, others for a bar; no more than one or two would remain in the building. None of us was a student of philosophy, but we had somehow stumbled on this practical answer to Berkeley's question: does a tree, falling in the forest, make a noise when there is no one there to hear it? Our answer was No. It was understood that if something happened that absolutely demanded reporting — say, a murder in the mayor's office — then whoever was still in the press room would get the news to all three papers. Otherwise, nothing would go out. As Ray solemnly explained to me, the most serious crime imaginable at City Hall was Breaking the Truce, a crime no one had so far dared to commit.

On other occasions we found a simpler method of curtailing the news: we could simply leave the room where a meeting was taking place, thereby making it — for publicity purposes — a non-meeting. Late one afternoon three of us sat at the press table in the parks committee meeting as a headline-hungry alderman harangued his fellow committee members about issue after issue. He wasn't making a great deal of sense but there seemed no way to stop him. Finally, one of the other committee members — Alderman Donald Somerville, later the mayor for a short time — came over to the press table and, *sotto voce*, addressed the three of us. "Look, that guy's just talking for you fellows. He doesn't believe any of that crap. But the way he's going, we'll be here till midnight. If you boys were to leave, I bet he'd shut up." We glanced at each other, silently gathered pads and pencils, and adjourned to the press room next door. A few minutes later the meeting ended.

Reporters routinely protected politicians from their own excesses in those days, but occasionally a reporter who wandered over from another beat would upset this arrangement. It was commonplace for Frederick G. ("Big Daddy") Gardiner — the first chairman of Metropolitan Toronto and effectively the creator of that level of government — to get drunk at evening meetings and do a good deal of shouting. This would always be ignored in the next day's paper. I didn't know about this arrangement when, replacing the regular Metro reporter, I covered a dinner meeting at which Gardiner addressed some citizens disturbed by plans for an expressway near their property. No alcohol was served before or during dinner, but after the plates were taken away and the talk began, Gardiner continued to drink from his coffee cup. Indeed, he was still drinking from it an hour and a half after every other cup in the room had been removed by the waitresses. As he drank he grew steadily louder, more abusive, and less coherent. The next morning my report in the *Globe* began: "'You're full of wet hay,' screamed Metro Chairman Fred Gardiner last night in reply to a…" I didn't mention alcohol — after all, I had seen none — but I went on to describe his behaviour at some length.

This caused much more of a stir around Metro headquarters than I had anticipated. The day it appeared our regular Metro reporter commended me for what he called my "courage," and reported that Gardiner had become hysterical when reading my piece. A few weeks later, though, one of his assistants passed along the word that he was no longer drinking quite so much on public occasions.

In the 1950s City Hall reporters often ate lunch with the mayor, Nathan Phillips, at Diana Sweets restaurant on Yonge

Street. I was young enough to be rather in awe of someone holding that title, but most of the reporters refused to hide their contempt for him. They agreed with Fred Gardiner's assessment that Phillips was silly and sentimental and that his approach to the voters (he always claimed services could be improved without raising taxes) was dishonest. Nate, as everyone called him, was a spectacular beneficiary of the name-recognition system, having spent two decades as an undistinguished but omnipresent alderman before floating finally into the mayor's office. He was the first Jewish mayor of the city and during one mayoral campaign marked himself as something of an original by coming out strongly in favour of the right of Christian churches to place a Christmas creche bearing a likeness of the infant Jesus on the plaza in front of City Hall. Most Gentiles at City Hall, believing in the separation of church and state, opposed the idea; but with Nate behind it, the creche was accepted and became an annual ornament at City Hall.

Everyone ackowledged that Phillips was a duffer, incapable of running anything, and that the city government was really directed by another member of our lunch group, Controller Ford Brand. A former printer and a member of the CCF, Brand belonged to that Depression-bred generation of cigarette smokers who would smoke half a cigarette, extinguish it carefully, and replace the butt in the pack for later use. He was thoughtful and shrewd, and he spent much of his time keeping Phillips and the city government out of trouble. Those who know nothing of human nature will assume that he found this work — well-paid and socially useful as it was — satisfying. In fact, I believe he spent some part of each meeting asking himself: how is it that this idiot is mayor and I am not? Eventually emotion conquered prudence, he ran against Phillips, lost, and retired from politics. By then Phillips — who loved to call himself "the mayor of all the people" — was a beloved figure, everywhere except at City Hall. But we who regarded him as a bumpkin didn't

ttawa; they, not I, would naturally be assigned to write a
olumn. Besides, I was getting old. I was twenty-two, and for
ome reason my twenty-second birthday was the most
oubling of my life, before or since. It seemed to signal that
dolescence was finally over, and that it was no longer enough
ust to be both faster and younger than most of the people
round me. I had to get going, and do something. All that
made a bit of sense, but the course I then chose made no
ense whatever. I went to work editing material I didn't care
bout for a magazine that I'd never before read and wouldn't
even have picked up if I hadn't been paid to do so.

understand that he had a larger vision tha
was beavering away, all those years, at his pe
City Hall, and he left behind not only Viljo
1965 City Hall (a building that was as respon
the revival of downtown Toronto) but also tl
ful Nathan Phillips Square in front of it.
Gardiner's ghost, on the other hand, has to t
the Gardiner Expressway, the ugliest highway

I THOUGHT of Nate, Big Daddy, and Ford
young woman from the Carleton University jou
came to interview me one day in 1983. She
paper on the lives of journalists, and at the m
pre-occupied with the word "glamour." Seve
had sternly informed her that, contrary to wh
ple might imagine, there was nothing at all gla
journalism — it was, they said, mainly a life c
argued the opposite case. True, there's some c
there's also drudgery in the life of all those pe
cians, movie stars, novelists — whom the publi
orous. The fact is that a newspaper reporter wi
all will come into frequent contact with some
manding figures of the day. Those men I had l
the 1950s were preparing the Toronto of th
1980s, the place that foreign magazines are a
miraculous; I had the great good luck to eave
they did their work. What could be more gl
more interesting, than that?

Even so, I must have found newspaper work u
because on four separate occasions I quit my ne
and went elsewhere. The first time this happ
because, after two years or so on the *Globe* i
began to think that in the near future the edito
likely to let me do anything I hadn't already d
were many reporters with better education and
— they, not I, deserved to cover the Ontario gov

FOUR

*M*y life as a hack

WHEN I THINK of the life I lived in the 1950s, the word "hack" appears in bold type before my eyes. In truth, much of what I did in those years of apprenticeship was as honest as I could make it, but the material that gives the period its peculiar flavour in my memory is the work I did without believing in it for a second. Once, for *Canadian Bride* magazine, I ghosted a young wife's account of decorating her first apartment with little money but much flair — and loved doing it, incidentally. (Ever since, I've envied professional ghost writers their ability to dart anonymously through the shadows behind their employers.) I wrote a profile of Foster Hewitt, whom I never met, for a magazine that an oil company gave away free to truck drivers. I wrote most of a travel magazine that never appeared, about places I had never been. I have a slip of paper indicating that in 1955 *Design Engineering* magazine paid me $23 for something — I think it was an article on developing a tougher form of cellophane. That same year, when I was between jobs, I ground out for *The*

Globe and Mail an entire section of what journalists now call advertorial — twenty pages of outrageous puffery about the retail jewellery business, a form of enterprise to which I otherwise have given not a single moment's thought. When the articles editor of *Maclean's*, Ian Sclanders, suggested that I write on the pressing national problem of level crossings ("Bob, the one in Saint John is a *scandal!*"), I did not question his sanity but instead accepted the assignment. I didn't complete it — there are subjects so boring that even the most desperate young writer finally can't face up to them — but I did write for the house organ of the Royal York Hotel and the company magazine of Canadian Industries Limited. I stopped just short of signing on with a cousin of mine who proposed to start up a tout sheet for buyers of penny gold stocks and wanted me as editorial director.

All these things I did for money, for fun, or because someone asked me and I was curious. I was, to put it mildly, available. But surely the oddest interlude of all those years was the eleven months I spent working full-time on (it seems peculiar just to set down the title) *Canadian Homes and Gardens*. As my father sensibly pointed out at the time, in the light of my interests *Canadian Homes* was the worst possible place for me. In 1954 I had no home except the one I lived in with my parents, no garden, and no immediate plans to acquire either. I wasn't even interested in house plants. But when Jim Knight, a fellow *Globe* reporter, mentioned my name to an editor at *Canadian Homes*, Frank Moritsugu, and Moritsugu offered me the job of copy editor, I accepted.

Between my beginnings at the *Globe* in 1950, and the day in 1968 when I became editor of *Saturday Night*, I held eight different full-time jobs — nine if you count freelance writing a full-time job, which I did during the one delightful and mildly frightening year I devoted to it. In those days journalists tended to move from place to place faster than they do now, so I didn't acquire any particular reputation as a job-hopper, but there were two odd things about my employment record. One was was my habit of going to work everywhere twice. I worked twice on the *Globe* (1950-54 and 1955-56), twice at Maclean-Hunter (1954-55 and 1962-64), and twice at the Toronto *Star* (1958-62 and 1964-68). I even worked twice for *Mayfair*, once (1955) when it was owned by Maclean-Hunter and once (1957) when it briefly sailed the dangerous seas of independent publishing before sinking forever. At the time, each change seemed logical, but as I glance back at the list of my jobs a speeded-up silent-movie scene appears before my eyes — a man is dashing through the same revolving doors again and again, forever being toasted at farewell parties and then, soon after, showing up again in the same office. Sometimes, when I left a job, the boss would generously say that I'd be welcome to come back if things didn't work out. But even when no one said that, I usually came back anyway.

In those years I was fired just once, when Maclean-Hunter sold *Mayfair* and the new owner said he wanted only the magazine, not the staff (a year later he changed his mind about me, and I went to work for him). Even then, Maclean-Hunter didn't throw me out on the street. I was offered either a job writing circulation-promotion copy for *Maclean's* or the assistant editorship of *Canadian Aviation*. I had the sense to know that neither could possibly lead to anything interesting, except by the most circuitous route: editors, being ruthless snobs, immediately write off anyone who does something second-class, like turning out promotion letters or working on a trade magazine. That year, though I was planning to marry soon, I decided not to accept either of Maclean-Hunter's offers and instead try to get on the *Globe* for the second time, which I managed to do in a couple of months.

The other oddity about my life as an employee is that I seem never to have had just one job. There was always, in the background, some other work I was doing in the hours when I wasn't earning my regular salary — a bit of magazine writing when I worked on a newspaper, some newspaper writing when I worked on a magazine, always a certain amount of broadcasting for the CBC, often something in the book business. I was habitually over-employed.

My family responsibilities naturally had a good deal to do with the pace of my work. In 1956 I married Jocelyn Dingman, who was then, like me, a reporter on *The Globe and Mail*. We had two children, James in 1958 and Margaret in 1960. We divorced in 1970 and that year I married Geraldine Sherman, a radio producer at the CBC. Our daughter Rachel was born in 1971, Sarah in 1974. Jocelyn died in 1976. These were, of course, the truly important events in my life, as compared to the events of my career that are the subject of this book. But they influenced my work for the obvious economic reasons that anyone with a family will understand. Perhaps my frenzied activity was also influenced by anxiety over the future, or boredom in my main job. In any case, I eventually elevated this practice to the level of a principle. By the early 1960s I firmly believed that it was unwise for any journalist — certainly it was unwise for someone with my ambitions — to have only one employer. I decided that those whose working lives extend beyond a single corporation are much more likely to perform independently and honestly, because they aren't owned by one boss. Put bluntly, they can quit when they need to. Twice in my life, I've found it necessary to resign from an excellent job for professional reasons, and on both occasions I was grateful that outside assignments made me far less anxious than I might otherwise have been. Moreover, working outside the office — moonlighting, as it's sometimes called — gives a journalist a chance to shape his own career. When I worked on the *Globe* in the 1950s, it had no use for me as an art critic, but there were other publications — *Mayfair, Canadian Art* — where I could begin writing about painting and sculpture.

Even so, there were moments, particularly in the 1970s and 1980s, when I wondered whether this lifelong course had been wisely chosen. When I was working on *Saturday Night*

I never felt I gave the magazine less than a normal week's labour, and often I spent fifty or sixty hours on editing and writing for it. But what if I'd dropped my weekly newspaper column, my radio show (in the early 1970s) or my TV show (in the 1980s), and the contributions to books and other odd jobs? What if I'd spent *all* my time obsessively working on *Saturday Night*? Would that have produced the financial success that the magazine so spectacularly failed to achieve? I'll never know, because I was too shrewd or too frightened — or both — to make a total commitment to any institution.

I LIKE TO THINK I took the *Canadian Homes* job in 1954 because of the challenge offered by the new world of magazines, and that was true. It was also true that there was a twenty-dollar raise involved, which moved me up from fifty-five to seventy-five dollars a week. And there was another attraction, one I had forgotten until I recently came across a letter I wrote at the time: my new position was a day job, the first of my lifetime and a novelty I looked forward to.

A conversation I had that month illustrates how much the world has changed for the better since the 1950s. On the street I ran into Frank Tumpane, then one of the best-known newspaper columnists in Toronto. He said he'd heard about my new job and he asked if it were true that the editor of *Canadian Homes* was a woman. I said she was. He said: "I could *never* work for a woman." I could, but working for this particular woman presented pleasures and problems of an exceptional sort. Jean McKinley, the editor of *Canadian Homes and Gardens*, ran her thin and unsuccessful service magazine in a style that wouldn't have been inappropriate for some lush American publication like *Vogue* or *House and Garden*. She had an imperious manner with her staff, she walked the halls of Maclean-Hunter like a queen, and she delivered opinions on almost everything with a confidence that would have made Simone de Beauvoir blush.

Jean believed in modern management. She believed in

memos, and lines of authority, and carefully supervised staff
development. A linguistic pioneer, she spoke of *relating* in
an *insightful* way and rarely delivered a sentence that did not
contain the word "concept." Her dealings with the people
working for her were emotionally charged, and at some point
or other every man who worked for Jean fell in love with her,
if only for ten minutes. She was the first woman I ever saw
use chunky jewellery as a rhetorical device: in meetings her
gigantic rings and bracelets would come crashing down on
the board-room table, underlining her views and cowing her
colleagues. She fascinated everyone who worked for her. We
gossiped about her constantly, and with happy intensity; I
have never known a happier staff.

Above all, we talked about her love affair with industrial
psychology. In the 1950s, a more innocent age, many employers and employees believed that psychologists could make
people happy and productive in their offices and factories.
This belief had no more passionate advocate than Jean
McKinley. Often it seemed that for days at a time she spoke
of little else, and that the minor details of putting out a magazine — covers, articles, photographs — were as nothing beside
the unfolding mysteries of group dynamics. She had a psychologist named Jim Hickling on a sort of retainer, and she
sent her senior staff to see him, one by one, for intellectual
and emotional assessment. Around the office his name
became a transitive verb, as in "Have you been hickled yet?"

The reports that came back from Hickling's firm, Canadian
Personnel Consultants, were theoretically confidential; in
fact their contents soon became known to just about everyone, and never failed to heighten the tension and excitement
in the office. One man was appointed managing editor just
before he went off to be hickled. His report, when it came
down a few weeks later, said he had many good qualities but
because of his personality should not be allowed to manage
anyone. This quickly seeped through the office and we knew
that he was certain to be reduced almost immediately to

something like gardening editor. I still have my copy of the memo to all staff — a masterpiece of its kind, everyone acknowledged — in which Jean explained that, while the chap in question would still be *called* managing editor, someone else was now to manage things.

Those who were hickled saw it as a badge of honour and a conversational subject of great interest; those to whom it hadn't happened yet were regarded with a certain pity, like virgins in a girls' school. A few years later I would have declined to be hickled, on the grounds that no corporation should be permitted access to an employee's private thoughts. But in 1954 I was still young and stupid enough to see this sort of thing as a creative experiment in personnel work.

So I spent two days in Hickling's offices on Bloor Street. I was given a Rorschach test and a thematic apperception test (where the stories you make up about illustrations reveal your innermost desires), some IQ tests, and many more. I even did an aesthetic appreciation test, and failed miserably. The tester displayed pairs of smudged reproductions of drawings which seemed to me uniformly uninteresting; I was asked to choose the better drawing in each case. By the standards of the people who made up the test, I picked incorrectly in most instances.

A couple of weeks later Jean McKinley called me to her office to discuss my report. I wasn't supposed to *see* it, she said, but I could glance at it. She handed it across her desk. Just then her phone rang and I — graciously respecting her privacy — stepped out of her office, report in hand, as if to read it in the hall. Instead I ran to my own office, quickly retyped it (the Xerox had not been invented), and returned, breathless, to her office. What she and I said about Hickling's conclusions is lost to me now, but as I write I have his report before me — the only written attempt, so far as I know, at an objective assessment of the twenty-two-year-old me.

We all laughed at it — of course I showed it around the office — and today it seems to me silly in some places and

crude in others. Having since written a few hundred thousand
words on art, I am naturally disinclined to agree with its view
of my aesthetic sense, though no doubt there are certain
artists who would be willing to endorse its judgment. In
general, though, this odd little document, now thirty-four
years old, seems to me more often shrewd than not.

"In intelligence, Mr. Fulford can be classified as superior."
This wasn't quite the compliment it seemed — most of the
staff tested high, and one chap (whom I didn't regard as
bright at all) smugly topped me by mentioning that Hickling
rated him "near genius." Of me, Hickling said: "He is very
alert and appears better at tasks which require quick, accurate
thinking, than sustained concentration." How did Hickling
know that? I've often felt I lacked the patience for long-range
work, and decades after Hickling's report people were still
saying that I was better in the sprints than the marathon —
in fact, a remark like that about me was attributed to Morley
Callaghan in a book published as recently as 1986. The Hickling report was positive about my language skills. "His strongest aptitude is in the use of correct English, where he scores
in the 80th percentile." Hickling enthusiastically discussed
my vocabulary, but then: "In both his ability to think in ideas
and numbers he is about average. This holds true for his
mechanical understanding and his spatial perception. His
eye for design is good, surpassing 88% of college non-art
students. In art appreciation he is surprisingly low..." Hickling suggested I might in the end be better suited to a magazine with some literary content, such as *Maclean's*.

All that having been settled, he got down to the interesting
stuff, the sort of thing I'd later work over in detail with the
gang at the office. "Mr. Fulford...is somewhat introverted —
is stimulated more by his inner life than by the environment.
While he shows a good degree of intellectual empathy, this
is probably not transmitted with the spontaneity and genuine-
ness which would make him a ready mixer." Guilty as charged,
Your Honour — I still find sincerity the hardest quality to

fake, and (to quote J.K. Galbraith) I never put in the spontaneity till the third draft. The report went on: "The impression is that he would be effective socially within a group sharing his vocational interests." I find it a little creepy that he was so right about me so early — in the years that followed, I almost never made a good friend of anyone who was not connected (at least by marriage) to my work. "With strangers and people in different walks of life he is probably reserved and somewhat withdrawn." All too true at that time, less so in later years.

Now Hickling moved to more dangerous ground. "A resentment to authority seems fairly deeply ingrained in Mr. Fulford. This resentment, however, is well controlled and he likely is not aware of it." I was entirely aware of it but thought it prudent to hide my views from a psychologist in the pay of my employer. "Rather he accepts authority fairly readily, but compensates by striving to excel." At this point Sigmund Freud was apparently called in as a consultant: "That is, instead of consciously resenting his father (the basis of his conflict) he accepts him, not merely as an authoritarian figure, but as a rival. Thus he has an inner striving or need to be more successful in the journalistic, publishing field than his father. As the resentment is deeply buried and well controlled, the result is a healthy ambition and need for recognition in his work. Apart from this, Mr. Fulford appears well adjusted..." In other words, what we have here is a neurotic whose resentment and anger have somehow been turned into ambition. It sounds, I admit, like Psych 1-A, but it also sounds more or less like the truth.

WHEN I ARRIVED at *Canadian Homes* I moved into a cubicle only recently vacated by Zena Cherry, who was then on one of the lower rungs of the career that culminated in her job as society columnist at the *Globe*. I discovered I had to buckle down to work right away, because the next couple of issues were behind schedule. In magazine work that's pretty well always the case, but at the time it sounded alarming, and I had to learn quickly how to write captions, heads, subheads, and something new to me, "copy blocks." Preparing copy blocks wasn't exactly writing, but it wasn't quite *not* writing either. What you had to do was fill some arbitrary space designed by the art director — for example, 17 lines at 35 characters per line, then nine lines at 21 characters — without making it obvious to the readers that there was nothing to say about whatever it was you were pretending to say something. At *Canadian Homes* I discovered truly what it means to be a hack. Someone who fabricates opinions for the benefit of an employer — writes editorials without believing them, for instance — is simply a liar. A hack is different. A true hack writes what he doesn't believe about something that doesn't interest him. I wrote or rewrote articles about recovering sofas, and baking bread, and what plants you should plant at which time of year, and how to build a birdhouse. It was fascinating to learn that one could do it, but after nearly a year I was ready for a real job.

I found one upstairs at *Mayfair*, another Maclean-Hunter magazine that no longer exists. The man who brought me there, saving me from articles about compost heaps and bungalows, was easily the most miscast editor in Canadian journalism. At Maclean-Hunter there was a widespread belief, totally without foundation, that any professional journalist could write or edit on any subject. That's why I was an appropriate copy editor for *Canadian Homes* and — though ignorant about aeronautics or airplanes — was offered a job on *Canadian Aviation*. But even within this bizarre context, the case of *Mayfair* and Eric Hutton was exceptional. *Mayfair* was an upscale monthly for women interested in fashion, society, travel, and culture. Eric Hutton was pulled off *Maclean's* to run it, and found himself editing a magazine he would not normally read, directed at people he would not care to meet. Hutton was intensely interested in women — in fact, the only aspect of him I didn't enjoy was his sexual boasting — but he knew nothing of fashion, society, or the kind of culture *Mayfair* was supposed to celebrate. He soldiered on, though, explaining along the way that he was an unsuccessful old hack — he used that word about himself, and never claimed to be a journalist — whose magazines were all eventually shot out from under him. When I worked with him two of the magazines in his past, *National Home Monthly* and *Magazine Digest*, were in the grave; by the time he retired in 1969, *Mayfair* and the *Star Weekly* had joined them.

For Hutton, magazine work was entirely a matter of technique; his highest praise always involved the word "craftsman." He claimed no expertise, in any subject, and had no message for the world. He wrote only for money, but he took a perverse pride in even his most squalid accomplishments. Once he was the ghost-writer for an American cancer doctor's book, and he loved to tell how the entire edition had been thrown into the Hudson River by U.S. public health officials; the doctor, it seems, was judged a dangerous quack.

Barbara Moon (who is now senior editor of *Saturday Night*) and I were both assistant editors to Hutton, and ever since then our friendship has been based partly on the strange time we spent with him. Barbara had less to learn from him than I did — she was already an accomplished *Maclean's* writer — but she enjoyed watching the interplay between the Falstaffian old pro and the wide-eyed, twenty-three-year-old innocent. In the style of the old journeyman, Hutton took a rather casual attitude to the facts and regarded "over-researching" as a danger to magazine work. Once he looked in on me while I was rewriting a freelancer's article about how all the lights in a theatre went out one night and a famous actor, Barry Morse, ad libbed eloquently in total darkness for fifteen minutes. I mentioned that I was about to call Morse to check the story. Hutton looked thoughtful. "I wouldn't call him," he said. "Some stories are too good to check. Just run it."

I, of course, came to *Mayfair* with grandiose ideas about what it might become. About that time I was friendly with

Paul Desmond, who played alto saxophone in Dave Brubeck's quartet. When Paul asked me what sort of magazine *Mayfair* was, I said — overstating things a little — that it was going to be a combination of *The New Yorker*, *Vogue*, and *Holiday*, the last of which was then a literate travel magazine. Well, perhaps that was our goal. The reality was less impressive, but some issues weren't too awful. And what seems important to me now is that at *Mayfair*, with Hutton's help, I started to figure out how to cross the line from reporter to writer.

Hutton made me realize that magazine writing, much more than the sort of newspaper work I'd done, involved literary standards and a certain literary ambition — though of course he'd never say "literary." He could point out, unerringly, where a passage of prose went dead, or where the writer delivered a certain fact at the wrong time, or where the purpose of the article got mislaid. He did this for all of the articles I wrote for *Mayfair*, and partly as a result my travel stories on Florence and Dublin, and my profile of the great Stratford Festival designer, Tanya Moiseiwitsch, were the first of my pieces that approached good magazine standards. Offhandedly and without pretension, Hutton conducted, day after day, the best seminar on non-fiction I've attended. By taking me into the techniques of writing he made me more conscious of the possibilities of my own work and at the same time helped me to think critically about literature of all kinds.

He also, by a fluke, gave me a chance to become an art critic. For a few years I'd been studying art on my own — in books, in European and North American museums, and in conversation with Toronto artists — and I wanted to write about it. *Mayfair* had a column, "Gallery and Studio" (earlier it was written by Zena Cherry), which now lacked a columnist. I volunteered, Hutton told me to go ahead, and I produced half a dozen pieces on current Canadian art. Years later, when I was fairly well-known as an art critic and had on one occasion even written a whole issue of *Canadian Art*,

Hutton said, "I created a monster." That was his little joke, but he did indeed have a great effect on me. I never shared his cynicism, partly because Gould was still a shining example of something important to me but also because in those years I was increasingly — and idealistically — influenced by the urgent moral passions behind the great jazz musicians I was also studying. It was Hutton, the ultimate hack, who helped me escape from hackery; but it was the musicians who told me why I should do so.

FIVE

Nights at the Colonial

DURING THE AMERICAN primaries of 1988, when a reporter asked Senator Paul Simon to name the most influential book of his life, he cited *Black Boy*, the autobiography of the American novelist Richard Wright. Reading Simon's reply, I remembered a moment in my own life. It was 1946 and I was giving an aural book report on *Black Boy* to my grade-nine class in the library at Malvern. I was describing Wright's life, and at one point I realized that — to the embarrassment of the teacher and my classmates — my eyes were filling with tears. The story I was telling them had to do with some southern rednecks casually inflicting danger on Wright during his childhood: when he was riding his bicycle a carload of young white men forced him off the road, nearly killing him. The cruelty of the life he had lived touched me, and for the first time I was emotionally caught by the idea of racial feeling as a malign force in human life; and, perhaps on a deeper level, of children and other innocents as the victims of that poison and others like it.

In the mid-1940s my political views, such as they were, reflected wartime liberal propaganda in pure form. The standard public line, adhered to by all newspapers and politicians, was that Good (the democracies and their allies, the Soviets) was defeating Evil (the Nazis and their allies) and that when this task was accomplished we would enter an era of world-wide peace, tolerance, and social justice. Our newspapers may have acknowledged that the Soviet system was imperfect, but we were led to believe that the imperfections were minor and certainly would be corrected in due time. The idea that a vast new empire was being built, and that the Soviets would come out of the war far more powerful than they had entered it, was so crazy that no one — at least no one I knew about — would have dreamt of stating it. There was little mention in public of the further bad news, that many millions of people and large sections of Europe — formerly Central Europe or Middle Europe, now called Eastern Europe — had just been condemned to at least two generations of foreign oppression. In that period, with the war finally over, peace was a gleaming and perfect thing. Not to be an optimist was close to treason.

I was old enough to receive the everyday nonsense of propaganda through the newspapers and the radio stations, but not old enough to see it for the wishful thinking that it was. In my mind, at least, it was as if history were coming to an end — a happy end. I looked forward confidently to a time of progress and racial amity. By then I was certainly a liberal, but — in the curious way of many Canadians in that period — I was an *American* liberal who happened to have been born and to live in Canada. I had read *PM*, the radical New York daily, which my father brought home from the office for a couple of years; it had taught me the American meaning of words such as "intolerance" and "discrimination," and had implanted in me a juvenile version of the Rooseveltian liberalism that dominated American politics. *Black Boy* took me some distance toward the reality behind that vision, and I've never since lost my interest in its subject. Years later I reviewed all the early books of James Baldwin, and for a time regarded his *Notes of a Native Son* (its title echoing Wright's famous novel) as the most powerful book of modern American essays. I met Baldwin, interviewed him on television, and liked him. Behind the grave, stately essays of his early years there was a small, ugly, and clearly loveable homosexual, who gesticulated wildly as he talked and had an unusual way of closing the social distance between himself and anyone he might be speaking to: in the middle of a conversation he would suddenly seize your hand to empha- size the point he was making.

But it wasn't race itself that turned out to be a major obsession of mine. It was a subject linked to race: jazz. Wright's book, embodying the black experience, was one way into that subject, and others appeared about the same time. Over the years I came to understand that my affection for jazz was historical, biographical, and social as well as musical. The life of every great jazz musician could be studied as a parable of modern history, and through such lives I learned about deprivation, courage, compromise, and personal integrity — and about how art can express these things.

The names of the musicians entered my life through a curious book called *Really the Blues*, a notoriously unreliable but evocative autobiography by Milton Mezzrow, an obscure clarinetist who knew Louis Armstrong, Sidney Bechet, and other major figures. Mezzrow's book, lent to me by a friend of my father's, introduced to me the disturbing but tantaliz- ing idea that the popular music I knew about — the big- band records of Benny Goodman, Glenn Miller, Tommy Dorsey, and the rest — was no more than a pale shadow of something grander and far more authentic, something whose edges I had barely glimpsed. Mezzrow made me hungry to know more about this phenomenon, and I had the great good luck to make a friend at Malvern who was an admirer of Duke Ellington. He informed me that Ellington was not, as many assumed, a band leader like the others. He was, simply, incomparable — or, at least, had been recently. My friend explained that the greatest days of the Ellington band were now a few years in the past, and then conducted me through a detailed study of the 1940 and 1941 Ellington records. Over and over we listened to them, till the names of the great men playing in the band — Johnny Hodges, Jimmy Blanton, Ben Webster, Cootie Williams — became as familiar to us as the names of our friends. I was an eager pupil, because everything I heard — sitting in his parents' basement recreation room, playing his 78 rpm records till they turned white — sounded good to me. The solos were of course improvised, but they and the orchestrated material came together in a way that sounded whole, the inevitable product of a great ideal.

I had to know where that ideal came from, and what it meant. I began reading everything I could find on jazz, and pursued the subject so relentlessly that when I was reading a newspaper or a novel the word "jazz" itself would jump out of a column of type with the urgency of my own name. Many years later someone remarked, "Jazz fans are like children — they want to be told the same story over and over again, about how jazz came up the Mississippi." I was one of those children. I wanted to know all about the origins of jazz among the slaves, about its flowering in the New Orleans whorehouses, and about its startling new life as bebop on 52nd Street in New York. I had simply never heard a story so moving and so attractive. There weren't enough jazz magazines for me to read or enough books on jazz in the library or the bookstores.

At Malvern a new friend, Don Priestman, turned out to be not only a jazz fan but a musician too — a clarinet player who had worked with some Dixieland bands. He didn't share my enthusiasm for Ellington, but he had a lot to tell me about the King Oliver and Louis Armstrong bands of the 1920s. He mentioned that he and some friends were putting together a band to play that kind of music, to be led by a trumpet player and law student named Ken Dean.

At rehearsals I met the other players. Somehow it was decided that I would, in a vague way, manage the band, obtain some publicity for it, and work out the details of its concerts. Organizing them gave me experience that proved useful when I managed New Music Associates a few years later. We put on several jazz evenings at unlikely places like the Polish Canadian Hall or the Balmy Beach Canoe Club. They were called "concert dances" — we wanted to be serious *and* popular. I played the role of MC, my lines being fed to me by Dean or one of the other musicians, and I followed the then common practice at jazz concerts of burdening the audience with rather more pretentiously phrased historical information than the occasion required. Though we were well publicized in the newspapers, the public response was uneven. The appearance at the canoe club was a sellout, but we were then curtly informed that we couldn't rent the place again because our success might interfere with attendance at the club's own dances. At the Polish Canadian Hall the audience was so sparse that I was able to use an ancient joke, possibly descended from burlesque. "Lady," I said at the beginning of the performance, "and gentleman." For that event I had the posters made up by a printer named Leslie Saunders, a staunch Orangeman whom I would later cover as a politician and whose time as mayor of Toronto was to be cut short by his insistence on issuing a municipal proclamation celebrating the anniversary of the Battle of the Boyne, an event noted mainly by Orangemen.

My record as booking agent for Ken Dean's Jazz Band was even less impressive than my performance as an impresario. I arranged a one-night stand at what was then called the Toronto Men's Press Club, but that was about it. Briefly I thought I had a booking at the Colonial Tavern, the main jazz bar in Toronto, but it fell through; apparently the owners were merely using us as a stick to brandish over another band whose demands the owners found unreasonable. Soon my career as jazz promoter and agent came to an end.

MEMORY TELLS us convenient lies, and over the years my memory has tried to persuade me that I was too knowledgeable about my own lack of knowledge ever to function as a music critic. Oh, perhaps I wrote a review here or there, but just to fill in for someone — nothing to be taken seriously. The truth is that, more often than I should have, I wrote pieces about jazz that passed judgement (usually respectful judgement, to be sure) on great musicians.

In 1980 an American who was writing a biography of Art Tatum called me to ask whether I'd met Tatum during his Toronto visits and picked up any interesting information. I replied that I had heard him play but unfortunately had never spoken with him. I asked how the biographer had come across my name.

"Why, because of the review you wrote about his concert at Massey Hall."

"You're mistaken. I never reviewed him."

"I have it here in front of me. It was in *The Globe and Mail*, April 2, 1952."

"No, I think someone else must have written it."

"It's signed 'Bob Fulford.'"

And so it was: he sent me the clipping. My memory had erased that occasion as a way of supporting my contention that I was really just a reporter when it came to music, a humble interviewer writing amusing little feature stories. My memory was trying to save me from a retroactive charge of outrageous chutzpah: someone with my lack of musical knowledge presuming to analyze the work of the most proficient pianist of his day!

My critical writing about jazz probably did no harm, but I doubt that I added to the understanding of my readers. For several years, beginning in 1953, I was the Toronto reporter for *Down Beat*, which was then essential reading for every jazz fan. As a *Down Beat* reporter I attended, on a May night in 1953, what may well have been the best jazz concert in history. At Massey Hall a Toronto promoter brought together, for the first and only time in their lives, Charlie Parker, Dizzy Gillespie, Bud Powell, Charles Mingus, and Max Roach. The record made that night, "Jazz at Massey Hall," has been re-issued several times, always to great praise. It seems strange to me now that at the time I had no idea how good a concert it was. I thought there were marvelous things about it (notably Powell's piano set, and a longish drum solo by Max Roach) but a large part of the music seemed almost routine. Today, when I listen to the record, I wonder how I could have heard so much magnificent playing and yet not heard it. Perhaps at the time I assumed this would be one of many occasions when I'd hear these men play together (in fact, Parker was dead within two years). In any case, I often think of that night when I tell myself to enjoy what is here and now, and depend not at all on the pleasures of the future. I also think of it when I hear the Joni Mitchell line, "You don't know what you've got till it's gone."

Like many of my jobs, the *Down Beat* assignment came to me because no one else wanted it and I asked for it. I still have the letter from Chicago making me a staff contributor and promising me "ten to twenty dollars apiece for personality features, depending upon lengths, content, etc." For every issue I wrote a longish paragraph of jazz gossip from Toronto for a column called Strictly Ad Lib. There was no fee for that at first, but in late 1953 the editor wrote with happy news: "From now on, you'll receive a minimum of five bucks for Strictly Ad Lib from your city, no matter what its length." Occasionally, if things broke right, fees might rise to an almost respectable level. Once I received $25 for an interview with Milt Buckner, the jazz organist. A few months later, just as I was leaving for a trip to Europe and was pulling together every available dollar, a cheque for $40 arrived from Capitol Records in Los Angeles, with no letter attached. I decided to cash it first and find out later why it had been sent. When I returned from Europe I discovered Capitol had used my piece as liner notes for Buckner's new LP. Thus the article brought $65, my record at *Down Beat.*

Of course money had nothing to do with my desire to work for *Down Beat.* What I wanted was some experience with subjects beyond the *Globe*'s normal range and some connection with the jazz history I'd been studying. Above all, I wanted a chance to observe the musicians at close range. All this was accomplished through *Down Beat* and through one of the great cultural institutions in my life, the Colonial Tavern.

The Colonial was a two-storey saloon on Yonge Street, a couple of hundred yards from City Hall. On the first floor a bar catered to off-the-street customers and offered an endless succession of lame lounge acts. On the second floor you could find bad food, surly waitresses, poor acoustics, and great art. The owners, two worried-looking men named Goody and Harvey Lichtenberg, brought in swing bands, Dixieland bands, and bebop bands. Here, for a few dollars, you could spend a long evening listening to Ella Fitzgerald, Miles Davis, Gerry Mulligan, or Sidney Bechet. The room held no more than 150, and seldom put on a cover charge, but somehow Goody and Harvey found the money to bring in even the big bands — Lionel Hampton's, Dizzy Gillespie's, Maynard Ferguson's. We were all squeezed in so tightly that the distance between performer and audience all but disappeared. One night Jack Batten, listening to the Gillespie band, was so close that he could look over the shoulder of a saxophone player and read his part. When Art Blakey came to the Colonial, local drummers would grab the table about three inches from his high-hat cymbal and sit there for hours, trying to figure out how he did what he did.

Because the Colonial's press agent — Dick McDougall, otherwise a CBC disc jockey — took a friendly interest in me, I was usually invited to the opening-night press table and introduced to the musicians. I got to know Dave Brubeck,

who came to the Colonial several times, and the first article
I ever sold to *Saturday Night* — "A New Leader for Jazz," in
the October 24, 1953 issue — was a profile of Brubeck. I
was paid fifty dollars for it by the editor of the day, Gwyn
Kinsey, but I had to sign it with a pseudonym, Robert Marshall,
because the *Globe* forbade its reporters to write elsewhere
under their own names.

What I liked about Brubeck was his eagerness to articulate
his purposes. As an artist to be interviewed, in fact, he was
almost perfect — he had (I now realize, and perhaps suspected
then) absolutely everything except genuine talent. He had
intellectual curiosity, learning (compositional studies with
Darius Milhaud), a taste for experiment, some showmanship,
and an urgent ambition to see himself among the great
figures of the day. But he lacked the ability to improvise at
the piano in a commanding way, write tunes anyone would
want to remember, or even play with routine charm. He had
the hands of a woodchopper and when he played loudly —
as he often did — he seemed to be hiding something, like an
orator who starts shouting when he ceases to believe what
he's saying.

At the Colonial I met Duke Ellington for the first time, on
the night of February 2, 1954: I know the date because the
next day I wrote to a friend in England to tell him about it. I
had first seen the Ellington band in the mid-1940s at a
Saturday morning concert for teenagers in Simpsons department store and I'd been to several later concerts. Ralph
Ellison, the novelist, first saw Ellington in the 1930s. "And
then," he wrote many years later, "Ellington and the great
orchestra came to town; came with their uniforms, their
sophisication, their skills; their golden horns, their flights of
controlled and disciplined fantasy...They were news from
the great wide world, an example and a goal." They were
that for the black boy Ellison was in Oklahoma City in the
1930s. They were much the same thing for me, a white boy
in Toronto in the 1940s.

Now the whole band was crammed into the Colonial, and the walls seemed to swell to hold it. Above all, the space between band and audience — no more than a table's width — had to expand, at least in imagination, to contain this titan who stepped down from the bandstand now and then to banter with the audience in his light and sometimes silly way. The 1954 band was far from his best, but that hardly mattered to me. That night I sat with Ellington and a few of the most devoted local Ellingtonians — Helen McNamara of *The Telegram*, McDougall and Byng Whitteker of the CBC — and felt blessed beyond my previous imaginings. I managed to get out a question now and then, but for most of the evening hero-worship kept me dumb. I doubt if I would have been more awe-struck if Beethoven had sat down and joined us.

I met Ellington a few times in later years, most memorably when I made a little radio interview with him in 1968. Louis Applebaum, who had supervised a recording on which Ellington played, re-introduced me to him, said some flattering things about my work, and introduced Geraldine Sherman, who was standing beside me with a tape recorder. At that point Geraldine was, officially, nothing but my producer at CBC radio; in fact, we were already embarked on the journey that has so far led us to marriage, two daughters, and nineteen years together. It took Ellington about a tenth of a second to understand our relationship. He turned toward Geraldine, nodded in my direction, and threw off one of those brief arias that provided most of the content of his conversations with women. "Is he *really* so great? Or is it just…the reflection of *your* beauty that makes him shine like satin?" Geraldine blushed. Ellington, having made yet another conquest, buckled down to our interview.

Many years later, on CBC radio, Ian Alexander asked me about my fascination with Ellington. I said that of course I loved the music he had made, but I also loved the way he had made it: spontaneously and co-operatively and in an atmosphere (most of the time) of mutual respect. Ellington understood talent and how it could be shaped — he was to jazz what Diaghilev was to ballet. He was an artist who both practised his own art and created spaces where others could practice theirs. Alexander said, shrewdly, "You sound like you're describing a magazine editor." Of course I was describing the editor I had always wanted to be, modelled on the leader Ellington had been. This ideal, presumptuous as it was, kept me going through some painful days.

That was only one of many lessons I took from jazz. Ten or so years ago I was talking with Michael Snow, who has been the most interesting painter of my generation in Canada and one of the most admired experimental filmmakers in the world. I mentioned that jazz had been the great teacher in my life, the mythic headwater from which my best impulses and my best insights had flowed. Mike said that was true for him, too — his real learning had started with jazz. In my case there was something else: one subject jazz taught me about was Mike Snow himself, the second genius I met in my youth. A student at the Ontario College of Art, Mike played with Ken Dean's band. Like Gould, he was a pianist, but he resembled Glenn in no other way. For one thing, the size of his talent — let alone its breadth — was not evident to anyone. He played piano well, but no one predicted all the other astonishing things he would do. Certainly there was nothing in my first dozen meetings with him to suggest that he would introduce me to some of the best Toronto artists, making it possible for me to be an art critic; or that I would spend several frustrating years trying (at last successfully) to persuade the Art Establishment of Toronto that he was a painter who had to be taken seriously.

SIX

Snow and Town, Art and Eros

"IF JAZZ IS CLOSE to any other art it is abstract painting, for the process of creation is much the same. The artist first learns the technique of the instrument or the brush and then forgets about it. To create he absorbs his material...and improvises, never knowing quite what the result will be." That's me, at age twenty-four, in the June, 1956 issue of *Mayfair*, trying to connect two subjects that claimed my intense affection and interest. The jazz soloist, alone in front of his audience, and the abstract painter, alone in front of his canvas, were coming together in my mind — and also in the mind of the subject of the article, Michael Snow. That was the first piece I ever wrote about him, I think the first anyone ever wrote. It was natural to analyze him in the beginning as both musician and painter because it was music that brought me to Snow and Snow, in a sense, who brought me to painting. He was the first Canadian artist I took seriously enough to write about often and the first artist who took me seriously enough to push me in an interesting direction. It

91

was Snow who called me one day in the winter of 1955-56 and said that his friend Avrom Isaacs, proprietor of a framing and art-supplies shop, was planning to become an art dealer in a serious way. Av was about to open a gallery on Bay Street, near Gerrard, on the edge of what some of us misleadingly called "the Village" — the closest thing to Bohemia that Toronto possessed in the 1940s and 1950s.

That Village disappeared long ago, and was replaced by hospital parking garages or office buildings, but even then it was hard to prove to a tourist that the place was much more than a fantasy. On two or three streets there were a couple of dozen ramshackle workers' cottages from the nineteenth-century, some of them converted into storefronts. Over the years I knew the Village, it contained a couple of restaurants (one of them certifiably French), some antique stores, a French-language bookstore, some artists' studios, a place that seemed to sell mainly hand-knitted neck ties (I bought several), and four or five different art galleries. One was the Gallery of Contemporary Art, where Harold Town had his first one-man show of paintings. Another was the Pollock Gallery, run by Jack Pollock, where the Indian painter Norval Morrisseau made his first big-city appearances.

In this tiny version of Greenwich Village, Av Isaacs, just out of university, set up an art supplies store and got to know some of the painters who bought paints and canvas from him, notably Snow and Graham Coughtry. He gave them their first commercial gallery shows and he therefore goes down in history as their discoverer; they, on the other hand, claim they discovered Isaacs, a humble storekeeper, and transformed him by their astute guidance into a great dealer. Av called his first place the Greenwich Gallery to acknowledge the district's grandiose dreams and catch an exotic echo of New York, which all of us were beginning to understand was now the art capital of the world. It was only when he was about to move to much larger quarters in midtown Toronto, five years later, that he changed the name to the Isaacs Gallery, "Greenwich" now perhaps seeming gauche and provincial.

The piece in *Mayfair* that touched on the relationship between jazz musicians and painters appeared not long after the opening of the Greenwich Gallery. A few months later I wrote the note published with the announcement of Snow's first one-man show, and fourteen years after that I wrote an essay for the catalogue that accompanied his first big retrospective. In between I wrote more than a dozen pieces about Snow in the Toronto *Star*, *Maclean's*, and *Canadian Art*, and many talks on CBC radio. At the beginning he was a favourite subject because, as a friend whose language I spoke, he was one artist I could begin to understand. But after a year or so that mattered far less than the fact that Mike was turning out to be as interesting a painter and sculptor as any on the scene, and far more so than most.

For a young critic, finding his way, Snow was stimulating but also frustrating: he wanted attention, but he didn't want to be entirely understood. He knew that critics were essential in some way, but he didn't trust our assumption that we could tell the public what was going on. "I'm interested in doing something that can't be explained," he once said, implying that if his work could be entirely explained it would probably be too simple-minded. Living in an era that placed a high premium on being articulate, Mike was almost willfully *in*articulate. His conversation, in any public forum, was illusive and fragmentary, something like the half-heard voices on the sound tracks of some Snow films. I interviewed him on radio once and decided never to try again.

At the Isaacs Gallery one night about a quarter of a century ago there was an occasion that seemed to require a speech from Mike. He agreed to give it, wrote a text, and then had a friend of his read it into a tape recorder. Mike stood up before the crowd at the gallery and played the taped, lip-synching with intentional incompetence; he started each sentence too late or too early. The effect, like many of

Snow's effects, recalled the Dada-ist absurdities of the 1920s and the experiments of Marcel Duchamp.

When Snow and his wife, Joyce Wieland, were living in New York in the mid-1960s, he was developing variations of his Walking Woman theme, using the same cut-out female figure in hundreds of different ways. He was also exploring the idea of the fortuitous in art by placing the Walking Woman in places where she might be randomly encountered — on subway cars, on construction hoardings, in a news-paper ad, on T-shirts worn by friends. He had a rubber stamp made of the Walking Woman and used it to create a drawing that was purchased by the Museum of Modern Art. When MOMA showed the drawing, Mike made small Walking Woman images on paper and left a trail of them through several art galleries in New York. The trail led to the museum and the room where the piece was shown. On the floor beneath the drawing he left a pile of the images.

Snow was intellectually restless, a man in motion, and his art demonstrated it — again and again he produced a one-man show in which every picture had a distinct purpose. The habit of most artists, as abstract painting grew popular, was to show together some fifteen or twenty paintings that were slight variations on the same theme — in a show by Jean-Paul Riopelle, for instance, one painting would look much like another, and each of them would be offered not as a separate achievement but as a kind of chip off the artist's personality.

Snow was capable of producing a dozen paintings that reflected a dozen different ideas. I remember saying of an early show of his that there were enough ideas in it for the careers of four or five ordinary artists. In later years I never had much to say about his highly regarded films (I often found them boring, a reaction that annoyed and disappointed Mike), but I had the enormous pleasure of seeing his paint-ing and sculpture flower. At Expo 67, which I covered for four months for the Toronto *Star*, Snow was the most accomplished artist on the site, his Walking Woman sculptures providing an unending series of aesthetic surprises in the Ontario pavilion. And at Expo 86 in Vancouver he was again the most impressive artist, this time filling a whole building with his experiments in holography, a technique he quickly assimilated within his own style.

Snow, Coughtry, and the other Isaacs artists were a wonderful gift to me. Just when I wanted to be an art critic, some first-class artists appeared. The greatest excitement in a young critic's life (and the largest challenge) is writing the first reviews or articles about artists of consequence. There was a period in the late 1950s and early 1960s, as I covered the art galleries every week — first for a local CBC radio program, "CJBC Views the Shows," then for the Toronto *Star* — when I had many of these artists more or less to myself. The critic on the *Globe* didn't pay much attention, the guy who wrote sometimes for the *Telegram* didn't care, but I was there week after week. Snow and Coughtry were followed by Gordon Rayner, Wieland, Dennis Burton, Robert Markle, John Meredith. Sometimes I wrote the first piece that appeared on an artist, and occasionally the second, third, and fourth pieces as well. I can remember my first glimpse of William Kurelek, the day his debut show was hung (he was a framer for years in Av's back shop), and my excited review of him that Saturday. What impressed me was not the quality of Kurelek's art (though some of the paintings were beautifully worked) but the fact that he was so clearly an original presence.

Av Isaacs never claimed to be an intellectual or a theorist, but he turned out to have a nose for talent as good as any in Canadian art during my time. The only other Canadian I knew with an instinct equally sharp was the publisher Jack McClelland, and the two of them — both shaping forces in Canadian culture — shared another quality: once committed to an artist, or a writer, they stayed committed. But Isaacs, unlike McClelland, was also a born businessman: he had the natural entrepreneur's easygoing ability to laugh at his failures

as well as his successes. He learned a great deal from Snow
and Coughtry, but in a few years he saw their work as only a
part of the art he wanted to handle. His ability to exhibit
Kurelek, a fanatically Christian painter, in the same stable
that included erotic artists like Markle and Burton, demonstrated the breadth of his imagination. In the thirty-two years
I've watched him, Isaacs has shown dozens of artists; I don't
think he's made more than one or two embarrassing mistakes.

If innate feeling for talent and a business sense made Av
an art dealer, what made me an art critic? First of all, the
desire to be one; second, the luck of living in a place where
such a writer was needed. The desire came out of my slow
discovery of painting, beginning in mid-adolescence with
Impressionism studied in books borrowed from the library
— then as now, Impressionism was the art most accessible to
a sentimental sixteen-year-old. At eighteen or so I was in the
Museum of Modern Art in New York absorbing that collection in the way its great director, Alfred H. Barr, wanted it
absorbed — as a didactic history of modern visual culture
rooted in Cezanne and the Cubists. (It was another decade,
at least, before I realized that Barr's account was just one
man's vision, even if a great man's, and that there were
several other ways to look at the art of this century.) In 1953,
when I was twenty-one, I spent three months touring the
museums of Europe. I returned to Europe in 1955 and
again in 1957, and in between I was an eager reader of art
books and a devoted follower of current art criticism.

By 1957 I felt confident enough to review the galleries
every Sunday afternoon on the CBC, receiving $30 for a
nine-minute script. By 1958, at age twenty-six, I was — according to a brochure published by The Centre for Adult Education, housed in the North Toronto YMCA — giving a
course called "Looking at Modern Painting...from Paul
Cezanne to Jackson Pollock, including an investigation of
such schools as cubism, surrealism, German expressionism
and the recent American non-objective painting...in several

The author as imaginary hockey
star with a boyhood friend,
circa 1943

A.E. Fulford of the
Canadian Press,
in the early 1950s

To Mr. Fulford
from Glenn and Nick

Glenn Gould, circa 1944, in one
of his favourite poses

Orfeo

Agency for Fine Artists
1231 St. Catherine West
Montreal — BElair 9823

Oct 16, 1954

New Music Associates,
c/o Robert Fulford,
Business Manager.

re Maureen Forrester $50.00

To concert services rendered

Monni Adams, Representative.

The Gould-Fulford partnership staged Maureen Forrester's Toronto debut in 1954, but did not pay lavishly

Four Toronto jazz enthusiasts of the 1950s, with two musicians from San Francisco. *From left:* Dave Brubeck; the author, representing *Down Beat*, disc jockey Phil McKellar; Helen McNamara of *The Telegram;* Alex Barris of *The Globe & Mail;* Turk Murphy

The new assistant editor of
Mayfair, 1955

West Cornwall
Connecticut
September 7, 1959

Dear Mr. Fulford:

I think your criticism of "The Years with Ross" is one of the very best of the hundreds I have seen. I am showing it to my good friend and neighbor, Kenneth Maclean, an American, but a professor at the University of Toronto. I think you two would enjoy each other. Your ideas on the subject of Ross as the original badgered man are interesting and agree with the theory recently mentioned to me in conversation by Edmund Wilson. Of course, I don't know for sure about its having started there, all right. I think maybe maturity, or childhood there, all right. I think maybe Bob Benchley and Don Stewart had done similar things earlier than the rest of us, and in 1923 I ran a half page in The Columbus, Ohio, Dispatch, and one of my continuing characters was a private detective who got everything wrong and was badgered by the police and his clients, too. He once said, "The actual solution of this mystery turns out to be less interesting than my own." He was smarter than the cops, but they were always right. Thanks again for the review and all best wishes.

Cordially yours,

James Thurber

JAMES THURBER

Mr. Robert Fulford
Toronto Star, Ltd.
80 King St. West
Toronto 1, Canada

JT/ek

A letter that hangs, framed,
in the author's home

Quitting day at *Maclean's* in
1964: Peter Gzowski, the author,
Ken Lefolii. Partially shown in
background: Alexander Ross.
Photo: Don Newlands

A publicity picture for "This
Hour Has Seven Days," issued in
September, 1964. The item
never made it to air.
Photo: Robert C. Ragsdale

cases students will attend and discuss important current shows in the Toronto galleries." Two of my students, Percy and Jesse Waxer, became important collectors, and were always nice enough to say I'd influenced them.

The most striking difference between art in the 1950s and art in the 1980s is not quality but quantity. In the 1950s, and far into the 1960s, there were only a few dozen regularly exhibiting artists in Toronto and seldom more than five or six art galleries of any interest. The opening of a new gallery was celebrated, the closing of an old one mourned. Today galleries come and go by the score, and only a few are ever noted outside a small circle of artists and patrons. As for the exhibiting artists, a platoon has grown into a regiment. When I started reviewing art galleries no one saw it as a full-time job — my employers considered it a sideline, and so did I. Around 1960 I could cover the new shows every Thursday between lunch and five o'clock, then sit down to write my column for that Saturday's paper. Today a full-time critic working for *The Globe and Mail* can barely begin to suggest the range of art exhibitions; I, on the other hand, often found myself short of material, and would scurry to any corner of the city to find a new artist, however obscure.

LOOKING FOR SHOWS to write about, I often climbed the stairs to the Picture Loan Gallery on Charles Street and talked to Douglas Duncan, the most eccentric dealer of his time. Somehow, Duncan knew everything about Canadian art and knew it before anyone else — he discovered David Milne, for instance, and he first showed the work of Paul-Emile Borduas west of Montreal. Duncan rented pictures to his customers and then, if they wanted to keep them, applied the rental fees to the purchase price. For some dealers this arrangement might have been simple to manage; for Douglas it was impossible. He was always far behind on his accounts, and it was never clear — to Douglas, the artists, or the customers — who owned how much of which painting. Nevertheless, he was an astute guide for many collectors, he brought into the light some artists who might otherwise have waited longer for exposure, and when he died he left the public museums some excellent pictures.

I wish I could say I liked visiting him; in truth I dreaded it, as I dreaded my visits to many dealers. I loved the art (or a lot of it) and I liked writing about it; I didn't enjoy the painful little roundelay of conversation with the dealer that had to be endured at each new show. Dealers, with a few exceptions, couldn't leave a reviewer alone — leave me alone, anyway. Av Isaacs, perhaps out of inborn tact, simply said hello and nothing more, offering information only when asked for it; Dorothy Cameron, another major dealer in the 1960s, would avoid talking about the exhibition or indeed the art business and substitute some pleasant gossip. But most of the others relentlessly pursued me around the gallery, explaining that the exhibition marked a great moment in the artist's career, that this painting was the highlight of the show, or that this kind of art (as opposed to the garbage in the gallery down the street) was the wave of the future. The dealers were critics *manqués*, desperate to write reviews, or at least the reviews of their own galleries. I sympathized with them — in some cases a review was their only chance to get the exhibition or the artist known beyond the clients on the gallery's mailing list. A negative review could have a mildly harmful effect, and no review at all might throw the artist into a paranoid rage.

There were times when I entered a gallery and knew in ninety seconds that the work was of no interest to me and could not possibly be the subject of even a paragraph. Did I bravely stride out of the gallery? No, usually I hung about for ten minutes or so, hands jingling the change in my pocket as I stared at the pictures and tried to give an imitation of a conscientious art critic. This problem is unique to art reviewing: literary critics, drama critics and music critics all have difficulties, but none of them has to face, week after week, in small rooms, often without any other human present, the people whose livelihoods depend partly on what the critic says. When I stopped writing regular art reviews, in 1968, that was the part of it I missed least.

At the Picture Loan Society there were things I wanted to know about Douglas Duncan, already in the 1950s a legendary figure — for instance, was he in fact the original of a character in *Self Condemned*, the Toronto novel by Wyndham Lewis, and if so, how did he feel about it? They were not the things he wanted to tell me. He wished to speak, in a monotonous drone, of obscure business matters, of small coups carried out years earlier. When I went into one of the little exhibition rooms to look at some new show of prints or drawings, Douglas would follow me, take a position in the corner, and begin slowly sliding down the wall as he spoke. By the time he was in a crouch, his limbs gathered like a spider's, he would have completed some unbearably tedious anecdote about a collector I'd never heard of; and I would be wondering whether the exhibit on the walls justified the pain of the visit. In fact he was old enough and knowledgeable enough to demand attentiveness of a critic so young and inexperienced, and with more patience I could have learned a great deal from him. Patience, however, was not my outstanding characteristic.

IT WAS AT the Picture Loan Society in the mid-1950s that I first saw a show by Harold Town, a collection of the elegant and ingenious prints that helped establish his reputation. I missed the exhibition during its run and saw it because Town thought I should and asked Douglas to take it out of the cupboard and show it to me, with Harold there to comment. I had met Town at a party in Rosedale, and we had argued loudly about something I now can't recall. That was how Town introduced himself in those days: in fact, what I remember most clearly about all those nights of joy and gin and anger is the argumentative voice of Harold, denounc-

ing whatever opponent was handiest, often me. Town was
and is enormously talented, but in those days his desire to
impose himself and his views on the world around him was
even larger than his abilities. In the 1950s and 1960s he
shot off in a dozen directions — as printmaker, muralist,
set designer, painter, columnist in *Toronto Life*, sculptor,
opinionmonger on every subject under the sun. Town could
tell you, and would, what was wrong with modern medicine
and suburban sex, what was right with Laurence Olivier or
Laurel and Hardy. I found him as stimulating as he was
talented, but I also understood those who were intimidated
not only by his conversation but by the almost unbelievable
range of the material he exhibited. He ran through styles
and manners at amazing speed, pumping out hundreds of
canvases and drawings in now this and now that manner —
look away for six months and you could miss an entire Town
Period. Some of the work was wonderful, some good, some
inadequate, but I never heard Town admit that a piece of
his was less than sensational.

I sometimes wrote introductions or notes for Town shows
or catalogues, always with enthusiasm but sometimes with
difficulty. In 1969 I spent some summer afternoons in the
ghastly factory then inhabited by McClelland and Stewart,
working on a book to be called *Harold Town Drawings*. I was
to write the text, but first it was necessary to choose which
hundred or so among all the drawings of Town's already
lengthy career would appear in it. This proved arduous.
There were five of us involved — Jack McClelland, a promising young editor named Anna Szigethy (later Anna Porter),
the art director, Frank Newfeld, Town, and me. We had
small photostats of all the drawings under consideration,
and we spread them out before us to plan the book. Much
later I realized that I had approached the question in the
wrong — democratic and open — spirit. I should have (or
someone should have) gone away with all the drawings and

returned with a ruthlessly pruned selection, prepared to defend each choice to the death and also prepared if necessary to declare each of them a work of genius. Instead, we sat around the board room table and tried to work in the opposite direction, by elimination. One of us, never Town, would gently and tentatively say, "I think, uh, we might drop this little group here..." Instantly, Town would reply, "You can't cut *those*," his tone suggesting that to do so would be a work of vandalism. He would then explain that they were crucial to his development because they led up to, etc., etc.

That idea defeated, someone else would propose another cut, with the same result. After an hour it became clear that every one of those drawings — there must have been twice as many as any reasonable book could contain — was the precious child of the artist. It also became clear that cutting even one of them would cost us at least half an hour and cutting the book to the size we hoped for would take years. Eventually, out of exhaustion, we put out a book that contained far too many drawings to be attractive: often two on a page, sometimes three, occasionally four. *Harold Town Drawings* was in its way a lovely book (and looks even better in 1988 than it did in 1969) but it had nothing like the success it deserved.

Perhaps better editing wouldn't have helped, though. In 1963, after winning every available prize, selling out a huge show of his biggest oil paintings, and appearing on the cover of *Maclean's*, Town said, "I think it's about time for me to become unpopular." And quite soon, he was: a few curators, a few critics and a good many collectors maintained their interest in Town, but for the most part the attention of the Canadian art world passed to other painters. For a while the media had made him the designated great Canadian artist of his day — once *Time Canada* carried a quote that compared him to Michelangelo. But now editors and producers, taking their cue from the art world, lost interest. All this didn't seem to make a great deal of difference to Town. He continued to produce as much as before, racing through style after style, following his peculiar vision.

Some of his ideas had been worked out in discussion during the 1950s with his fellow members of Painters 11, a group of non-objective artists who were to the 1950s what the Group of Seven had been to the 1920s. My friend Joan Murray, the art scholar who runs the McLaughlin Gallery in Oshawa (and with whom I wrote a book on Lawren Harris) has told, in a series of catalogues, how the group was established when abstract painters had no other way of exhibiting and how it gave confidence and a sense of accomplishment to members as diverse as Town, Jack Bush, and J.W.G. (Jock) Macdonald. I happened to see a Painters 11 show before I ever wrote about art; it was February 13, 1954, my twenty-second birthday, and a colleague took me to the opening at the Roberts Gallery. I loved some of the pictures, thought the quality amazingly uneven, and came away with a sense of new life in Canadian art.

What I did *not* recognize was that one of these artists, Jack Bush, was destined to be, in international terms, the most successful Canadian painter of his generation. Had I been forced to rank the painters in that show I would have put Bush fifth or sixth. I didn't begin to like his work until about 1961, and even then I seldom wrote about him: his art was so simple that it seemed beyond comment. When he asked me to write a note for the invitation to one of his New York shows, I told him I was too busy; the truth was that I couldn't imagine what I'd write. Like many critics (including some who wrote often of him), I respected the mature Bush but really had nothing to add to what the pictures said. By the time I began to admire his work I was nearly thirty years old and had learned at least one rule all critics should follow: when you have nothing to say, try to say nothing.

I FIRST HEARD the voice of Dorothy Cameron over the telephone one day in 1955, when she was a young society lady named Dorothy Cameron Moes and I, an assistant editor at *Mayfair*, was delighted to receive phone calls from young society ladies. She was on the junior women's committee of what was then called the Art Gallery of Toronto, which is to say that she had already — through charm, breeding, social connections, a good marriage, and a respectable trust fund — reached what her peers regarded as the summit of Toronto society.

There are those who complain that today the Art Gallery of Ontario (which it became in 1966) is dominated by the rich and the well-connected, and there may be some justice in that view. But in the 1950s the social side of the gallery's life was far more obvious — so obvious, in fact, that at times it appeared to be the main purpose of the place, the pictures being there to provide an appropriate background and a sense of cultural uplift. The permanent collection was mediocre and the temporary exhibitions only occasionally interesting, but that seldom bothered the trustees. The parties were what counted, because they provided the Toronto rich with a chance to display themselves and confirm their own significance in a genteel atmosphere. The fact that the gallery included the Grange, where the Family Compact met in the 1830s and directed the affairs of the young colony, added an element of delicious irony. The history books, written by liberals, depicted the original Family Compact as a villainous Tory clique; now, on the same piece of property, the winners of the 1950s were happily at play. And on the gallery's board of trustees, young lawyers and accountants could advertise their personal excellence to potential clients while their wives on the junior women's committee solidified the social position of their families.

I don't think I ever resented the influence of these people. After all, most of the great museums of the world are dominated by the rich. What I did bitterly resent — and found rather baffling — was that they bought their status so cheaply. Many of them hung about the gallery for years, preening, and left without making the slightest impression on the financial statement or the collection. Bankers, beer barons, and department-store owners would float through the board of trustees, maybe even reaching the chairman's job, and then depart, satisfied with a job well done, perhaps having mistakenly believed that they had been recruited for their management expertise. They didn't seem to understand that their function was to provide money and art, and so far as I know not one of them even considered becoming a truly ambitious international art collector, on the level of several dozen Americans in this century. Of course, we know the real stature of collectors only when they give their art to public institutions, either at their death or earlier; by that standard it's clear that the Canadian upper classes, for all the money they've accumulated, have so far produced not a single great collector. Our rich people have tended to be rather easily satisfied with themselves — and perhaps never more so than in the 1950s, when I first saw them up close.

In this atmosphere of sublime complacency, Dorothy Cameron Moes was unusual. At the University of Toronto, in the post-war years, she had been part of the generation that included Robert Weaver of the CBC and the poet James Reaney; she used to say that she took one creative writing course and ended up the only member of it who didn't become famous, a condition she eventually corrected. Those years at the university — the years when Northrop Frye was simultaneously creating his own international reputation and directing his acute critical intelligence at Canadian poetry — left her with a restless ambition for Canadian culture and a need to be part of it.

The voice that I heard on the phone in 1955 — she was calling to ask that *Mayfair* write a piece about a show arranged by the junior women's committee — was in some ways

Standard Rosedale, but there was something else coming over the line too: a laugh that held a hint of intimacy, as if she were saying that she and I understood each other or would at our first face-to-face meeting. I don't remember when that finally occurred, but when it did I realized that Dorothy was much more serious about art, and her potential place in it, then anyone else I met at the gallery. She also took me seriously, which of course pleased me. I still have a fan letter she wrote in the spring of 1958 to the producer of "CJBC Views the Shows," describing me as "an articulate, honest and constructive spokesman of a calling sadly mishandled generally in this country" and our program as "the sole source of real art criticism in our city." That was typical. She was an enthusiast, a fervent champion of whatever she admired. She was also a romantic who believed passionately in love and art and never forgot the intimate connection between the two. She was imaginative and naive, sensually alive and girlishly innocent. All of those qualities were to come together in the most celebrated, the most bizarre, and the most distressing event of her professional life, her trial for obscenity.

In 1960, when she set herself up as an art dealer, Dorothy carried some of the ambience of the junior women's committee with her. The opening-night parties at her two galleries — first the Here and Now Gallery on Cumberland Street, then the Dorothy Cameron Gallery on Yonge Street — were social as well as artistic events. The husband of one junior women's committee member became Dorothy's lawyer, the architect husband of another designed her gallery. Old friends from the committee became her clients, and bought the work by Rita Letendre, Gershon Iskowitz, Yves Gaucher, Louis de Niverville, and all the other remarkable artists she showed. What set her apart from most dealers, then and now, was her national ambition. She showed Quebec art, B.C. art, Regina art, art from the Maritimes. At one point she mounted

a major show of sculpture brought at great expense from
across the country, even though there was almost no market
for Canadian sculpture.

Perhaps she was too ambitious, and perhaps her business
sense was underdeveloped. Possibly there weren't enough
Rosedale friends with empty walls. In any case, by the season
of 1964-65 the Dorothy Cameron Gallery was losing money.
What finally killed the gallery, and finished Dorothy's career
as a dealer, was Eros 65, an event I covered in minute detail
for the *Star*. I still own a print from that exhibition by Paul
Young, purchased for fifty dollars. It shows two naked lovers
embracing in the open air; around them, and above their
heads, are some not-quite-distinguishable shapes — leaves,
perhaps, or butterflies. The tone is joyfully innocent, which
is what makes it an appropriate souvenir. Though Eros 65
went into legal history as a criminal offence, it was founded
on an innocent idea and defended in court with an innocence that in retrospect seems breathtaking.

Dorothy's idea was to show publicly a side of art that had
been largely hidden. Artists often make erotic paintings and
drawings, but until the 1960s most work of that kind remained
inside the studios where it was produced. Now, Dorothy
believed, there was a new freedom in the air. The old rules
of taste had been dying, one after another, since the *Lady
Chatterley's Lover* court decision in England in 1960. We no
longer needed to hide our erotic impulses, or their expression through art. So she gathered a collection of paintings,
prints, and drawings by Canadian artists — Harold Town,
Dennis Burton, and Robert Markle were included — and
unveiled it one night in May as a springtime celebration of
love. Pierre Berton spoke at the opening, and said that the
exhibition demonstrated that Toronto had finally come of
age; only a few years before, he said, such a show would
have been unthinkable in Toronto.

Shortly after the opening two policemen came into the
gallery, shooed out the customers, and began inspecting

every work of art. They took away seven drawings — five of
them by Robert Markle — and charged Dorothy with seven
counts of unlawfully exposing to public view an obscene
picture. It was the first time since the 1920s that such a charge
had been made against an art dealer in Canada.

Five months later I was sitting among the prostitutes and
pimps in C Court at the old City Hall, where I'd covered
criminal trials for the *Globe* a dozen years before, waiting for
the arrival of my friend the accused. She entered grandly, in
High Rosedale style: black pillbox hat, navy-blue dress of
heavy linen with high neckline and flaring hem, pearl neck-
lace, her grandmother's enormous diamond circle pin. She
was making damn sure no one confused her with an ordinary
pornographer — as Kildare Dobbs remarked in his account
of the case for *Saturday Night*, "Though everyone agrees the
courts are not prejudiced against appearances, no one wants
to bet on it." When the clerk called her name, Dorothy
answered with a gay wave and a quiet "here," which the clerk
missed; he called it again, she said "here" rather more loudly,
and the clerk missed her again. In that courtroom she was
like a long-stemmed rose in a field of petunias, but for some
reason the clerk couldn't see her. He was turning regretfully
to the bench and saying "She's not..." when Dorothy finally
trilled "*Here* I am" in a loud voice and strode forcibly toward
the magistrate. That odd little exchange looked like the
funny beginning of a serious drama, but in fact it was a taste
of the judicial comedy we were all to watch over the next
three days, a comedy of mutual incomprehension that inad-
vertently summed up certain problems of art in the 1960s.

In 1965 all high thinking in art was formalist: what mattered
was not content but form. The ideas that descended from
Roger Fry in England and (much more recently) Clement
Greenberg in New York made the visible content of art largely
irrelevant — Cezanne, it was often explained, did indeed
paint apples on a table, but if he had painted tennis balls, or
testicles, the formal results and his place in history would

have been the same. In 1965 abstract art was the art that
mattered, and people who still painted identifiable subjects
were considered at best eccentric. Pop Art was at that moment
leading the long trek back toward subject matter and the
neo-realism popular in the late 1970s; but at the time of the
Cameron trial, Pop was only marginally legitimate.

Eros 65, of course, was a show of subject matter — everything in it referred in some way to love — but art criticism
was uncomfortable with subject matter. So the witnesses who
appeared for Dorothy Cameron were unable to say frankly
what the same witnesses would have said a decade later or
perhaps a decade earlier: that this was erotic art of high
quality and deserved to be left alone. Instead, four out of
five of them gave sworn testimony that — despite the title of
the show, the intentions of the artists, and the clear evidence
of every eye in the courtroom — this was not erotic art at all.
The detective sergeant who charged Dorothy said of one
Robert Markle drawing, "It purports to show a woman, nude,
laying on her back with her legs open and another woman
with her head face down in the other woman's female geni-
talia area." William Withrow, director of the Art Gallery of
Toronto, professed to see in the same drawing only "the
pattern of dark and light. The flame-like figures as they flicker
across the surface, the highly abstracted forms…an emphasis
on pattern." Later, when asked in cross-examination whether
he could not, in fact, see the sexual content of one of the
drawings, Withrow replied primly: "It depends on what one
is looking for, I suppose. I was interested in art." And art,
as the witnesses knew but the magistrate didn't, had nothing
whatever to do with content.

The crown prosecutor, pointing at what was clearly a drawing of coitus, said to Withrow:

"Is that not a position of intercourse?"

"Possibly."

One witness, the lawyer and sometime art critic Harry
Malcolmson, acknowledged that some of the art was "gamey"

and that there were people it would offend. The others — Withrow; Doris McCarthy, a painter and teacher; Stewart Bagnani, an art scholar; Ronald Bloore, a painter and director of the Regina art gallery (and later Dorothy Cameron's husband) — professed to see nothing but light, shadow, modelling of forms, and so forth. I have never in my life felt so powerfully the gulf between those who care about art and those who don't. And I confess that, as I listened to the nonsense coming from the witness stand, I occasionally forgot which side I was on.

The magistrate, a stolid fellow named Fred C. Hayes, maintained through the three days of the trial an expression that clearly said, "Are you people putting me on?" But they weren't: they had become so caught up in abstract theory that content had literally become invisible to them. What everyone else in the world could see, they could not. It reminded me of George Orwell's comment on some asininity uttered by a heavy thinker of his day: "You have to be a member of the intelligentsia to believe things like that — no ordinary man could be such a fool."

Magistrate Hayes found Dorothy Cameron guilty on all seven counts and fined her $350, or $50 per offensive drawing. In his judgement he went beyond the idea of obscenity in art and spoke of "the theme and activities" portrayed in the exhibits. These, he said, "are in no way accepted by the community and in fact some of the activity portrayed by Markle could, if practiced in the community, be the subject matter of a charge of gross indecency..." True, as far as it went: Pierre Trudeau was not yet justice minister, the state had not been ordered out of the bedrooms of the nation, and oral sex, however popular, was still an offence against the Criminal Code. But Hayes implied that depicting something illegal was in itself illegal, a notion that would put in jeopardy anyone who ever published a murder mystery. Hayes clearly thought the witnesses were too clever by half; cleverness was not among his faults.

Dorothy appealed to the Ontario Supreme Court, where the distinguished lawyer Walter Williston — assisted by, among others, the young Julian Porter — tried to get the verdict overturned. Now it was the turn of the law to be innocently obtuse. The splendidly gowned judges, sitting beneath their gold, red, and blue lion and unicorn and the "Dieu et mon droit" slogan, asked questions which indicated astounding ignorance of life in the 1960s. A few blocks from where they sat, a dozen Yonge Street bookstores carried material far more salacious than anything Dorothy Cameron would ever think of exhibiting. Yet they professed to find everything in the drawings shown them — *oral* sex? — not only scandalous but novel. Only one of them, Bora Laskin, a civil libertarian who later became chief justice of the Supreme Court of Canada, asked intelligent questions and seemed interested in Walter Williston's argument that erotic art was part of western cultural history. The others clearly believed they were dealing with a unique threat to the morals of Canada. As the appeal hearing ended one of the young lawyers whispered to me, "We'll lose, four to one. Laskin of course will *have* to vote for us — he owes it to his public."

That's what happened, and after the Supreme Court of Canada refused to hear her appeal, Dorothy Cameron was left with a criminal record. She later organized some exhibitions (including a lovely outdoor show at the new Toronto City Hall in the centennial summer of 1967) but she never returned to the business of selling art. In recent years she's become an artist herself, and has exhibited a series of charming autobiographical collages.

Her conviction didn't have quite the chilling effect on the art scene that some of us feared. I have a clipping from the Toronto *Telegram* in which Harold Town, having just been told about the magistrate's verdict, says: "The morality squad has been handed a club and they will use it. At what precise moment was the Gestapo born? Where did the Inquisition begin? Who first thought of Siberia and where does one go to get a degree in the certification of obscenity? To that dark corner of the mind where tyranny is born..." Things didn't turn out quite that badly. In fact, with the rise of neo-realism, art galleries across Canada eventually showed work far more abrasive and challenging than anything in Eros 65. But in the 1980s the issue came alive again, in a new guise: a new generation of puritanical civil servants and politicians, armed with the language of feminism and social pseudo-science, tried to put into law an obscenity bill far more threatening than the one under which Dorothy Cameron was convicted. Around 1960, Pierre Berton pointed out to me that I'd written three or four *Star* columns on censorship in the past month. "Fulford," he said, "if they ever eliminate censorship you'll be out of business." That day appears to be far in the future.

MY ART COLUMN in the Toronto *Star* for January 6, 1962, contained a light-hearted review of Alan Jarvis's exhibition at Dorothy Cameron's gallery. She was showing a selection of his portrait busts — his Peter Ustinov, his Kirsten Flagstad, his Samuel Bronfman — and offering to set up commissions for more. My column quoted the offer Alan made to the British rich, when he lived in England: "For 500 guineas, I'll do you as you are. For 1,000 I'll make you look handsome. For 2,000 I'll make you look honest." I also quoted his description of his own work: "I'm very quick, and very, *very* expensive.

That show was one of many pathetic gestures through which Alan tried — not very hard — to re-establish himself as a figure of consequence after the great disaster of his career. He had been a glowing young star at the University of Toronto in the 1930s, then a Rhodes scholar at Oxford who stayed in England during the Second World War and became private secretary to Stafford Cripps, the minister for aircraft production. After the war Alan was a sculptor, a social worker, a bit of a writer, and a great friend of the famous. Kenneth Clark, in his autobiography, described Alan as the most beautiful young man he had ever seen, but added that Alan's face was his misfortune. Everything, apparently, came too easily, including a series of well-placed homosexual lovers who introduced him to British society. In 1955, as a I understood it later, he was running out of jobs in England and — recommended by Clark and by Vincent Massey — accepted the directorship of the National Gallery of Canada.

A year or two later I first met him, in his office in the dark nineteenth-century Ottawa building that then housed the gallery's collection. He seemed, even then, a bit out of place; he talked almost incessantly of Britain and British artists, and in a brittle mid-Atlantic accent that made him sound like a naval officer in a wartime English movie. At that moment British artists and administrators were playing a major role in the building of Canadian culture — Tyrone Guthrie had founded the Stratford Festival, Celia Franca was developing the National Ballet, and Peter Dwyer was soon to be the key figure in the Canada Council. Nevertheless, the culture of anglophone Canada — like Canadian life in general — was shifting its attention from London to New York. and those who were shifting fastest were the painters, who had fallen in love with American abstract expressionism.

After fourteen years in England Alan had returned to a Canada he barely recognized. In Ottawa he was more or less at home so long as Louis St. Laurent was prime minister and civilized Liberals like Lester B. Pearson were in power; but when John Diefenbaker replaced St. Laurent in 1957, Jarvis was suddenly defenseless. He fought with the government over a plan to buy for the National Galley two European masterpieces, lost that battle, and was abruptly fired in 1959.

At that moment Jarvis had more friends than anyone else involved with the arts in Canada. Diefenbaker was widely loathed, and being discharged by him amounted to a badge of honour. Clearly, Jarvis would now move on to a wonderful career. But, as I came to understand only in slow stages, he didn't see it that way. He thought the firing was a disgrace, he believed he was broken, and he set about drinking himself to death. Along the way he gave every appearance of a man with a career. He briefly wrote a newspaper column, did a TV series, showed his sculpture, edited *Canadian Art* magazine, and ran the Canadian Conference of Arts. But everything was done half-heartedly, and after two or three luncheon meetings with him I realized that the important question on each occasion was not what was said or decided but how many vodka martinis he could get down before he was obliged to nibble a little food. I also understood that the new Canadian art world of the 1960s was outside Alan's understanding. He still spoke constantly of "K. Clark" and Henry Moore and Margot Fonteyn and dear Noel. The more he drank, the more he reverted to London in 1950. He was making every effort to turn himself into a ghost.

Alan's life appears, almost incident for incident, as the life of Alwyn Ross, the National Gallery director in Davies' *What's Bred in the Bone* (his lover, Douglas Duncan, may have inspired the hero, Francis Cornish). The only crucial difference between Jarvis and Ross is that Ross commits suicide almost immediately after losing his job; Jarvis took thirteen years. The last time I saw him was in 1972, at a dinner party he gave in the little town house he had in Clarence Square, a gentrified section of downtown Toronto. He ate nothing, was drunk before nine o'clock, and spilled a glass of red wine over the dress of one of his guests. On the way to the bathroom I noticed a gallon jug of vodka beside the bed. He was dead six months later, and as I prepared to write his obituary I was astonished to discover that he was only fifty-seven years old. The host of the dinner party had appeared to be at least seventy.

THERE WAS something pathetic about Alan's love affair with everything British; the pathos was even more obvious in the life of one of his friends from the generation before, Vincent Massey, who tried desperately to be both a civilized Englishman and a Canadian patriot and failed at both. But if either of them were alive now he could point out something equally pathetic about my generation, the one that learned to be professionals in the 1950s: we were over-awed by the Americans, and at times our work and our thinking must have looked like a parody of the American style.

Eventually we escaped from it — at least I think we did — but in the art world of the 1950s (and in journalism and literature too, though not so markedly) we were swamped by the Americans and totally unable to develop our own views. It was all right for me to learn the history of painting as Alfred Barr taught it at the Museum of Modern Art (one must start somewhere) but it was not all right for me to spend the next decade or so judging all of contemporary art with a sensibility trained by the Americans. Nor was it all right for most of the abstract artists in Canada to believe, year after year, that the final judgement on all their work would be made by New York.

In those days the Canadian painters knew that Clement Greenberg was the greatest American art critic, and sometimes they invited him to come to Canada and advise them on their work. In the roof bar of the Park Plaza one day in 1962 I met him with Jack Bush, whose exhibitions Greenberg sometimes edited. I found him an amiable and generous man with an increasingly narrow view of art's past and future. He believed that there was a mainstream in art and that those who didn't swim in it were crazy — it began with Cezanne, went through the Cubists, passed through certain New York abstract expressionists, then arrived at the "post-painterly abstractionists," such as Bush. Along the way there were diversions such as surrealism, expressionism, Pop Art, and Op Art, all of which were to be avoided. A former Marxist, trained in the *Partisan Review* school, Greenberg retained the confidence of a Marxist long after he lost his interest in Marxist doctrine — he was like an Anglican who retains the snobbery even after losing the faith. He was, putting it very mildly, a formalist — and in the view of many Canadian painters he seemed to hold the key to a place in art history.

In recent years Joe Fafard, a Regina sculptor — and definitely not a formalist — has made a sub-specialty out of doing satirical sculptures of Greenberg. In Fafard's mind, Greenberg, for over twenty years, has stood for everything wrong in theories of art. "I remember thinking," Fafard recently said, "'Who is this guy from New York coming up here and telling us how we should be making art?'" Greenberg came only by invitation, of course, and was invited because American art was so powerful and the Canadians yearned to absorb some of its strength.

In the early 1970s, when it was possible to put our collective infatuation with New York in a certain perspective, I came across a passage in which Jorge Luis Borges wrote about his youthful love for Walt Whitman. "For a time," Borges said, "I thought of Whitman not only as a great poet but as the only poet. In fact, I thought that all poets the world over had been merely leading up to Whitman, and that not to imitate him was a proof of ignorance." That's how we felt, for a few delirious years, about the American artists: only the very ignorant could afford not to imitate them.

SEVEN

*B*eland
and Nathan
and Me

IN THE SPRING of 1988 *The Financial Post* carried a feature under the headline, "Honderich Clings to Torstar Power." Never was a verb more grossly misused. The point of the story was that Beland Honderich, at seventy, was still showing up at the office at 6 a.m. and running the corporation he organized. But only someone who never met him could imagine Honderich in the act of clinging. Others cling to him, or bounce off him, or nervously live in his shadow. Honderich himself sits silently at the centre of his empire, unmoved by events around him, unchanging in his views: I don't believe he's altered one of his political ideas since the late 1950s. He's like a huge shoreline rock, against which waves of editors, writers, and executives fling themselves, year after year. In a few millennia waves will make an impression on a rock, but nothing has dented Honderich in the three decades or so he's spent at the head of the Toronto *Star* and the corporation that owns, among other sources of embarrassment and pride, Harlequin Books. Honderich is a wonderful puzzle for anyone who cares about journalism and public life in Canada — he is to my profession what Russia was to Churchill, a mystery wrapped in an enigma. I'm delighted that for a while I was close enough to observe him in action and I'm even more pleased that, despite a few temptations that were put in my way, I never got closer. As it is, I may be the only human being who worked under Honderich for some years, profited by it, and left without serious complaint.

It was at Honderich's newspaper — or, rather, his first serious try at creating a newspaper — that I was allowed to make my reputation. Part of it was made writing on art, but covering the artists and art dealers who appeared in my last chapter was never more than about a sixth of my work on the *Star*. I joined the paper as literary editor, and not long after became a daily books columnist. During the years I worked there — 1958 to 1968, with two years out on the staff of *Maclean's* — I usually wrote five daily columns on books during the week and a review of art shows on Saturday — about 5,000 words a week, or roughly 2-million during my time on the staff. It wasn't something you could do forever, but it was an enormous pleasure at the time, and an opportunity given to no one else before or since.

It was all a matter of luck; certainly long-range planning had nothing to do with it. In 1958 I was a twenty-six-year-old freelance writer, getting by with the hackwork I've described earlier and some interesting writing too — a CBC television documentary about Method acting, for instance, and a literary essay commissioned by Robert Weaver for "Anthology" on CBC radio. In the course of that year I made about $8,000, which was considered quite good for a just-getting-started freelance. I hustled earnestly around magazine and broadcasting offices in Toronto, picking up work here and there, turning down very little that was offered me. After all, I was a family man. Jocelyn and I, having married in 1956, were now parents: James was born on March 4, 1958. I was with Jocelyn during most of her labour but in the early stages I left her for an hour or so to dash over to the CBC radio building and do a live three-minute local broadcast in a series called "Town Talk," a twenty-dollar fee that we agreed was not to be missed.

One of my ambitions was to write about literature, and I looked around for places to publish occasional book reviews. I imagined that this would always be at best a sideline; certainly the idea that I might be hired to spend most of my time at it, and be given a platform by the biggest newspaper in Canada, was beyond my imagining.

At that point Beland Honderich, forty years old, had been editor of the *Star* just three years and was still consolidating his power and working out what sort of newspaper he wanted to run. At the *Star* nepotism was an established part of the management style. The founder, Joseph Atkinson, and the first successful editor, H.C. Hindmarsh (working for whom, Hemingway said, was like serving in the Prussian army under a bad general) were both dead; but they had left behind on the premises various relatives. A newcomer to the paper had to be instructed in the family connections of Atkinsons and Hindmarshes, any one of whom might be encountered on the elevator and each of whom would require a carefully calibrated degree of obeisance. In this atmosphere it must have seemed natural to Beland that he appoint (or let someone else appoint) as editor of the book page a graduate student of philosophy at the University of Toronto who happened to be his younger brother. This turned out to be not at all a bad idea. While Ted Honderich pursued the studies that eventually made him a major figure in British philosophy and the author of books such as *A Theory of Determinism: The Mind, Neuroscience and Life-Hopes*, he turned out some lively pages. Like earlier *Star* literary editors, he was hampered — fortunately for me — by the lack of a budget to pay writers. He was expected to produce much of the material that appeared on the pages himself and obtain the rest of it free from any staff members he could cajole into writing for him.

For a while his contributors didn't receive even the review copies of the books they read: there was a rule, handed down years before by God knows which executive, that review copies had to be passed on to the *Star* library and, if found unsuitable for its shelves, donated to the poor.

Ted Honderich was therefore receptive to someone who was anxious to write about books, who could lay at least a shaky claim to the beginnings of expertise, and who insisted he wasn't worried about money. During our first meeting he looked at me oddly, as if wondering just how crazy I was and just how far — he may have been working it out as a problem in moral philosophy — he should exploit my insanity.

"I won't be able to pay you more than, uh" — he paused — "five dollars." Perhaps I showed alarm, because he went on: "Or ten dollars, for a longer piece." It was a few weeks before I understood his hesitation. By then two of my reviews had appeared, one at what we had agreed was the five-dollar length, one at the ten-dollar length. I asked him when I would receive my money. He said, "Oh yeah," took out his wallet, and handed me one five-dollar bill and one ten.

Over the years I have heard many producers and editors complain about "my lack of a budget." Ted was one editor who wasn't fooling. Whatever he paid me came out of his own salary. He was also one editor who never complained about overly long articles. When I tried to stretch my muscles by turning what might have been a 400-word review into a 1,000-word attempt at an essay, Ted was grateful. He had a lot of space to fill, and once he told me that he sometimes filled it by scalping — that is, rewriting — reviews from the New York *Times*.

In the autumn of 1958, when he was about to leave the *Star* to work on his doctorate in England, he asked me whether I was interested in succeeding him. Interested? I still have a carbon of my letter of application to Borden Spears, the assistant managing editor, and I'm surprised by its moderate tone. At no point does it offer to assassinate

the enemies of Mr. Spears; it doesn't even pledge allegiance
to the Liberal Party. It does manage to strike that combination of sycophancy and ambition which I have since seen in
several hundred letters by other hands. "Right now I admire
the *Star*'s book page as the best in the country, but I think
that if I got the job my tendency would be to make it a little
lighter, both in layout and content, while trying to maintain
its present high standards." Present high standards? I'm sure
Borden, whom I later came to know and love, read that letter in exactly the same way I've read similar letters since;
but he gave me the job.

He also gave me a little money to spend on contributors,
something like fifty dollars a week to start. My own salary,
covered by the Newspaper Guild contract, was munificent.
I began at one hundred and forty dollars a week, more than
I'd been making as a freelance, and only a month or so later
a raise under the union contract came into effect. To my
astonishment, my salary jumped another fifteen dollars or
so. Then it was Christmas, and my bonus — the first I'd
ever received — was a full week's pay. This was as close to
prosperity as I had known.

AT THAT POINT, Beland Honderich was just beginning
his life's work, the eternal remaking of the *Star*. He didn't
like the paper he had taken over in 1955, and as I understand it he doesn't much like the paper he puts out today.
In the intervening thirty-three years, I believe, there have
been at most a few brief periods when he's read the *Star*
with wholehearted approval. He's a man of infinite dissatisfaction, and, in an odd way, a visionary. He seems to believe
that just up ahead there's a *Star* that will make him pleased
as well as rich, a really good paper the whole world, even
Honderich, will admire. What he doesn't understand —
though most of the people who work with him do — is that
he himself is the main obstacle between the *Star* and its
destiny as a great newspaper. Tinkering, carried to extremes,

demoralizes a newspaper's staff and erodes the authority of everyone but the publisher.

Early in 1959, all I knew about him was that he was ambitious: he wanted a new kind of *Star* for the new Toronto slowly being born. He seems to have had in mind a combination of populism and sophistication, a paper that could be read by large masses of people but could also impress the most knowledgeable readers. For a time, strangely enough, he had something like this within his grasp. First he hired Pierre Berton, who began writing a daily column that dazzled the city. Berton helped Honderich acquire a wonderful illustrator as political cartoonist, and within a few months Duncan Macpherson was the best in the country; in retrospect he seems to have been the best in Canadian history, though he always insisted he knew little about politics. Honderich hired Ron Haggart from *The Globe and Mail*, and during the next few years Haggart wrote a brilliant column about municipal affairs, a subject that has never since been so well analyzed. Honderich acquired (and soon made executive editor) the ragingly ambitious ex-evangelist, Charles Templeton, a man with no experience in journalism who nevertheless confidently took command of the newsroom. Honderich brought in a Soviet affairs specialist, Mark Gayn, and the *Star* became the only paper in the country where *Pravda* was read every day in the original. For the first time in many years the *Star* became essential reading.

One day, during this time of swift change, I heard an amazing rumour: Honderich was thinking of hiring Nathan Cohen as drama critic. Even then Cohen was notorious. Working mainly on CBC radio, he had earned a reputation as a flamboyantly abrasive critic, the scourge of everything in the theatre that was pretentious and mediocre. Alone among Canadian drama critics of his day, he treated the eminent and the anonymous with equal disrespect — Arthur Miller, Lister Sinclair, and the Stratford Festival were among his favourite targets. He had the audacity even to wonder aloud whether devoting most of our scarce resources to producing the works of a dead Englishman was the ideal way to create a vibrant Canadian theatre. He was a great admirer of Celia Franca and her ballet company, but he could write: "Ignore the complaint that there are far too few comic works in the repertoire of the National Ballet...For sheer humour, its full-length production of *Swan Lake* is hard to beat. Just because the humour is unintentional is no reason to amend that statement."

Nathan was one of those thick, heavy men whose shirts seem always to be one size too small and whose suits appear to rumple automatically ten seconds after emerging from the dry cleaner's polyethylene bag. He used his weight to create an aura of importance, pushing impatiently through crowds in theatre lobbies, creating a comfortable space around himself. In later years he usually carried a walking-stick, which gave him an old-world look. Arthur Hailey, the novelist, bought him a handsome-looking cane that concealed a sword; if pressed by his colleagues, Nathan would sometimes unsheath it and practice a few thrusts and parries, to the delight of all.

I loved him unreservedly. For years I had intensely admired his radio talks, and my first meeting with him, in 1957 — over lunch with Robert Weaver and another CBC producer, Gordon Babineau — was a great occasion for me. Nathan dominated the conversation (there was no occasion when he did not) but he did so with such tact and generosity that he made me feel honoured to be with him. He treated us as an audience, but he graciously allowed for a certain amount of audience participation. He drew each of us out in turn. Babineau had written some short stories, and Nathan — to Babineau's obvious pleasure — urged him to write more. Weaver had recently been responsible for a good program, and Nathan commented favourably on it. He had even read something I'd written, and he discussed it with a seriousness that enchanted me. Over coffee he told us he was writing a play. "Finally," he said, "I've recovered from the trauma of *Blue Is For Mourning.*" That was his first play (also his only one), which had been savaged by critics and ignored by audiences during a brief run a few years earlier. Now, he said, he was working on a backstage drama which would take place at the Royal Alexandra Theatre during a National Ballet performance. It sounded good to me, but I never heard him speak of it again.

In 1959 the idea of working beside Cohen on a newspaper was so exciting, and so unexpected, that I could hardly contain myself. And then there came further news: Honderich wanted me to come to his office and discuss this proposal with him.

I decided I wouldn't stride in with a banner saying "HIRE COHEN." I would wait respectfully for my editor's questions. When I entered — I hadn't been in Honderich's office before — he was sitting behind his desk, smoking a good cigar. Long before he became fabulously wealthy he had the shyness of an old-fashioned Canadian millionaire, and some of the habits too. He dressed in three-piece suits, which made his bullet-shaped head and his thick body seem even more impressive. He gestured toward a seat. He was, he said, thinking of making some changes. He wanted the *Star* to have more...authority. Somebody had suggested that we needed a new drama critic. Somebody else had told him he should hire, uh, Nathan Cohen. What did I think of Cohen's ability?

"I think he's a first-class critic," I said. "Good judgement, a good writer." No need to gush.

"Fine, but there's one thing that bothers me. Some people have suggested that he's" — Honderich tipped a little ash off his cigar — "well, a...*self-promoter*. What do you think of that?"

What I thought was that I had just heard one of the funniest questions of the year. Saying that Nathan Cohen was a self-promoter was like saying that Pierre Berton was ambitious or Peter C. Newman political. Cohen was an impre-

sario who devoted his life to creating one star, Nathan Cohen
— and, as I was to learn later, Nathan understood this as well
as anyone. But I could hardly say anything like that to
Honderich: the man appeared to be in earnest. (So far as I
know, he has never been anything else.) He seemed to be
suggesting that the *Star* — the paper that gave the world
Gordon Sinclair and a dozen other exuberant public egos —
disapproved of self-promotion.

"Well, I, uh, perhaps there's…well, Mr. Honderich, I think
that anyone in, you know, show business, as Nathan is, in a
way, has to develop a sense of publicity and…"

My barely coherent waffle apparently satisfied Honderich.
A couple of days later I heard that Nathan was coming on
the staff.

MY ENTHUSIASM for Nathan's arrival was not shared by
the veterans in the *Star* newsroom. To them he looked like a
trained seal, the old reporter's contemptuous term for an
expensive specialist brought in to do a job that any real
newspaperman could do just as well or better. To the old
timers, the appointment was one more proof that Beland
Honderich really had no idea what he was doing and was (I
heard the word often) "ruining" the *Star*. So far as I was
concerned, he couldn't ruin the damn thing fast enough —
I'd never thought it much of a paper. Naturally, I concealed
this view from my colleagues as best I could.

The old timers also sympathized with Jack Karr, who had
been both movie and drama critic; when he learned that he
was now to cover only films, he resigned in humiliation and
spent the rest of his working life as a press agent. Nathan,
installed as drama critic, began spraying in all directions the
opinions that had made him infamous at the CBC and that
contrasted sharply with Karr's muted, easygoing reviews. And
then, to everyone's surprise but his own, Nathan also made it
clear that covering the theatre wasn't the limit of his ambition. He wanted to run the entertainment department as

well. This was viewed as a curious ambition. Until then, at the *Star*, "entertainment editor" was hardly a title at all, just a slot filled temporarily by someone detached from the city desk. It was a chore, not a position, and I doubt that anyone had ever asked for it — certainly the fellow Nathan abruptly displaced made no great show of resentment.

Nathan turned it into the throne of an emperor. In handling Honderich — who looked on him with both awe and amusement — Nathan proved an adroit office politician. He asked for a bigger budget, more staff, and more space in the paper — and got them all. He became a jealous protector of his turf and his prerogatives. When thwarted by an incompetent or officious executive, he sometimes deployed a force of histrionic rage that surprised everyone around him. Clearly, he was taking all this newspaper stuff seriously.

I saw him, in the beginning, as an intellectual who might be a bit lost on a big daily, and might find it distasteful to deal with the everyday trivia of the entertainment pages. All to the contrary, Nathan thrived on Hollywood gossip, fought ferociously for scoops, and always knew as much about soap operas, horror movies, and trashy fiction as the writers who covered them from day to day. It was as if he and the *Star* — or, at least, the exciting, unpredictable *Star* Honderich wanted to create — were made for each other. In no time he transformed himself from a broadcaster with a rather marginal place at the CBC (he had chaired an on-again-off-again panel show, "Fighting Words," and edited scripts for a TV drama series) into a newspaperman who seemed to be standing at the core of the biggest paper in the country. And he became, almost overnight, a fierce *Star* partisan, curling his lip in contempt at the feeble efforts of the *Telegram*, barely deigning to notice the *Globe*.

Soon he made the *Star* the place where everyone learned first about anything of importance in Canadian show business. In the early 1960s a CBC executive said to me, "Nathan's sources are amazing. He knows what happens around here before I do." One of his secrets — I didn't learn this for several years — was a close friendship with the CBC casting director, who saw each performer's contract well before any program was announced.

Nathan accepted as his due the fawning attention of every Toronto press agent, and took it for granted that out-of-town press agents would offer him his choice of appointments with the stars whose time they organized. At one point he announced that his writers would no longer, under any conditions, attend press conferences. "Why," he asked at a meeting, "should *I* spend *my* time thinking up the best questions for *my* writers and then have *their* writers get the same answers?" From then on, until he changed his mind, *Star* writers interviewed their subjects only in private.

No matter how much gossip he published, Nathan wanted his pages, and his own column, taken seriously. He often said, before coming to the *Star*, that he was not just the best drama critic in Canada but the only one. Now he had the forum where, day after day, he could prove himself. He covered not only the theatre but also ballet and, from time to time, movies. Sometimes, after the *Star* movie critic had reviewed a film, Nathan would run his own opinion, contradicting his colleague. There were those, like me, who regarded this as a healthy form of debate, but the reviewers sometimes thought it vicious. On a few occasions Nathan also wrote about jazz, incompetently, until I threatened to form a committee whose sole purpose would be to get him to stop.

There was no question, however, of his authority in the theatre — actors, directors, and producers bitterly resented his criticism, but recognized that he knew what he was talking about. Provided with a handsome travel budget by Honderich, he became the first national theatre critic in Canadian history. He knew Vancouver and Winnipeg theatre, and he was often in Montreal or Ottawa. When Leon Major set up the Neptune Theatre in Halifax, Nathan was there to cheer him on. He couldn't always praise the productions, but his presence was a gesture of support.

He said he wanted to surround himself with similarly effective critics in the other arts, but he managed to do so only occasionally. He found it impossible, for instance, to hire a TV critic and leave him alone long enough to let the poor wretch make a reputation. Since Cohen rightly believed he knew more about TV than anyone he might hire, he couldn't keep himself from interfering. Luckily he professed to know nothing of classical music, so he was able to employ an excellent critic, John Beckwith, a composer who later became dean of the Royal Conservatory. For a while, he had Wendy Michener as movie critic, but she resigned in rage and frustration over his interference and eventually made her reputation at *Maclean's* and the CBC.

And then there was my case. When Nathan became my boss I was running the book page and writing the art column; he turned me into a five-a-week book columnist. Later he claimed it was his own idea and I claimed it had been mine all along, but in any case Nathan piloted this very un-*Star*-like idea through management. He took me to a meeting with Honderich and Harry Hindmarsh, the grandson of Joseph Atkinson and the son of H.C. Hindmarsh, who at that point — not yet reconciled to seeing Honderich run everything — was still nominally managing editor.

After Nathan introduced the subject, I outlined my column. Hindmarsh, who seemed to think book reviews were called "book reports," wondered how I could read a new book every day and write about it. I explained that I wouldn't be doing that — there would be a couple of new books a week, an interview, a collection of news and gossip, maybe a piece about a re-issue in paperback of a book I'd read years before. Hindmarsh didn't quite follow. "Well," he said, "what the hell — those you haven't time to read, you'll just skim." We left it at that, and set the date for my column to appear.

In our time together I found Nathan stimulating, infuriating, insecure, smug, brilliant, and bloody-minded. But I never found him unkind, and though I listened in sympathy to colleagues who regarded him as a martinet, I could never match their complaints with my own. He treated me with delicacy and paternal affection. This father of two daughters saw me, for a while, as something of a son. Though he was only nine years older, he insisted on calling me "My boy," and "Robert, my boy…" He would instruct me on some point and then close the conversation by saying, "Thus endeth the first lesson." He noticed my tendency toward hero-worship, and tried to prevent me from being taken in — Saul Bellow wasn't the titan I believed him to be, *The New Yorker* wasn't the model everyone should follow, and the Tyrone Guthrie productions which had launched the Stratford Festival were essentially hollow. Nathan explained Guthrie's failings to me in such detail that I almost believed that I'd had a rather miserable time during the first few seasons at Stratford.

Not surprisingly, Nathan Cohen, up close, was less heroic than the magisterial Nathan Cohen I had heard so often on the radio. For one thing, he never learned to write well and never realized what he needed to learn. He trusted his first drafts, always a mistake. When he expressed his views powerfully on something that mattered to him, his columns could be quite wonderful; more often, they were poorly constructed and crammed with clumsy sentences. They were also strewn with factual errors and misspellings. He wrote his column in the middle of the night — after going to the theatre he might watch a couple of TV movies before sitting down to the typewriter — and sent it in by taxi, close to the deadline. His copy was messy, with changes scrawled here and there and sometimes extra sentences typed sideways in the margin. This naturally led to a great many errors in the paper, which Nathan once ascribed to anti-Semitism among the linotype operators. For all I know the composing room was crawling with neo-Nazis, but they didn't need to be bigots to make a mess out of the copy Nathan sent them.

I enjoyed defending him against the constant attacks of theatre people (many of whom began to speak lovingly of him after he died), and I was no more than mildly uncomfortable when members of the staff called him arbitrary or mean. But something much more troubling began to show up. One by one, those who worked for him came to realize that they could not always depend on the truthfulness of what he said. When a TV critic Nathan inherited, Dennis Braithwaite, was being pushed out of the *Star*, Nathan told me that Dennis had been offered in turn to each section of the editorial department — the rewrite desk, the city desk — and turned down. That's why he had to go. I repeated this as fact and was challenged by the head of the rewrite desk, who informed me that he hadn't been offered Dennis and would be delighted to get him.

On that occasion Nathan may simply have been misinformed, but another kind of fiction also cropped up in his conversation. Once Nathan and I talked with the American literary critic Leslie Fiedler, who told us of certain unimportant but interesting experiences in little theatres in Paris and Rome. A couple of months later I heard the same stories coming out of Nathan's mouth, as if they had happened to him. Could this be forgetfulness?

Then, at a party, I was drawn into a corner by David Cobb, an expert feature writer in our department, whom I knew only slightly.

"That Cohen is a marvellous character, isn't he?"

"Sure as hell is," I said.

"Amazingly knowledgeable about damn near anything."

"Truly amazing."

"But can you tell me something, Bob? Can you explain why he's a pathological liar?"

I demurred — surely not pathological — and Cobb began

citing chapter and verse. Nathan had said this or that, which
Cobb had learned was untrue. In each case the story didn't
matter all that much to the listener or, indeed, to Cohen.
Cobb and I shook our heads in wonderment and rejoined
the party.

Over the years, a pattern emerged. Most of the stories in
some way enhanced Cohen's stature. Once, after seeing the
press baron Roy Thomson, Nathan told me that Thomson
had begged him to move to England and run the entertainment pages of all his newspapers. Nathan had held out for
drama critic of the *Sunday Times* of London, and negotiations had broken down. Well, that *could* have happened.
Later Nathan reported that he had been approached by the
New York *Times* to become drama critic. At another point he
was being courted by *The New Yorker* to replace Kenneth
Tynan, on Tynan's recommendation. William F. Buckley Jr.
wanted him to write regularly for the *National Review*. He
was offered the editorship of *Maclean's*, but turned it down.

He told that last story so often, and to so many well-
connected and loose-lipped people, that I felt called upon
to figure out what it was all about. I was working on *Maclean's*
at the time, and Ken Lefolii, the editor, was annoyed when
several acquaintances informed him he was about to be
replaced by Cohen, or had narrowly escaped being replaced.
Eventually I heard from Cohen what had actually happened.
He and the publisher of *Maclean's* had met over lunch with
a woman who did public relations for the magazine. Cohen
had told the publisher he didn't much like *Maclean's*, and
the publisher — a man with no say in these matters — had
asked what Cohen would do with it if he were editor. Cohen
had described the sort of magazine he would like to edit,
and the three of them had gone their separate ways.

From that acorn, Cohen had grown the oak of a firm offer
and a possible major career change. This made me think
about all the other offers he reported receiving. Probably
there was *something*, however small, behind every one of

them — maybe Tynan had once said that Cohen should write something for *The New Yorker*. Nathan was not a liar, really; he was what the English used to call a romancer — he improved his stories, sometimes changing them beyond recognition. A poor shopkeeper's son from Cape Breton who had made his way to the head of a difficult profession, he was still unsatisfied, and given to dreaming of distant offers, tantalizing alternate futures. He told his friends, including me, what *should* have happened to him, and I think that at the time of telling he believed every word.

To the end of his life he also retained some of the style of the boyish show-off; he wanted everyone within hearing to understand not only that he knew more than they did about any subject that might come up but that he knew a lot more. Around 1967, when he was drama critic but no longer editor, he still attended story meetings of the entertainment department and handed out ideas and advice. At one such meeting someone raised the possibility of a piece on the early Warner Brothers movies, to be written by a staff writer — in my memory the writer is Ralph Thomas, who later directed *Ticket to Heaven* and other films. Thomas wondered aloud which actors appeared in the Warners pictures of the 1930s and 1940s.

Nathan, who had said little that day, took this as some sort of challenge.

"Well, you know the obvious ones — Cagney, Bogart, Bette Davis, Edward G. Robinson, but there were also — "

Ralph (scribbling notes): "Yeah, thanks Nathan…"

"Ann Dvorak, Dorothy Dare, George Arliss…"

Ralph: "Gotcha, well…"

"Beulah Bondi, Arthur Treacher, Paul Muni…"

Peter Gzowski, who was in the middle of his brief career as entertainment editor, began chuckling. "Go, Nathan," he said. Nathan didn't see anything funny, or pretended he didn't. He pressed on.

"George Brent, Ruth Chatterton, Lyle Talbot…"

Nathan was picking up speed, naming them faster than Ralph could get them down.

"Ruby Keeler, Franchot Tone, Hardie Albright…"

A secretary poked her head in the door. Someone went out to take a phone call.

"Frank McHugh, Joan Blondell, and oh, of course, Dick Powell…"

On it went, a virtuoso performance. Nathan kept reciting long after Ralph put down his pencil. Finally he stopped. Perhaps he had mentioned everyone who ever worked at Warners above the level of bit player — or perhaps he had come to the end of his prodigious memory. He allowed himself a chuckle and sat back. The meeting moved to other subjects. Later Gzowski and I agreed that we could probably have gotten Nathan a place in the Guinness Book of Records, if someone had thought to keep an accurate count.

Nathan and I stopped working together when I left the *Star* in 1968 for *Saturday Night*, but we were in touch from time to time. One day in 1971 I heard he was in the hospital with a heart ailment, that he didn't want visitors, and that the prognosis was bad. The next news came only a few days later: he had died in the night, just forty-seven years old. I had more than the usual chance to mourn him in public. I gave a written talk about him on the CBC radio network that morning, and discussed him with Bruno Gerussi (who then did a program rather like the one Gzowski does now). That week I devoted the ninety minutes of my own program, "This is Robert Fulford," to interviews about Nathan. I wrote a little piece in *Saturday Night*.

All this was accomplished calmly, or perhaps numbly. A few days later, I was working on something — an article, or a program — and the words "Nathan will *love* this" went through my mind. When I realized that Nathan would neither love it nor hate it, I began to feel genuine, heart-stopping grief. I remembered going through precisely the same sequence of emotions only once before, following the death of my actual father in 1957.

AS A REVIEWER — conducting my education in public, in the phrase of one celebrated critic — I both copied Nathan and reacted against him. Consciously I tried to emulate the breadth of his knowledge and interest. I agreed with him that a critic's worst sin is ignorance. He believed that no one could ever know enough about anything, and he encouraged everyone to read widely and look into every corner of movies and television and public affairs. Once I made the mistake of admitting to him that the mere idea of a book on Social Credit in Alberta bored me; he sat down and delivered an impromptu lecture, at the end of which I understood that, political journalists to the contrary, there was absolutely nothing inherently boring about the history of Social Credit.

We never agreed, though, on the business of reviewing and criticism. To Nathan a critic's duty was to uphold the standards of whatever art form he wrote about. I thought this idea laughable, and still do. On important matters critics have been as often wrong as right, and I didn't have any reason to think that on Judgment Day my final score would be any better than the international average over the last two centuries. Of course I gave my honest views of whatever I wrote about, and I spent a lot of time reading earlier critics and trying to develop my own standards; but I knew that my opinion was the least important part of any review I wrote. The core of my work was discovery — searching through the books and art galleries for what was interesting and possibly important, then describing what I found accurately and engagingly. I also understood that, no matter how carefully I honed my standards, the most compelling artists would set their own standards — and sometimes would produce art that was significant even though it didn't please me. Leonard Cohen's second novel, *Beautiful Losers*, was the perfect exam-

ple, a book that was a lot more significant than my opinion
of it. I disliked it, and said so, but I saw it as fascinating and
important. I think I wrote three pieces about it in the first
ten days after it appeared.

I was trying, all those years, to apply everything I knew
about journalism and storytelling to the business of practical reviewing. And early in my *Star* career I received a letter
that suggested I was on the right track. "I think your criticism
of 'The Years with Ross' is one of the very best of the hundreds I have seen," James Thurber wrote from West Cornwall,
Connecticut on September 7, 1959. He went on to discuss
briefly, but with great charm, the thesis of my review (that
Thurber and other *New Yorker* writers based many of their
fictional characters on their irascible editor, Harold Ross).
His letter, with the blind man's signature scrawled across the
bottom in soft pencil, hangs on a wall in my house today.

The *Star* column provided by Honderich and Cohen
turned out to be the perfect platform for me. Day after day I
wrote about what I thought were the important books of the
time — I enthusiastically tracked all the early émigré novels
of Vladimir Nabokov as they came into English, read every
word of Isaac Bashevis Singer that was translated from the
Yiddish, reviewed J.D. Salinger and Truman Capote when
they first appeared in *The New Yorker*, told my readers about
the Two Cultures battle between F.R. Leavis and C.P. Snow
in England, followed every move of Philip Roth, Kingsley
Amis, John O'Hara, and Saul Bellow. My affection for O'Hara
in those years was boundless (it is now bounded), which
disturbed Morley Callaghan. "O'Hara," he said to me once,
"has the mind of a cab driver."

Callaghan, whose reputation was slowly emerging from a
mid-career dark period, became a great subject for me. Of
course I described with enthusiasm the unfolding careers of
Mordecai Richler, Margaret Laurence, and Brian Moore,
but I also wrote about every other Canadian novelist who
appeared in English. Strange as it seems now, it was possible

in the early 1960s for one critic to review every new novel in the country — and to write about the important non-fiction, the literary magazines, and many of the poets as well. (Today it would take a platoon of reviewers.)

Most of those writers would have had their successes or failures without me; all I could do was try to create a climate in which their work might be taken seriously. But in the 1960s there was one book, and one writer, whose destinies I seem to have shaped. In the spring of 1965, in a hall at CBC radio, I ran into Stephen Vizinczey. I'd known him for several years and had written for *Exchange,* the magazine he briefly edited in Montreal. Now, having been a producer at the CBC for three years, he was resigning.

"I've written a novel," he said. "Everybody says you should write about what you know, so I've written about sex."

I gave him a that's-nice smile, wished him luck, and went on my way. Meanwhile, he was showing *In Praise of Older Women,* or parts of it, to publishers. Jack McClelland of McClelland and Stewart wanted to publish it, but the advance he offered was in the low hundreds. Vizinczey was making an outrageous demand: he wouldn't sign for anything less than $2,000. Neither McClelland nor any other publisher was interested in laying out a fortune like that, so Vizinczey decided to publish it himself. He invested $6,000 and formed Contemporary Canada Press (which turned out to be a one-book company). When he had the bound proofs from the printer, he called me.

I went over to the Rosedale apartment he shared with his wife, Gloria, whom I had known earlier as Donald Harron's first wife. Vizinczey showed me some of the pre-publication quotes he had assembled from eminences he knew — F.R. Scott, Hugh MacLennan — and I interviewed him about his background in Hungary, his part in the 1956 revolution, his progress from Hungary to Canada. I didn't like the title he had chosen, I didn't much like the sound of the quotes he showed me, and I decided the book wouldn't be much good either. For one thing I knew that an immigrant, new to English, couldn't possibly write a good novel on his first try. But out of charity, and admiration for his nerve, I decided to forego reading the book while I prepared a column on his life and his self-publishing project. Reading the novel first, I feared, would sour me on the whole business.

Headed "A Novelist all on his own," my piece began: "Stephen Vizinczey is a Hungarian-born writer who plans to become Canada's first socialist millionaire. A country is not really sophisticated until it has socialist millionaires, Vizinczey argues. He plans to provide us with one by the least promising of all possible schemes — publishing his own novel."

I wrote that column, delivered it to the *Star*, and then went home to open the novel. Twenty pages into it, I realized that Vizinczey was a fresh voice — cool, distanced, and witty — with a great deal to say. I started a one-man campaign for *In Praise of Older Women*. By the end of the year I had written three more newspaper columns about Vizinczey, had talked about the book on the radio several times, and had written a profile of him in *The Canadian*, a national newspaper supplement. That fall *In Praise of Older Women* led the Canadian best-seller list and a New York publisher paid an advance of $40,000 for American rights. Eventually it sold some 2.5-million copies in several languages. Before he left Canada to live in Europe, Vizinczey sent me a copy of the first edition, inscribed "To Bob Fulford, with gratitude — for I only wrote this book, it was he who *made* it."

ALMOST EVERYONE whines about working on Beland Honderich's *Star*. While I've always complained about the quality of the paper, I've seldom found cause for serious complaint about my own treatment. But there was one day when officious editing threw me into a wild rage and provoked the only really silly resignation in my career.

The first edition of the *Star* for October 20, 1967, carried my account of John MacGregor's exhibition at the Isaacs

Gallery. The third paragraph began: "MacGregor turns zippers, vegetables and mountains into sex symbols. In one of his drawings a necktie turns into a penis…." Martin Goodman, the editor of the *Star* and Honderich's second-in-command until his death, read that passage in the paper and immediately cut the second sentence. I got to the office soon after the second edition appeared, and glanced over my column. When I saw what had happened my reaction was, putting it mildly, extreme. A hangover may have been involved, since in those days I tended to drink a good many more martinis than were good for me. In any case, I loudly demanded to know what filthy-minded censor had attacked my innocent little column just to cut out a perfectly clinical word. When I found out it was Goodman I called his office.

"He's on the third floor," said his secretary. For the moment I forgot that this was a euphemism for Honderich's office.

"What local?" I demanded, and she told me. I called, and Honderich picked up the phone. Only after I said "Put Martin Goodman on" did I realize whom I was ordering about. But still I didn't settle down.

"Goddamit, Martie, I don't want to work on a paper where people think 'penis' is a dirty word. I just can't do it — and I don't need this goddamn job."

"That's how you see it, but I have to take the phone calls from readers and believe me, they…."

"Martie, I quit!"

I looked down at the phone, now resting on its cradle. What had I done?

The next twenty-four hours or so were devoted to finding ways in which I could climb down to safety with dignity and yet not damage Goodman's own position. Peter Gzowski and Ron Haggart talked reasonably to me, somebody else talked to Goodman, I spoke privately with Honderich and finally a senior editor produced a memo promising that in future my column would be changed only after consultation with me.

Gratefully, I rejoined the staff, never having missed an issue.

At that time Gary Dunford (much later the gossip columnist of the Toronto *Sun*) was producing, on the office Xerox machine, a sort of underground paper for members of the *Star* staff. He gave a florid account of the entire incident, and ended it with a made-up quote he attributed to me: "You'd quit, too, if your penis were cut off between the first and second editions."

Perhaps that incident was a sign of what was coming: certainly the *Star* was getting duller and more cautious, and Goodman himself was remaking his rambunctious personality in the image of the paper he imagined Honderich wanted to create. Goodman was the longest-lasting of all Honderich's editors, and by the end of his life he was — at least theoretically — in charge of the whole newspaper. But he knew, and everyone else knew, that there was only one man in charge of anything, and whatever title you held — editor-in-chief or president or executive this-and-that — meant nothing at all when you were in the presence of Beland Honderich.

Most of the men who went to work for him anywhere near the highest levels of the paper (I don't think there were ever any women) obviously believed they would be exceptions. The weaklings preceding them had fallen by the wayside, sure, but they would somehow find the freedom to manoeuvre within the Honderich system. So far as I know, none has ever succeeded. One by one they fell out of favour with Honderich, or grew tired of the struggle. In my fantasy I see them — the guy who was once told to reorganize the whole editorial department, the guy who was brought in from the States to punch up the front page, several guys who used to run the editorial page — stacked up like cordwood outside Honderich's office.

In many sections of the *Star*, morale has been low for a long time — sometimes, walking through the office with my once-a-week column in the 1970s and 1980s, I saw the editorial room as one giant depression ward. But the executive suite is filled with an even deeper melancholy. The reason, beyond question, is Honderich's personality. The same attention to detail that made him a powerful executive in the first place has spread despair among senior editors and ruined his chances of creating the newspaper of his dreams. He can't keep his hands off anything.

I understood how deeply this compulsiveness ran when a city editor, Patrick Scott, told me what happened on the day in 1971 when Honderich bought the circulation of the *Telegram*. Honderich himself wrote the announcement, took it to the news desk, and gave instructions about how it was to be handled. This was the great triumph of his life; his competition was now eliminated and his paper would likely dominate Toronto and southern Ontario for the rest of his life. He turned to walk out of the newsroom, but stopped as he passed Scott's desk and picked up a piece of paper from the floor. "Patrick," he said, "I've spoken to you about this before. I'd like the city room to be a lot neater."

Honderich speaks with such confidence, and makes his points with such persistence, that whatever he says becomes amplified in the re-telling and in the minds of underlings acquires the force of Holy Writ. A couple of years ago, when he was driving home through a snowstorm, he was annoyed by how much the radio stations were making of this event. He was only twenty minutes late getting home, and he thought the radio people were overplaying the storm. He phoned the city desk to say so; and this impressed the editors so deeply that they didn't run anything at all on one of the biggest storms of the year. Once, so the story goes, Honderich said he liked to see red in colour photographs in the paper. For years — and long after Honderich himself had forgotten the whole notion — photographers were required to deliver pictures of people wearing red jackets and red dresses; some carried red sweaters in the trunks of their cars, to thrust on subjects who lacked proper apparel.

Honderich speaks quietly and mainly stays out of sight, but the effect is the same as if he were running across the newsroom, shouting through a megaphone.

Several times, while I was at the *Star*, I was offered promotions that would have sent me in the direction of the executive suite and the human cordwood. On another occasion I was interviewed by headhunters for the job of editor. But only once was I offered outright a senior position and forced to turn it down clearly. That was in 1963, when I was working on *Maclean's*. Robert Nielsen, an accomplished journalist and a good man, took me out to lunch and said he had Honderich's authority to offer me the position of co-editor, with Nielsen, of the editorial page. Bob predicted that he and I would work well together, he being strong in subjects where I was weak and vice versa. I agreed with that part. It wasn't Nielsen who worried me.

EIGHT

*T*he boys *at* Maclean's

ON A MONDAY afternoon in the middle of December, 1963, I faced an exceptional problem. In the next twenty hours or so, I had to write a cover story for *Maclean's*, from scratch. Normally it takes me at least three weeks to produce a magazine piece of any length, but this case wasn't normal. There was no opportunity for anything you could properly call research, there would be precious little reflection, and there was no possibility of a rewrite. The article had to go to the typesetter the next morning, and all I had was a pile of blank paper. I hadn't met the subject of my article, and didn't know anyone who had.

A few weeks earlier, after the assassination of John Kennedy, we had decided to publish a cover story on the new president, Lyndon Johnson, and our Washington staff writer, Ian Sclanders, had agreed to write it. Peter Gzowski, who was running the magazine — the editor, Ken Lefolii, was in Europe — had bought Canadian rights to Yousuf Karsh's recent colour portrait of Johnson. The photograph was being prepared for the cover, and the necessary space inside the magazine was set aside. The article, however, didn't show up. Sclanders missed his deadline by one day, phoned to apologize, then didn't deliver the next day. He promised it again, adding that large parts of it were done. Again he didn't deliver.

The press date was getting close, but there was still a weekend to spare and that was cause for hope. All writers and editors cherish the belief — despite abundant contrary evidence — that wonderful things can be accomplished when "a clear weekend" is available for writing. But on Monday morning no article came on the wire from Washington. Gzowski phoned Sclanders and learned that it wasn't ready and wasn't going to be. He asked Sclanders to dictate what he had to a secretary. A few minutes later she typed out about 250 words, all he could provide. As I discovered later, Sclanders always found Christmas a painfully difficult season, perhaps because of an unhappy childhood experience. He had begun drinking heavily around the time he accepted the assignment, and hadn't stopped. He apparently had done no work at all on Lyndon Johnson.

The incident illustrates, in extreme form, the atmosphere of desperation common in magazine offices. Some readers may imagine that an editor's job is simply to read the manuscripts submitted to the magazine and choose those suitable for publication; more sophisticated readers may understand that the editor's main work is to generate manuscripts by suggesting ideas to writers, then carefully sifting the material that results. But the truth is that in many cases editors find themselves publishing the least bad material available on the day the final list of contents is made up. Sometimes, when an editor is asked why this or that article was published, the only honest answer is, "It was all I had."

On that day in 1963 the situation was much worse than usual. We didn't have a bad article to run: we had no article. Those who haven't worked for magazines might assume that editors routinely prepare alternative articles, particularly cover articles, and that these can be inserted when scheduled stories fall through. That's how it should work, and all editors dream of a day when it will. Unfortunately, it never does. Sometimes there are articles awaiting publication — "the bank," editors call them — but they tend to be pieces no one really wants to publish. And in this case a back-up article wouldn't have helped anyway. It was too late to put another cover through the colour printing process.

An article had to be written in the office, and I was elected, perhaps because I was the fastest typist on the staff. I talked about it briefly with Gzowski, then went around the office collecting reference books and magazines that carried material on Johnson (a trip to the public library would have eaten into my writing time). I set to work. When Gzowski poked his head into my office on his way home I was desperately banging away at my Underwood. At three o'clock in the morning I put a 3,500-word manuscript on his desk and went home to sleep.

At *Maclean's* late the next morning I found a large sign on my wall. Maclean-Hunter's company slogan was "Fear Not When Doing Right." Gzowski had lettered, "Fear Not When Writing Other People's Articles (Superbly)." Beside the sign hung the largest and most expensive cigar that Gzowksi's secretary had been able to find, a Churchill corona. The piece went in the magazine under the byline "Grattan Gray," the name *Maclean's* traditionally used for articles of mixed or dubious authorship. It won no prizes, but neither did it attract any accusations of incompetence. I didn't read it again until the autumn of 1987. A quarter century later the prose seemed amazingly confident, considering that the author had never been in Johnson's presence and had not even visited Washington. The content, on the other hand, looked wonderfully stupid. In the early weeks of Johnson's presidency, American liberals had concocted the hopeful but unjustified view that he was at heart a genuine liberal and

potentially a statesman of Rooseveltian qualities. Grattan
Gray clearly bought this newly hatched wisdom and passed
it on to the readers of *Maclean's*. Those who believed what
they read in their national magazine must have been startled
when Johnson turned out to be one of the most loathsome
politicians in American history.

WHEN KEN LEFOLII came back from Europe I had enough
sense not to ask him what he thought of the Johnson piece,
and he had enough grace not to tell me. A judicious silence
was part of Lefolii's style. He could inform you, better than
anyone I ever knew, what was wrong with an article and how
it might be put right, but he didn't waste time on work that
couldn't be altered. He fixed his attention on what we were
doing, or about to do, and he had a very clear-sighted notion
of what was possible. He had worked for years under Ralph
Allen, the famous editor of *Maclean's* in the 1950s, and no
one spoke of Ralph with more respect; but Lefolii rightly
wanted to make a better magazine than the one he had
inherited from Ralph and Ralph's immediate successor, Blair
Fraser. Lefolii imagined a mass magazine that would be
intelligent, surprising, irreverent, and amusing. I think he
briefly achieved something like that, but what I can say for
certain is that Lefolii — and Gzowski, his managing editor —
created a working atmosphere as good as any I've ever known.
     Lefolii was sympathetic and yet demanding, funny but
also, in his way, stern. The *Maclean's* editors of the day spent
many of their social hours together, exchanging gossip and
insults in the roof bar of the Park Plaza, but on the morning
after an evening of amiable drinking Lefolii was still a tough
editor. He was as hard on his friends as he was on strangers
— harder, perhaps, because he held such high hopes for us.
Under his encouragement, some of the best journalists of
the period blossomed. Harry Bruce, a good young newspaperman, turned into an excellent magazine writer. Jack
Batten, challenged by Lefolii's sharp criticism, developed

the fluency that became the basis of a remarkable career. Barbara Moon's writing, always impressive, acquired a new depth and confidence. Alexander Ross, David Lewis Stein, and half a dozen others did work that surprised even themselves. My own writing — a 1963 cover story on Lester B. Pearson, for instance — became more ambitious, largely because of Lefolii's confidence in me. In the summer of 1964, in my last weeks on *Maclean's,* I wrote what I think was the first cover story anywhere on the new version of feminism; that was the beginning of my long engagement with that subject.

Some of the pieces Gzowski wrote in that period, such as his article about prejudice against Indians in the North Battleford area of Saskatchewan, still read extremely well in anthologies. Those were good years in other ways for Gzowski. He had been hired by Allen, off the daily in Chatham, Ontario, but he had developed into a more serious journalist under Lefolii and now he deferred to Lefolii's superior talent as an editor. Otherwise, he saw himself as the equal or better of just about anyone around, and since many of those who worked for him were older than he was, they often found dealing with him uncomfortable. He became managing editor at the early age of twenty-eight — Berton, something of a boy wonder in his own day, had been thirty-three when he got the same job — but Gzowski gave no sign that he thought his youth was an impediment.

As those who worked with him immediately noticed, Gzowski had the habit of turning everything from writing articles to mixing martinis into a contest. At any moment he might be found demonstrating — always in a laughing way, and at the same time always in a serious way — that he was better than someone else at something. Once, at a bar in Regina, we were playing checkers — the bar was called "Checkers" — and I was winning. Something distracted me, and I suggested we stop playing. "Don't do that, Fulford," Gzowski said, "this may be the only game in the world you can beat

me at. Make the most of it." Competition between the two of
us, though seldom at games, became one of the foundations
of a friendship that has now lasted a quarter of a century.

I'm not at all immune to feelings of competitiveness, but I
like to believe I mask them. In Gzowski's presence, however,
the mask sometimes slips. In the 1960s, when Gzowski, Bruce,
and I had summer cottages on the Toronto Island, we managed to turn our pick-up volleyball games into ferocious
battles of will. Once I was so carried away that, about to
smash the ball with my right hand, I actually lowered the net
with my left so as to facilitate the ball's passage into the
enemy court. Gzowski never let me forget that shot. In more
recent years we have pretended to care, or perhaps not
pretended, who got the first honorary degree (he did) and
who was first admitted to the Order of Canada (I was).

Lefolii took his writers and his magazine seriously, and
though we've since gone off in different directions, he's still
with me — internalized, a permanent reproach to whatever
impulses encourage me to settle lazily for my second best.
By questioning everything I wanted to write, and always in a
way I could respect, Lefolii made me think harder about my
work than I had before. His sense of humour was one of my
chief pleasures in those years, and I enjoyed him even when
he took lightly my own minor misfortunes. On October 22,
1962, the night John Kennedy announced the blockade of
Cuba and the Cuban missile crisis, the most threatening
event in the history of the Cold War, I had a tiny accident.
When Kennedy finished speaking on TV I walked across my
living room to turn off the set and twisted my ankle. I ignored
it, but in the middle of the night I awoke in some pain.
Eventually I went to the hospital, using a cane that a previous tenant had left in my house. When finally I got to the
Maclean's office the next morning, I was still supporting
myself with the cane. As I passed the open door of Lefolii's
office, he looked up and said, "Never saw a man declare
himself a non-combatant so early in a war."

For a time I served as articles editor of *Maclean's* which made me third in the rough chain of command, after Lefolii and Gzowski. I found this less agreeable than either writing for the magazine or editing the reports-and-reviews sections at the front and back. I can't say that I discovered even one journalist of any note, but I had the pleasure of playing a walk-on part in the career of Malcolm Muggeridge, a writer I'd always admired. Someone mentioned to me one day that Lord Beaverbrook, the newspaper baron, was turning Fredericton, N.B. into a personal shrine. Fredericton had a Beaverbrook Hotel, a Beaverbrook Theatre, a Beaverbrook Art Gallery, and a floodlit bronze statue of the Beaver in the park. There was even a Beaverbrook birdbath. I knew that Muggeridge was amused by Beaverbrook's pretensions, and I asked him to visit Fredericton and describe what he saw. The result, "The Cult the Beaver Built," was as delightful as anything we published. "Lord Beaverbrook," Muggeridge wrote, "has conferred many benefits on New Brunswick, but not by stealth." Beaverbrook had honoured himself with monuments "which might have been considered excessive if accorded to Napoleon on Corsica, or to Shakespeare in Stratford-on-Avon." At the time Muggeridge was writing a weekly column on books for Beaverbrook's London *Evening Standard,* and when the *Maclean's* article reached England, he was sacked. "This is the only occasion in my life when I have been actually fired," Muggeridge wrote in his autobiography. Graceful as always, he told me he didn't mind; he was sick of writing the books column anyway.

IN OUR MOMENTS of self-congratulation, which probably occurred more often than reality justified, some of us cherished the notion that we were changing Canadian journalism. We were not only improving *Maclean's*, we were bringing a new level of literacy to the profession. This was largely a delusion, so far as the editors and writers in Toronto were concerned: I don't think we seriously affected any journalism except our own. But someone close to us, someone we didn't take nearly as seriously as he took himself, was in the process of working a big change indeed. Peter C. Newman, our Ottawa columnist, was preparing the book that would make his reputation — a scandalous (by the standards of the time) biography of John Diefenbaker.

Newman had been on the staff since 1956, but in 1962 — when I was editing the column he sent from Ottawa — he stood apart from the rest of us. On his visits to Toronto he was stiff and overly solemn, the kind of young man who never quite gets the joke — I remember thinking that he seemed more like a writer for *The Financial Post*, where he had started out. His manner conveyed the belief that where he came from, Ottawa, was the centre of important matters, which we in Toronto understood only in a superficial way. I don't think he approved at all of the fact that we were having such a good time.

Newman was just beginning to generate the legends that would make him, by a wide margin, the most gossiped-about journalist in the country. My first conversation with him left me with the impression that he had a good many enemies, or thought he did. One of them was Blair Fraser. For years Fraser and Newman worked side by side as Ottawa correspondents in what was clearly, perhaps inevitably, an uneasy partnership. They represented not only different generations and different approaches to journalism but different views of Canada. Fraser was the quintessential Ottawa Man, a good friend of Liberal cabinet ministers and senior public servants. Articulate and supremely self-confident, he was also the best broadcaster in Ottawa — he could make literate and effortless good sense under deadline pressure, and when he appeared on CBC radio or television he seemed to speak from the very heart of Ottawa. Newman, by contrast, was a Czech-Jewish immigrant who continued to see himself as an outsider long after he had reached the head of his profession. Fraser casually assumed that he was welcome anywhere, from Lester B. Pearson's office to Buckingham Palace; Newman believed, with some reason, that official Ottawa was unwilling to accept him. Something else set them apart, a matter of energy. There was a touch of the elegant amateur about Fraser — certainly no one ever caught him trying too hard — but Newman brought to his work the furious energy of the immigrant. Fraser wrote only one book, a minor piece of popular history, and that after years of procrastination. Newman set out to produce a shelf of books, and did.

Like his friends among the mandarins, Fraser probably despised Diefenbaker as much as Newman did, but it was Newman who hustled around Ottawa collecting the Diefenbaker gossip and cobbling it together into *Renegade in Power*. At moments his book achieved a certain literary grace, perhaps through the editorial influence of his richly talented wife, Christina McCall. But there was also something awkward about it, beginning with the title — I never understood in what sense, if any, Diefenbaker was a renegade, and I never met anyone else who did. Newman apparently reached for a catchy title, found one, and decided that his readers wouldn't care what it meant. He was right. *Renegade in Power* became the first hugely popular book on Canadian politics, and opened the way for dozens of others; no book until Newman's own *The Canadian Establishment*, in 1975, attracted so many imitators.

More important, *Renegade in Power* brought investigative journalism to Ottawa. Newman exploited what most journalists knew but chose to ignore: executive assistants to politicians, the chatty eunuchs in the political harems of Ottawa, loved trading stories about their ministers. With their help Newman became the first journalist to describe recent cabinet meetings and party caucuses in detail. His account of Diefenbaker's uncontrollable paranoia, particularly during the last year of the government, was the best Ottawa gossip Canadians had ever been allowed to read: unlike every other

political journalist of the day, Newman wrote in public the
way everyone in Ottawa talked in private. His frankness
changed Canadian journalism, and helped change the way
Canadians saw their government. By the time *Renegade in
Power* finished its run on the best-seller lists, the era in
journalism exemplified by Blair Fraser was over and the
Newman era had begun.

There are those who wear success with ease, and grow
more comfortable as their reputations flourish. Not Newman.
The more success and influence he achieved, the more
anxious and self-conscious he became. As editor of the
Toronto *Star* and then of *Maclean's*, he became increasingly
sensitive to criticism and particularly hated analysis of his
work by university professors. No academic, he often said,
would ever be fair to him, would ever recognize his contribution to the public understanding of public affairs. Newman
yearned to control not only the way his work was presented
(every journalist's legitimate goal) but the way it was received
as well. In the 1970s he suggested to me that in magazines
such as *Saturday Night*, academics should not be allowed to
review the books of journalists. Later, in conversation, he
extended this notion: *journalists* should not write about journalists. It wasn't proper. When I said it seemed only fair that
those who scrutinized politicians should themselves be
scrutinized, Newman argued that public criticism of one
journalist by another was destroying the convivial atmosphere of the profession (it sounded like a point Blair Fraser
might have made). Having become a public figure, Newman
was now being treated much as he had treated other public
figures, and was discovering that in some ways being part of
the Establishment could be as unpleasant as being an outsider.

In private the criticism of Newman was even sharper.
People who worked for him at *Maclean's* discussed him
obsessively, and never (in my experience) with affection.
They could rage about him for hours — about his secretiveness,
for instance, or about the difficulty of working for a man

whose connections to power were so numerous and so complicated. Walter Stewart sometimes grew almost hysterical when discussing, in painful detail, the conflicts of his life as a *Maclean's* editor under Newman. I once suggested to Stewart that he lay off the civil servants and businessmen he usually wrote about and instead set down *My Years with Peter*, a book that would truly engage his passion. He apparently decided it wasn't a good idea.

Almost from the beginning, Newman was unable to imagine that criticism of his work was honestly intended and might even be justified. As soon as a word of criticism appeared, he looked for the hidden motive — and always found it. In my own mind I came to call this habit "Newmaning," and tried to guard against its appearance among my own responses to criticism. In 1980, in *Saturday Night*, Morris Wolfe wrote a negative piece about the new weekly *Maclean's*. Immediately, Newman was on the phone.

"Well," he began, "he's had his revenge at last."

Apparently, at some earlier date, Wolfe had been rejected as a contributor to *Maclean's*. To Newman that proved that his *Saturday Night* article was without merit and his views could be brushed aside. When Newman failed to receive the Governor General's Award for the first volume of *The Canadian Establishment*, he told me the reason: the people at the Canada Council were against him. Timothy Porteous, who ran the council, was a Liberal who could never forgive Newman's criticism of Pearson and Trudeau. I pointed out that the prizes were given by outside judges, far beyond Porteous's control. Newman declined to let the facts get in the way of his anger. "They'd give it to the Ottawa telephone book before they'd give it to me."

A particularly outrageous act of Newmaning brought him a libel suit. In 1979 Peter Brimelow, who had worked at *Maclean's*, wrote a negative review in the *Wall Street Journal* of Newman's book about the Bronfman family ("a scissors-and-paste job...profoundly derivative"). Newman's response was

a private letter to the editor of the *Journal.* "Mr. Brimelow,"
Newman wrote, "was business editor of *Maclean's* for a time,
until I had to fire him for incompetence and distortion of
news. I assume that his review was a form of 'revenge'..." This
was untrue: Brimelow had not been accused of incompetence
and had left of his own accord, in amiable circumstances.
When he received a copy of the letter from the *Journal,* he
sued Newman. The out-of-court settlement involved a cash
payment as well as a written apology from Newman: "I admit
that you were not fired from *Maclean's* and there was never
any cause for you to be fired." Brimelow told me he was
forbidden by his agreement with Newman to disclose how
much money he received; he did tell me, though, that he
had used the settlement to buy a Persian rug he could
otherwise never have afforded. If I knew what Persian rugs
were worth, he said, I could visit his apartment in New York
and estimate the cost of Newman's letter.

So far as I know, I was the object of Newmaning only
once. In 1981, when the second volume of *The Canadian
Establishment* appeared, I wrote an unenthusiastic review. I
couldn't see the point of this thick collection of anecdotes
about entrepreneurs whose effect on the life of the country
was no more than marginal. Newman and I had been on
friendly terms for about twenty years, and I had often
written admiringly of his work. Nevertheless, when we met
at a friend's party shortly after my review appeared, he took
one look at me and turned away in sullen silence — "Cut me
dead," as they used to say in English novels. I understood
why. He had sensed an evil purpose, a purpose so devious
and so well hidden that it was unknown even to me, and
remains so to this day.

THE BUFFALO, someone once told me, is a dangerously
unpredictable animal. It can be bred successfully, but only
through the exercise of eternal vigilance; at any moment,
after standing patiently at pasture for years, it may suddenly

turn angry and kick someone to death. At Maclean-Hunter we editors and writers were the buffalo, the managers of the company our wary keepers. They viewed us with suspicion, knowing that as members of a different species we could not be trusted. We viewed them as dolts.

To us "conformity," as expressed through conservative clothes and fawning deference to superiors, was something to read (or occasionally write) magazine articles about. To them it was simply the natural order. They spoke of "the company" with reverence, and followed its eerie customs with the devotion of cloistered nuns. As late as 1964 it was a rule that any male employee entering or leaving the Maclean-Hunter building on business must wear a hat. One executive used to travel in every day from the suburbs with a soft hat in his briefcase and put it on just before leaving the subway; he repeated the process when returning home at night. Apparently Donald Hunter, the son of the original Hunter, thought that men without hats lacked a look of serious purpose. I learned this odd regulation when the publisher of *Maclean's* took me out for lunch. As we left my office he paused, as if waiting for something. Then he said, "Oh, I forgot. You don't have to wear a hat, do you?" At some earlier date an exception had been made for journalists, those feckless, hatless people.

At the time I had never heard the phrase "corporate culture," but whenever I see it now I think of Maclean-Hunter, a place with a culture uniquely its own. The core of its ethos was a sense of mission that outsiders and newcomers found laughable. In the world beyond our building on University Avenue in Toronto, *Maclean's* and our other publications were regarded without undue reverence or gratitude, but inside the building it was agreed that what Maclean-Hunter did was crucial to the nation. People there routinely spoke as if Canada without *Maclean's* — and, by extension, our other publications — would hardly be Canada at all.

The source of this corporate self-hypnosis was the president,

Floyd Chalmers, a man of great simplicity who hoped to be thought complex. He was a former editor of *The Financial Post*, and in the early 1960s he was reshaping the company, pushing it into broadcasting and the other enterprises that eventually made it hugely profitable. In his spare time he was also the leading private patron of the arts in Canada. Chalmers more or less called into being the Canadian Opera Company, he raised the money to build Stratford's theatre, and he not only suggested the creation of the *Encyclopedia of Music in Canada* but provided $400,000 to get it going. One day in 1963, over lunch, he told me he wanted to commission an opera on a Canadian theme to be produced in centennial year. He asked me to suggest a subject, and I said that Louis Riel was the most operatic figure in Canadian history. I have no idea whether I influenced him — he may have heard the same idea from a dozen other sources — but Harry Somers' *Riel* was indeed produced in 1967, under Chalmers' patronage, with a libretto by Mavor Moore and direction by Leon Major.

Like many patrons, Chalmers seemed curiously lacking in passion or even enthusiasm for the art he sponsored. In conversation he might speak about the problems of running an opera company, but he seldom mentioned anything that happened on the stage. His autobiography, *Both Sides of the Street*, published in 1983, explained the workings of the arts organizations he helped, but said almost nothing about what they produced or why Chalmers thought it valuable. Apparently his long association with the arts failed to give him even the beginnings of a vocabulary that could be used outside the boardroom; in his mind, Shakespeare or Verdi productions were good in themselves and needed no further discussion. More important, perhaps, culture was an expression of his self-image as a leading Canadian. At times, his self-regard was painfully obvious — when a university gave him an honorary degree Chalmers directed that "LL.D." appear after his name on the *Maclean's* masthead, to the amusement of his employees. But if his approach to the arts was superficial, a matter of personal public relations, it was nevertheless a great improvement on the approach of most Canadian capitalists of his day. For them the arts were a nuisance, to be handled through minions in the corporate donations department.

By the 1960s Chalmers' view of *Maclean's* as an essential instrument of nationhood had grown to majestic proportions; it was hard to imagine any actual magazine that could have lived up to his stately ideal. Certainly the one that Lefolii, Gzowski and the rest of us were producing failed to satisfy him. He did not hesitate to judge us. He saw himself as a journalist and an expert manager of journalists, and he had good reason for pride. He chose Ralph Allen as editor of *Maclean's* in 1950 and helped him make it a first-class magazine. They didn't always agree, but to the end Chalmers respected Allen's talent and judgement.

Ken Lefolii, however, was another matter. My impression is that in 1962 Lefolii was chosen as editor for want of a better — in management's eyes — alternative. He was popular with the editorial staff, who knew his abilities intimately, but to the managers he was clearly an alien. They were afraid to offend anyone, especially anyone connected with a potential advertiser; Lefolii believed, rightly, that if a magazine offends no one, it's worthless. His view of businessmen was sardonic, he showed no reverence for the company, and he barely pretended an interest in the earnest plans of advertising salesmen. He sometimes came to meetings without a tie, and he routinely wore the sort of shoes that good Maclean-Hunter people wore only at their cottages on Georgian Bay. Chalmers didn't even like Lefolii's byline. He thought "Ken Lefolii" too informal for the editor of so august a magazine, and suggested that he become "H.K. Lefolii." Ken decided to stay Ken, which provided another irritant.

These differences would have produced tension at the best of times, and we were not living through the best of times. *Maclean's* had been losing money for years. The advertising agencies had little affection for us, and even our own ad salesmen were not impressed with what we did. The chief salesman didn't like the magazine and I suspect didn't spend much time reading it. When I suggested to one of his associates that this rather undermined his effectiveness — could you sell Chryslers if you thought Chryslers weren't good cars? — I was told that I didn't understand these matters, he was really quite good at his job. He understood demographics, apparently, and cost-per-thousand. The space buyers in the agencies liked him. Once he came into my office and flicked his lighter. It emitted a little tinkling sound, the notes of "Smoke Gets in Your Eyes." He explained that this was one of his devices for getting the attention of space buyers, making his visits to their offices memorable.

His boss, F.G. Brander, the publisher of *Maclean's*, was an amiable man, a layman of some eminence in the United Church and a former ad salesman. He was anxious to please but seldom knew what to think. He seemed a melancholy figure, caught between the official Maclean-Hunter ethos and editorial decisions that he found incomprehensible. As the months passed it became clear that what we thought was best about the magazine, Brander thought regrettable. We were delighted to have Mordecai Richler's articles, for instance; he was distressed. "I don't like Mordecai Richler," he confided to me once. "Never did." He said it with the brave satisfaction of a man who has finally got something off his chest. Richler's prose was abrasive, he felt, and that was bad. We were pleased with an article by Sidney Katz which thoughtfully developed the view — commonplace now, but fresh then — that aggressive marketing by the drug companies was encouraging doctors to over-prescribe drugs. This annoyed the drug companies and appalled our managers. There was a tense meeting in Lefolii's office at which the editors were required to explain solemnly to representatives of the pharmaceutical industry that Katz — certainly the most experienced medical writer in the country — knew what he was talking about.

In this atmosphere, even a trivial anecdote could precipitate a crisis. The most memorable was the Schick saga, which the managers regarded as momentous and the editors as ridiculous. To advertise its razor blades, Schick published — not in *Maclean's* — an ad showing the sixteen players on the Toronto Maple Leafs; all of them, the ad said, had shaved with the same blade. Peter Gzowski, in a 1964 article on the money-making activities of the Leafs, mentioned that this was a fiction. The players had not participated in a mass shave-in, but had simply received $50 apiece for the use of their picture.

At this revelation Schick was outraged, its advertising agency mortified, and our managers thrown into despair. Schick was not an advertiser, but its agency had placed ads for other clients in the magazine and Schick itself was said to be on the verge of advertising with us. Gzowski was forced to prove his astounding charge, and he did; but our managers were left wondering why journalists would publish such a damaging story, even if true. The fact that it illustrated the point of the article was of no interest to them; the fact that it was also amusing was even less persuasive. The incident increased the uneasiness between the editors and the businessmen. As Gzowski said later in a *Canadian Forum* article, "This event became known as the time the Schick hit the fan, I being the fan."

THE CASE of Pierre Berton was much more serious, and more troubling. It raised a delicate issue that has bothered journalists before and since: what do you do when your boss is right for the wrong reason? In 1962 Berton left the Toronto *Star*, where he had been writing the best general column I've ever read in a daily newspaper. It seemed natural that he should once again contribute to *Maclean's*, and we happily signed him up to write the last page of every

issue. But what seemed to be a coup turned out to be a
mistake. Perhaps because he was too busy elsewhere, or
perhaps because he had lost interest in magazine work,
Berton's pieces were almost always disappointing. After a
few issues we began to wonder how we could gracefully get
rid of him. No answer presented itself, and he went on
writing the column until he wrote his piece for the issue of
May 18, 1963. "It's time we stopped hoaxing the kids about
sex," said the headline. Berton expressed the view that sex
among teenagers was not necessarily a bad thing and might
be preferable to the tortured frustration endured by many
adolescents.

I read that column in manuscript, thought it might stir up
some arguments, and sent it off to the typesetter. No one in
the office, so far as I can recall, considered it scandalous. But
when the advance copy of the issue reached Floyd Chalmers
he made it clear that he thought the piece immoral and
improper. After it was published indignant letters from
readers began arriving by the dozens and advertisers (so we
heard) began threatening to withdraw their ads. Chalmers
told Lefolii to stop running Berton's column.

This presented the editors with a dilemma. It breached
what was then a clear agreement: that the editors, while
willing to take management's views into account, would
make every final editorial decision. In the end, if management
didn't like the decisions, it could fire the editor. The
principle was worth defending. But could it be defended
from such shaky ground? We were unwilling to stand
behind a columnist whose work we had come to dislike and
wanted to drop anyway.

Neither keeping Berton's column nor eliminating it would
have been easy. Lefolii eliminated it, and I don't believe
anyone on the staff thought he had done the wrong thing.
But Chalmers had lost patience with *Maclean's*, and soon he
found a new way to handle us. In 1964 he put *Maclean's* and
some other magazines under the control of a vice-president

named Ron McEachern. Like Chalmers, McEachern was a former editor of *The Financial Post*; unlike Chalmers, he had no particular reputation for editorial acumen. When he took over, Peter Newman — who had worked for him at the *Post* — predicted that we would find him impossible. Newman soon announced that he was leaving to become Ottawa columnist of the *Star*, where his old mentor, Ralph Allen, had recently gone as editor.

Not long after, in July, 1964, six editors — Lefolii, Gzowski, Barbara Moon, Harry Bruce, David Lewis Stein, and I — resigned. I would love to say that the cause of this event, which changed the lives of all of us, was an article so devastating that it terrified the timorous executives of Maclean-Hunter. In fact, it was something of no great importance, a 1,000-word item by Harry Bruce on the Toronto newspaper strike. Like most of Bruce's pieces it was intelligent, well researched, and deftly satirical. But McEachern did not like it. As he wrote to me later that week, "It said nothing new about this Toronto affair and...would only serve to infuriate the partisans of the unions and the partisans of the publishers. A piece which does nothing except stir up animosities in both these big camps seems unnecessary." He decided to exercise what he called his "moral responsibility" and eliminate it. He didn't call Lefolii, however; he sent orders directly to the printers to kill it.

For a few hours I thought about the implications of this move. Obviously, it meant that, for the foreseeable future, the independence of the magazine was gone. If a vice-president could kill an article on a whim, the editors were no longer in charge. Sad, but hardly a new development in the history of journalism. Like everyone else, I had worked for difficult publishers before and expected to do so again. Everyone operates under some sort of constraint. Why not accept this one and stick around? I loved *Maclean's*, and only two years before I had achieved one of the goals of my life by joining its staff. It might be silly to throw that away.

But something equally bothersome was running through my mind. McEachern's intercession would make working on *Maclean's* even more difficult, and I already found it taxing. I was working harder there than I had at the *Star*. The writing and rewriting and arguing and planning consumed up to sixty hours a week, sometimes more. McEachern had added a new level of decision-making to the process, and a new difficulty. Each piece would now have to satisfy not only the editor, which was hard enough, but also management. I could imagine large chunks of prose being excised by the vice-president at the last minute because he found them "unnecessary"; other chunks would then have to be prepared, no doubt in an atmosphere of hysteria, to replace them. The prospect made me weary.

In the end my decision was practical as much as it was principled. When I wrote to McEachern I didn't go into detail. I just said that issues such as those he had mentioned in his letter had traditionally been left in the hands of the editors and I had understood this to be a condition of employment on *Maclean's*. "This condition having now been changed, I feel I must resign." My colleagues felt the same way, but most of us went to one more meeting in the Maclean-Hunter board room to discuss our grievance.

Chalmers presided, now blandly casting himself in the role of peacemaker. He said he valued all of us, he acknowledged that perhaps McEachern's decision had been arbitrary, he hoped we would withdraw our resignations.

"What about Ken Lefolii?" someone asked. "Does he come back too?"

This was the first acknowledgement of a fact that was sitting uneasily in everyone's mind: Lefolii had not been invited to the meeting.

Chalmers paused, as if the question required some thought.

"I have accepted Ken Lefolii's resignation," he said. "That's final."

Clearly, he was offering us what he imagined would be a happier, less stressful future, without Lefolii. The meeting was civilized, but there was an undercurrent of anger among the editors. Certainly I was mad. Chalmers didn't know, or didn't want to know, that in important ways Lefolii was the best journalist some of us had ever worked with. If we were loyal to him, that was a way of being loyal to our own best instincts and our best hopes for the magazine. Smugly, obtusely, Chalmers saw our affection for Lefolii as a youthful foible that had nothing to do with our lives as professionals. We declined his offer, and went our separate ways.

A year later the greatest American literary critic of the day, Edmund Wilson, wrote a generous epitaph for our version of *Maclean's* in his book *O Canada: An American's Notes on Canadian Culture*. Wilson said we had "succeeded in transforming *Maclean's* from a rather inferior version of the kind of thing that we get in *McCall's* or the *Saturday Evening Post* into an outstanding journalistic achievement…It is regrettable that a change of management which involved putting a curb on the free expression of the findings and views of these writers should have resulted in the resignation of almost the whole staff and converted the magazine back again from a serious venture in reporting to an exploit in the higher pulp." It was the best review, from the best source, that any of us would ever get, and easily worth quitting for.

NINE

*T*he Age of McLuhan

LIKE MOST journalists, the people at *Maclean's* in the 1960s regarded Marshall McLuhan as a remote and incomprehensible theorist at best and an intellectual con man at worst. The *Maclean's* editors knew something about McLuhan and his ideas — after all, they were running a mass-circulation magazine and he was a theorist of mass communications who taught English about half a mile from their office, at St. Michael's College on the University of Toronto campus. But they saw no reason to take seriously anything he said or wrote. From the early 1950s to the mid-1960s it was fashionable among journalists and broadcasters, as it was among academics, to sneer at McLuhan. Again and again, people in our business said — each of them delivering the line with smug delight, as if it were freshly minted — that McLuhan was an expert on communications who (indulgent chuckle) couldn't communicate. Among academics the favoured *bon mot* was another paradox — on every possible occasion, professors would go out of their way to note that McLuhan was so devilishly clever that he'd managed to sell copies of a book declaring (slap of thigh) that books were obsolete! I heard this twenty-five-year-old remark spoken in a hall at the University of Toronto as recently as February, 1988 — McLuhan is long dead, but the tired jokes about him live on. Of course he never said books were obsolete. He merely pointed out that they had lost their central place in our culture, a fact that — like many of his views — seemed startling when he first said it but became conventional wisdom long before his death.

His work was a subject on which I differed sharply from my colleagues at *Maclean's*; in fact, I was probably the closest thing to a McLuhanite you could find in an editorial office. I'd begun reading him around 1952, when a friend pointed me in the direction of his first book, *The Mechanical Bride*, a flippant and inconsistent but outstandingly original attack on mass culture. I'd collected the whole run of *Explorations*, which McLuhan and his friends edited at the university in the 1950s and which I still regard as one of the great journals published in my lifetime. In fascination I had followed McLuhan's progress from the stern critic of commercial society in 1951 ("Today the tyrant rules not by club or fist, but, disguised as a market researcher....") to the benign pop seer of the 1960s, who insisted he had no point of view at all and appeared to smile on even the most grotesque excesses of mob culture. I had read *The Gutenberg Galaxy* with excitement — by the year of its appearance, 1962, McLuhan's inelegant but rich language seemed almost natural to me.

I saw McLuhan often, I went to parties at his house, I attended the wedding of one of his daughters. I interviewed him many times on radio and television, I wrote about him often, and from time to time I claimed with some justice to understand what his books said. But I never for a moment pretended to understand Marshall himself. He was everything his enemies claimed: paranoid, arrogant, and often rude. He was one of those people who in conversation seem never to listen to what others say but wait impatiently for the chance to resume their own monologues. This wasn't necessarily true — later one often realized that he had absorbed everything said — but it was disconcerting. McLuhan always wore a distracted air, as if several conversations were buzzing inside him. Those who felt he wasn't listening to what they said were sometimes mollified to realize that he didn't appear to pay much attention to what he himself was saying either.

He had a genius for the arresting phrase that wasn't altogether clear, and sometimes it brought to life an occasion that would otherwise be flat. Most TV panels, for instance, are dead even before the cameras switch on, but with Marshall on hand there was always at least the semblance of life. Once he and I were summoned to the CFTO studios in suburban Toronto to talk about contemporary culture. It was the early 1960s, and the Twist was a new dance form. We were asked what we thought of it. Marshall, clearly prepared, said, "I believe it means we have slipped another disc socially and revealed in anguish the Africa within." For the rest of the program the audience was entertained by the spectacle of the other panelists trying to deal with that one.

Marshall was a publicity hound, and his constant need for attention was embarrassing. He thought nothing of calling up a journalist to demand coverage of some half-baked idea he had just concocted — usually an aspect of his work that few readers could be expected to care about and that he himself might forget a month later. He had little tolerance for those who sought to interpret him (my humble role, from time to time) and less for those who disagreed with him (which I often did). He wanted journalists to be what the New York reporter Jack Newfield says politicians want us to be — stenographers with amnesia. We were to write down or broadcast what Marshall said, but on no account were we to ask him how his most recent idea squared with something he'd said a year or two before.

He enjoyed sycophants, and he found them in great number among the growing hordes of "futurists" who were then appearing on the campuses and in the television studios. These people had no idea that McLuhan's views were Catholic and essentially medieval, based on his idealized vision of communal life in unified, pre-Gutenberg Christian Europe. His followers simply picked up a few of his phrases and notions, parroted them, and ignored both his cultural background and the style of his thought. Often they signed on as his followers even before they became his readers. In the mid-1960s a Toronto journalist told me she "understood" McLuhan and appreciated him, though so far she hadn't got around to reading any of his books.

"You don't need to," she said. "It's in the air."

And so it was, in a sense. For a year or so you could hardly turn on television or open a magazine without encountering McLuhan in some form or other, almost always hideously distorted to serve the purposes of the writer quoting him.

He was an easy man to distort, of course, because his prose was so tortured. He was also an easy man to satirize. As his enemies never tired of pointing out, he was by no means an expert on the mass media. So far as I could tell from conversations, he watched only a little television, saw movies only now and then, and had no more than a passing acquaintance with the popular press. Often he was embarrassingly out of date, as when he announced a piece of cultural news (that the Beatles were influenced by Indian music, for instance) six months after everyone else had grown tired of hearing about it. His jokes were always a long way from funny, and sometimes entirely off the point. In 1967 Polish jokes were a fashion, and as I sat with McLuhan, Norman Mailer, and Malcolm Muggeridge in a restaurant on the Expo 67 site, waiting to chair a television panel, Marshall said: "Have you heard the latest Polish joke — it's about Alexander Graham Kowalski, the first telephone Pole!" Aside from its simple-mindedness, that wasn't even what people meant by "Polish joke," a point which clearly eluded Marshall. Mailer and Muggeridge stared at him with looks that clearly said, "Can this bumpkin be the famous guru we've been reading about?" I chuckled nervously, and we went in to do the TV show, a non-meeting of minds.

McLuhan aroused in me a powerful strain of ambivalence, as if in some way he challenged my identity. Many of his readers found him unsettling: he proceeded from assumptions we didn't share toward conclusions we found frightening. But in my case there was a special reason for unease, and a careful reader of my articles — full of enthusiasm for his ideas and apologies for his style — might have guessed it. McLuhan was discussing two worlds which lived in ignorance of each other — the high modernist culture from which he drew so many insights (Pound, Eliot, the Cubists, and above all Joyce) and the world of mass culture in which those titanic figures were no more than distant and exotic brand names.

In the same way, my own life in the 1960s was following two lines that often ran parallel and seldom converged. To over-simplify it a little, I was an intellectual among journalists and a journalist among intellectuals. In the mid-1960s I was still only a dozen years away from covering high-school basketball and my professional life was already more enriching than I had ever hoped it would be. Yet I wasn't satisfied. I wasn't willing to settle for a conventional career in journalism. I wanted my work to range wider than journalism normally did — I wanted it to be large enough to deal, on some level, with all of modern culture. Why did I want that? At the time I couldn't have explained, but from this distance it seems clear that Glenn Gould and Michael Snow — artists who refused to recognize limits to their intellectual development — were still forces in my life. In my way I was loyal to journalism and its simplicity, its need to strip away nuance and present itself with confident clarity. At the same time I was also loyal to modern culture in all its ambiguity and mystery.

In practice this meant that I was always telling journalists and broadcasters that McLuhan had a lot to say to us because he could look at what we were doing through the prism of modern culture. When he compared the front page of a newspaper to a Symbolist poem, he wasn't trying to annoy us by being obscure; he was trying to show how mass culture, like Symbolism, puts disparate ideas side by side and produces an unexpected effect. At the same time, though, I was telling intellectuals — McLuhan among them — that it wasn't enough to toss off grand insights, stripped of context, in the vague hope that someone out there might understand.

Did I imagine, in my arrogance, that I had achieved some sort of golden mean, the stillpoint at which these extremes could be modified and these questions resolved? I certainly imagined that I was good at explaining such matters. My colleague Doug Fetherling once threatened to write a piece about me called The Great Explainer, "great" in this case being ambiguous at best. As it happens, Fetherling first came to know me at the height of McLuhan's fame, around 1967, and it occurs to me now that my anxious desire to explain everything arose because one of my best subjects was a man who notoriously refused to explain anything.

Given my interest in mass culture and the history of ideas, McLuhan could hardly have been other than an obsession for me. But there was much more to it than that. Again and again, he seemed to go to the heart of Canadian intellectual life, even when he scorned the ideas of his fellow Canadians and even when he implied that Canadian nationalism was hopelessly parochial (nationalism of any kind, he kept telling us, was a dead nineteenth-century idea, blithely ignoring the fact that it flourished in the twentieth century as never before).

More important, McLuhan's central concern was broadcasting, and in Canadian public life for the last fifty years there has been no cultural issue so potent. It was no coincidence that this great theorist of communications appeared in Canada: communications, after all, has been the central Canadian problem from the beginning.

The most misleading of all our national clichés holds that the Canadian Broadcasting Corporation plays in this century the role that the Canadian Pacific Railway played in the nineteenth, linking the country from sea to sea. The flaw in that idea is that a railroad is pure communication (you can carry anything on it) while the CBC is both medium and message, an institution that not only carries sounds and pictures but creates them as well. Even so, the fact that we routinely speak of broadcasting in those terms — and endlessly wrangle about it in public — indicates how much it means to us. McLuhan's presence in Canada gave another dimension to these debates, even if he was in no position to say what a broadcasting system could or should do.

McLuhan's religion, aside from Christianity, was technological determinism. He saw history as a series of unfolding inventions, each of which reshaped humanity according to its own new rules. Television, he thought, had an inner logic (or illogic) that would defeat all attempts to impose order or purpose on it. Most of what I've seen, as broadcaster or critic of broadcasting, has reinforced that idea. Everyone who works in television can explain how the power of the picture swamps the words that appear with it; everyone who has ever worked in the executive offices of the CBC can tell you that a television network is an uncontrollable monster. But the effect of McLuhan's views has been pernicious. Accepted even by people who don't know their origins, these ideas have become an excuse for thoughtless and lazy work, for pointless sensationalism and meaningless provocation. A producer, accused of committing some crime against journalistic ethics or broadcasting material that the public can't possibly understand, will say in defense: "But it's good *television.*" That excuses all. And this notion that there is some inherent value in "good television" — something quite separate from information and analysis — began with McLuhan.

SO FAR AS I KNOW, the first important producer who consciously put into effect McLuhan's ideas was Patrick Watson, who in the mid-1960s created "This Hour Has Seven Days," the most famous of all Canadian television programs and one with which I had a marginal connection. In September, 1964, I heard from Douglas Leiterman, a CBC producer whose work I admired. That season, as everyone in broadcasting knew, he and Watson were preparing an ambitious and expensive public-affairs show to run for an hour on Sunday nights, right after Lorne Greene's western series, "Bonanza." Leiterman and Watson were perilously close to their first program, and they still lacked a host. Would I audition for the job?

I was again writing a daily column for the *Star* and also chairing a CBC network radio show on Sunday called "The Arts This Week," but I was delighted to audition. I understood, of course, that I wasn't the only candidate, but I didn't learn the names of all the others until the appearance of Eric Koch's definitive book, *Inside Seven Days*, in 1986. They included Peter Gzowski (we were rivals again, this time unknowingly), Peter Jennings (who now anchors the ABC news from New York), the Montreal actor Percy Rodriguez, Bernard Braden, and James Sinclair. Braden was a Canadian actor and interviewer who had been hugely successful in Britain. James Sinclair was then running the Fisheries Association of British Columbia; he had become well-known in the 1950s as a minister in Louis St. Laurent's government and would become even better known in the 1970s as the father-in-law of Pierre Trudeau. Trudeau himself, a McGill law professor, was offered one of the hosting jobs and turned it down — as he had earlier turned down Watson's suggestion that he host another public affairs show, "Inquiry." He did agree to appear occasionally, however, and at one point interviewed René Lévesque, with Larry Zolf as his co-interviewer. Zolf had to do most of the talking because, at least on that day, Trudeau wasn't prepared to engage Lévesque.

My audition was directed by Leiterman in the CBC television building on Jarvis Street. First he told me to read a passage from the TelePrompter, which I did competently enough. Then he asked me to improvise for two or three minutes, as if I were filling time, on a topic that he chose. I don't know how good I was, but the fact that today I can't even remember the subject suggests that it wasn't a triumph. Nevertheless, Leiterman came down from the booth, congratulated me, and sent me home with the astonishing feeling that the job was mine. I spent the evening thinking about how I could reconcile this new assignment with my other commitments.

I needn't have worried. The next day Leiterman tracked me down by phone at the CBC radio building. "We've decided on someone else. We've decided to use a fellow named John Drainie." I hadn't heard that name associated with the program, but "a fellow named" was just Leiterman's cute phrase: Drainie had been the greatest actor of the radio age (not the greatest in Canada, but the greatest) and a well-known figure on Canadian TV. Leiterman and Watson now provided him with a new career, co-hosting (with Laurier LaPierre) "This Hour Has Seven Days."

Putting an actor in that job may have, in some way, fulfilled Watson's strategy. Leiterman was the driving force behind "Seven Days," but Watson was the theorist — and his theories were cousins to McLuhan's. Through their friendship, and through reading McLuhan, Watson had come to the firm belief that what mattered in television was the visual impression made rather than the information conveyed. Television of every kind — a public affairs show no less than a play — was drama: Watson and Leiterman would create a program that would satisfy the audience that had just watched "Bonanza," and satisfy it in a similar way — with engaging stories, attractive personalities, and thrilling encounters. In that light, an actor as host made perfect sense, at least in theory, but I'm not sure Drainie got the point. He gave a performance as an old-fashioned CBC public-affairs host, avuncular, friendly and thoughtful, while Leiterman and Watson surrounded him with sensational and hard-edged material, much of it the antithesis of the CBC style. They were determined to get a huge audience, an audience larger than any public-affairs producer had dreamt of before. They would do almost anything — put on an American Nazi; interview some hooded members of the Ku Klux Klan and surprise them by bringing a black man onto the set; send a camera crew to ambush a former cabinet minister who was accused of sleeping with an East German spy. They always had a rationale: these things were done in pursuit of truth and justice, never for the base purpose of grabbing an audience. Even when they carried an item on a topless go-go girl in San Francisco, Leiterman intoned solemnly that it "says something about our society," though he didn't explain what.

Drainie never looked comfortable, and as I watched him I gave thanks to whatever kind deity had saved me from sitting in his place. "Seven Days" didn't really come into its own until Drainie — who became terminally ill in the spring of 1965 — was replaced by Watson himself.

In the winter of 1965-66, even those of us who had found the first season silly and self-indulgent were impressed. In its last six months on the air, "Seven Days" was not only the most popular public-affairs show in the history of the CBC, it was also the best. But it carried out Watson's theories of dramatic TV so well that it offended many politicians and most of CBC management. In the spring of 1966 management tried to change the direction of the show, the producers publicly fought back, and the result was the noisiest controversy in the history of Canadian broadcasting. There was a parliamentary inquiry and a one-man investigation commissioned by the prime minister's office; a "Save Seven Days" group was formed; there were hundreds of newspaper and magazine articles. In the end the death of "Seven Days" destroyed the career of the CBC president, Alphonse Ouimet, and shadowed the subsequent working lives of Watson, Leiterman, and almost everyone else connected with the program. Certainly no one who worked on "Seven Days" ever again did anything so impressive.

Before "Seven Days" went on the air I taped a piece on Ian Fleming and James Bond, and the pre-season publicity releases included a photograph of me delivering it. Perhaps fortunately, that item never got on the air. Nor did my long interview with Susan Sontag, which deserved to be shown but died with the program. The third piece I did appeared on the fiftieth and last edition of "Seven Days," on May 8, 1966. It was an interview with the man who inspired the program, Marshall McLuhan.

SIX YEARS LATER, in 1972, McLuhan appeared on a CBC radio show called "This is Robert Fulford" to speak an improvised obituary on Ezra Pound in response to my questions. Getting him into the studio took some persuasion, because he was concerned about his fee ("What kind of budget have you got?"), but the result was perfect. The death of the mad poet he had known, admired and studied for decades brought out something I hadn't seen before: the rich chaos of his thought was replaced by an ordered sense of urgency. He gave our audience a fresh sense of Pound's significance.

That was one of several dozen occasions when I was deeply grateful my program existed. For most of his life McLuhan was a stranger in the halls of the CBC. Certainly he was interviewed from time to time, and I can remember one half-hour TV documentary during his lifetime, but I don't think that our leading theorist of broadcasting ever collaborated with our public broadcasting system on a series or even a major program. The reason was an instinctive antipathy between McLuhan and the people who ran the CBC. Most CBC executives regarded him as an oddball whose ideas were only occasionally interesting. He looked on them the way he looked on most media executives, as dinosaurs collaborating in their own extinction. He was, in truth, far too rich for their blood. He leapt casually from subject to subject and era to era, like a one-man Department of Interdisciplinary Studies.

CBC executives, on the other hand, divided knowledge into sharply defined spheres — treating "news" and "public affairs" as two different departments, to cite one spectacularly stupid case — that had to be defended bureaucratically as separate pieces of turf. In McLuhan's view, that was a perfect example of the filing-cabinet mentality that the post-industrial era would bring to a well-deserved end. Moreover, his view of the world was Catholic, theirs Protestant. He was looking at all of history for answers to the question of how we should live — and, like a writer he enormously admired, G.K. Chesterton, he was as likely to find answers in the Middle Ages as anywhere else. The CBC people, coming out of the Methodist-CCF tradition that produced the National Film Board as well as the early CBC, were earnest progressives, committed to a liberal, modern, secular world.

In a way that I didn't understand at the time, "This is Robert Fulford" was a response to McLuhan and the intellectual atmosphere he created. At the same time (I *did* understand this part), it rejected the tightly-controlled CBC style of the past, with its careful categories and its nervous reticence. On its best nights it was a program without barriers.

"This is Robert Fulford" — the title wasn't my idea, but I agreed to it, no doubt blushing modestly — was invented in the summer of 1967 by Geraldine Sherman, a former town planner who had become a CBC producer the year before. About six years later, when TIRF (as Geraldine and I privately called it) went off the air, I told the audience: "I'll always think with affection of this program because its creator and first producer was Geraldine Sherman, who is now my beloved wife and the mother of our daughter." She had to withdraw from the program when we married in the fall of 1970. A CBC executive's memo insisting (correctly, I guess) on a change of producer was headed "Re: Mrs. Robert Fulford," a large error indeed since Geraldine did not change the name she was given at birth. After she left, the program became less interesting to me, not only because we had worked so happily together but because it now missed her original ideas and shrewd judgements. Somehow, both of us understood what it was all about without quite articulating it. Later producers didn't quite see the point, and after a while neither did I.

I think our budget was $375 a show, including my own fee, so there was never any danger of over-paying our contributors. McLuhan received $100 for his Pound obit, a miserly sum by ordinary standards but a bit on the high side by ours. Our goal, of course, was to make up in ingenuity what we lacked in cash, and certainly we took the time of night — 11:30 p.m. to 1 a.m., once a week — as a license to experiment with forms and subjects. A documentary on an incomprehensible underground film might be followed by an interview with Margaret Laurence, which in turn would be followed by an obituary, with music, of Jimi Hendrix. Sometimes, as with *Fortune and Men's Eyes*, we had the whole cast of a new play on at once, along with the playwright. Ivan Reitman and David Cronenberg came to talk about films they'd made, and Bob Rae — now the NDP leader in the Ontario legislature — showed up to promote a festival that he and some other University of Toronto students were organizing. We made a documentary on the opening of an A.J. Casson show at the Roberts Gallery, where collectors lined up for an hour outside and then bought out the entire show in a hysterical frenzy that lasted no more than two minutes. (That night I left my art critic's badge at home and didn't mention that every picture in the exhibition was boring.) One time we rigged up the phone-in equipment and for ninety minutes asked our listeners to explain the meaning of the new film, *2001: A Space Odyssey*, drawing in (through the CBC Windsor station) a great many esoteric views from distant corners of the American Midwest: it was the first time I had any hint of the range of our audience.

We brought on a long list of eminences — Moshe Safdie, Duke Ellington, Jerzy Kosinski, Neil Young, Kate Reid, Bruce Cockburn, Pauline Julien (who denounced me for failing to show sufficient sympathy towards Quebec separatism). When the great Scots poet Hugh MacDiarmid visited Toronto, Geraldine and I went to interview him at the home of his friend, Barker Fairley, the Goethe scholar and artist. We soon learned that MacDiarmid, who was otherwise a healthy seventy-eight-year-old, could hear you only if you shouted at him at the top of your lungs. On the spot, we invented a system for dealing with this problem. I would ask a question in a normal tone: "What was the reason for the revival of Scots language?" MacDiarmid would look at me with patient incomprehension. I would then draw a deep breath and, with all possible force, shout, "*What was the reason...*" He would answer normally, and later Geraldine simply snipped out the shouting. I felt a little silly, but was reassured by MacDiarmid's benign gaze. Later I discovered that upstairs in Barker Fairley's study, while this was going on, Alan Walker from *Time* magazine was interviewing Fairley about some milestone in his life. Every couple of minutes, Walker told me later, their discussion was interrupted by my hysterical scream, coming up through the floor.

We never claimed that all we did was serious: once we brought in from New York (return air fare: $72) a strange little man named A.J. Weberman, a self-proclaimed "garbologist" who had achieved his moment in the sun by stealing and analyzing the garbage of Bob Dylan. Often the show was done live, which was sometimes exciting. In 1970 the novelist Hugh Garner, a notorious drunk, showed up in what seemed to me reasonably good shape but turned out, once we were on the air, to be not only drunk but angry — at me, I think, and everyone else in what he thought of as the literary

Establishment. He raved on for quite a while, which would have been embarrassing at an earlier hour but didn't seem a problem in the middle of the night. The program was intended to be informal, and Garner's performance was no more upsetting than the appearance of a drunk at a party. Patrick Scott, in his Toronto *Star* column, once described the tone of our show: "What I like about the Robert Fulford show is that, although much of the time I don't know exactly what the hell it is all about, it invariably leaves me feeling virtually awash in culture...Fulford is inclined to address his guests by their first names alone. Thus, if you are a minute or two late tuning in, you are apt to find yourself puzzling through an hour or more while your host discourses eruditely with someone known to you only as 'Gail' or 'Gael' — and, once you have established to your reasonable satisfaction that it is not Gale Sondergaard or Gail Storm or even Gale Gordon in drag (which, on the Fulford show, is a distinct possibility), this can be frustrating." Scott must have switched on when I was talking to either Gail Dexter, the art critic, or Gale Garnett, the actress. In any case, after that piece appeared I tried to insert an occasional last name or word of description in mid-conversation. But the idea of the show (however often it bogged down in panels that led nowhere or interviews that didn't work) was to break, McLuhan-style, whatever rules were there for the breaking.

"WRITERS," Russell Baker has said, "have to cultivate the habit early in life of listening to people other than themselves." This is not the easiest habit to acquire, and — as I'm sure various witnesses will point out — I'm far from a perfect listener. But I've been working on that skill for most of my life, and never more consciously than when trying to turn myself into an interviewer for radio and television. This craft requires that the interviewer be curious, friendly, and well-read in whatever is to be talked about, but above all it requires focused attention. Other things being equal, the program will be better or worse in direct relation to how much energy the interviewer puts into encouraging the subject. Ideally, of course, the energy is invisible: the perfect interview seems to be without strain, unplanned, the interview that *had* to happen. Like the best prose, it appears inevitable.

I know an interview is showing signs of success when my guest says something that surprises me, something I didn't know was in the mind I'm confronting. And I grow even happier when I realize that what's coming out is also something of a surprise to the person being interviewed. Occasionally she will confess as much, as when Susan Sontag paused during our interview (we spent most of a day in New York taping a series of radio shows) and said, "You know, I've never *thought* this way before." More often it's something unspoken but sensed, a wonderful moment when everyone realizes that — against all odds — the person being interviewed is actually thinking. Those moments repay all the effort of broadcasting, but the interviews I remember most vividly, sometimes in the early hours of the morning, are those that went painfully wrong.

My radio interview with one of my favourite writers, Alice Munro, was a broadcaster's nightmare, though not for lack of preparation. Geraldine and I planned to record about half an hour and I, as usual, came equipped with far more questions than I could possibly use — enough for forty-five or fifty minutes, at least. In a box-like studio in the CBC building, Alice and I exchanged greetings, Geraldine pointed at me, and I asked my first question. Eight minutes later, I asked my last question. In between, Alice had given not a single answer longer than a dozen words; some ran three or four words, and I think there were actually a couple of "Yes" and "No" answers. The more complex responses were along the lines of "I never really thought about that."

In the control booth, Geraldine looked desperate. We

weren't broadcasting live, but we were recording the show that was to go on the air that night; we needed half an hour. Geraldine stopped the tape and came into the studio.

"Is there," she asked Alice, "anything you would like to talk about?"

"Not really," Alice said. "I don't think so."

I wiped my forehead, thanked Alice, and said goodbye. We filled the time with records and Alice and I never spoke of it again. Later she grew adept at answering the questions of Peter Gzowski and others, so in 1987 my producer at TVOntario asked her to come on our show. Alice replied that she loved the program but didn't want to be on it. She added that she really had nothing to say, and I wondered if she, too, was still shuddering at the thought of the time we spent together, eighteen years ago.

But that non-interview seems like a pleasure when set beside my encounter with W.H. Auden. In 1970 a producer for a CBC television show, "Man Alive," noticed in the clipping files that I'd often written with enthusiasm about Auden. He asked me to go with him to New York and interview Auden in his apartment on the Lower East Side.

No assignment could have pleased me more. At last I was to meet one of the heroes of my life, the poet whose work I'd read since adolescence, the essayist and seer I'd followed for decades. With the producer and the film crew beside me, I knocked eagerly on the door of his old walk-up apartment. When he opened it, everything was as it should have been. Auden wore floppy slippers, baggy pants, and a black turtleneck of some synthetic material. With the gesture of a lord inviting tourists to inspect his stately home, he waved us into precisely what we had been told to expect — a grease-spattered cave that looked like one of those places where eccentric millionaires are found dead, their money in piles under the bed.

The crew set up while Auden finished his lunch and I fidgeted with my notes. Finally the lights went on, I cleared my throat to ask the first question, and the lights went out. Our equipment had blown the building's electrical system; we could still see each other only because a little light came through a window opening onto the street. Well, I was used to that sort of thing, and I imagined Auden was, too — he'd been involved in filmmaking as early as the 1930s, when he worked with John Grierson in England. The two of us sat waiting as the producer and the crew huddled in the background. Then I heard someone say "need an electrician" and glanced over my shoulder. To my horror I saw my producer *looking in the Yellow Pages*. Auden, who made the same observation, began to show unmistakable signs of grumpiness.

It took ninety minutes for an electrician to come; it felt like a century. Naturally I wanted to talk to Auden, for all the usual reasons and because I hoped his mood might improve before we started shooting. But nothing I said was right. I mentioned *Runner*, the National Film Board documentary about Bruce Kidd, made a few years earlier by Don Owen. Don had commissioned a poem for the sound track from Auden.

"Have you thought about publishing that piece?" I asked Auden.

He glowered. "It was in my last book."

Apparently there was a recent book I hadn't seen, and I had found almost the only possible way to betray my ignorance. But I pressed on. Had he any thoughts about writing other films?

"I hate movies. Hate seeing them. Hated working on them."

Well, maybe we could talk about the interview a little. It had been agreed that he would read a few poems into the camera. I asked if he would read the one that begins "Lay your sleeping head, my love," the most famous of his love poems.

"My policy is not to read old warhorses."

Battered and bruised, I moved on. Most of his readers had known of Auden's homosexuality for years, but it had been publicly discussed only recently, in profiles published by *Life* and *Esquire*. I hoped to interview him on this central fact of his life, and I assumed the magazine pieces were written with his approval. He informed me they were not.

"Oh, they were very liberal, very tolerant, of course, but I don't like that sort of thing at all." He stared at me, his great watery eyes looking solemnly out of a face that resembled a dry valley through which powerful rivers had once flowed. Clearly, we were not to speak of homosexuality.

My next question, whatever it was, drew only a grunt. Obviously, he did not feel that the $1,000 he was receiving from the CBC for the afternoon's work covered conversation with total strangers. Abruptly he waved both hands with exasperation and whined, loudly, "Waiting around is such a bloody bore!" It was a short-term temper tantrum, and he repeated it several times before we got to work. I confess (my gay friends will have to forgive me) that the words *flagrant* and *queen* flickered through my mind.

Finally, with the power restored, I began to ask my questions. I'd noticed that in all printed interviews, Auden made the same points. Asked why he didn't live in England, for instance, he'd say that the English were like a family and he didn't want to live with his family. He'd say it again six months later, and again a year after that. If asked about the uses of poetry he'd point out that all the poems written in the 1930s and 1940s hadn't saved one Jew from Hitler. He had made this point a dozen times.

I decided I'd ask questions others hadn't asked, and get a fresh interview. But no matter what I asked, he twisted the question around so that he could give his prepared answer. If I asked about American life, he'd say he lived in the U.S. because the English were like a family he didn't want, etc. When I raised the subject of politics, he gave me the line about poetry and the Jews. The interview amounted to a recitation of sentences and even paragraphs I'd read in old London *Observer* articles. All of them were delivered with reluctance and annoyance, as if he were a politician under indictment.

We left with our cans of film and, at a restaurant around the corner, tried over martinis to convince each other that it wasn't terrible. It was finally broadcast — little slivers of interview stuck between old newsreel stock shots, with a lot of narration and some poems read voice-over. It looked pretty awful to me, and I think the producers shared my opinion. "Man Alive" remains on the air, but I have not since been called by any of their producers. I imagine they still have me on a little list in their office.

A few weeks after the interview I wrote to Joan and Paul Fox, who were in England: "The whole business left me with the desire to meet no more heroes. Bellow and the rest can go uninterviewed by me, the hell with them. I'll just read their books and cherish my dreams. Meanwhile, I'm trying to get to like Auden's poetry again." Time passed, the memory dimmed. Well before Auden died in 1973, I found that I could once again read his poetry and essays with pleasure.

In 1982 I heard from Stephen Patrick, an executive producer at TVOntario whose earlier work — in print, and at the CBC — I had noticed. Stephen wanted to know whether I might have time to do some work for him. I assumed he meant something like the script for a documentary, and I said I'd be glad to see him. Over lunch he said he was thinking about an interview show, with me as co-host. He had the idea that I was a good TV interviewer, and I made no effort to persuade him otherwise. Then, as if to justify his opinion, he said: "I loved that Auden interview you did."

My blood froze, and the horror of that long-ago day in New York returned. I suppressed an impulse to say, "Then you must be some kind of idiot." Instead I sat silent, like a stone Buddha, and in a few minutes we were joined over coffee by two quite exceptional people, both of whom quickly became major figures in my life — Moira Dexter, who is now producer and director of "Realities," the program that was then being born, and Wodek Szemberg, the story producer. Stephen Patrick left TVOntario some time ago, but Moira, Wodek, my co-host, Richard Gwyn, and I have since made about three hundred programs in nine cities across North America as well as in London and Paris.

If I was surprised to find myself working regularly on a TV show, I was even more surprised to discover how it was done. At the beginning no one explained that I might sometimes find myself doing five half-hour interviews in a day. Low-cost television is now done in batches — a day's work by the crew costs so much that the producer must make the most of it. There's more pressure when the program moves out of town, still more when we go to Europe. In 1984 Richard and I made more than two dozen shows in the course of about five days in London; that was half of our 1984-85 season. There have been moments when I've worried that, carried away by the excitement of the moment, I'll mix up the material and ask a theologian about Shakespearean stage production or a psychologist about Vatican II.

"Realities," in fact, has turned into one of the great pleasures of my life, which should hardly be a surprise. After all, when people take you to England, put you up in a good hotel, ask you to spend half the afternoon with Stephen Spender, and pay you, it's difficult to find grounds for complaint. The subject of the program is ideas, and my job (or Richard's when he's the interviewer, which is about half the time) is to elicit from the people we talk to the ideas that rule their lives and their work. I've interviewed Mavis Gallant and Hans Kung, Robertson Davies and David Hockney, Joy Kogawa and Jonathan Miller. My favourite subject, and apparently the audience's as well, is Allan Bloom, the Chicago philosopher whose views of education — tried out earlier on "Realities," among other places — turned into the astonishing 1987 best seller, *The Closing of the American Mind.*

It's possible that if pressed I could imagine a television

series I'd enjoy more, and people I'd prefer to work with, but I doubt it. Being educational TV, "Realities" provides no great sums of money for anyone, but my passionate and selfish wish is that it will last forever, or at least until I reach the point when I'm too infirm to lean across the table, gaze into my guest's face, and utter what one viewer calls my most annoying phrase: "What you're trying to say is…"

LONG AGO I absorbed what must be, for broadcasters, the central fact of the McLuhan age: television leaves us with feelings and impressions rather than facts and arguments — though facts and arguments must be there as well. As an educational broadcaster I can't hope to teach in the way universities and schools do. What I want to provide is the intellectual and emotional environment of an issue or a personality: I want to surround the subject rather than spell it out.

McLuhan would understand this approach without necessarily subscribing to it. He rarely gave his assent to anyone who claimed to be using his ideas, and in any case he never thought that I understood him. In *Maclean's* in 1964 I wrote a review of *Understanding Media* that concluded: "I'm as aware as his enemies are that his work is disorganized and erratic, but he has taught me more about his subject than any six well-organized, consistent writers." His letter in reply said that he valued my friendly approach, but: "It's amazing that you got anything out of my writing at all, since you misconceive my entire procedure. I do not move along lines. I use points like the dots in a wire-photo." That was why his book was repetitious and inconsistent. He wanted me to know that he had no fixed point of view on anything: "I am interested only in modalities and processes." Fourteen years later, in 1978, he said something similar in a letter to the editor of the *Star*, responding to a few words I'd written about him: "I do not use any ideas at all, but perceptions only." He was interested, he said, not in elaborate theories but in the patterns of media: "I prefer to study the pattern minus the theory. This is what confuses Fulford."

Long before McLuhan died, in 1980, his vogue was over. The sort of intellectual who had once been anxious to write about him had moved on to other phenomena. Among media people, who were once so flattered by his attention, his central ideas were now conventional wisdom, so totally absorbed into the mainstream of discussion that they no longer seemed to be McLuhan's. In that world his reputation now resembles Voltaire's — no one talks about him because no one any longer disagrees with him; he's a historical artifact. He's what Auden called Freud, not a man but a climate of opinion.

Just as Freud never became a Freudian, McLuhan was never a McLuhanite. It was his misfortune to be misunderstood at almost every turn, above all by those who worked in television and wanted to use what he said. Most of them believed that he enjoyed and admired the electronic world that he discussed. Far from it. On the last night of "Seven Days" he said to me, and to the largest audience for a public affairs show in the history of Canada: "I'm resolutely opposed to all innovation, all change. But I'm determined to understand what's happening because I don't choose just to sit and let the juggernaut roll over me. Many people seem to think that because you talk about something recent you're in favour of it. The exact opposite is true in my case."

TEN

Mythology, politics, and Atwood

MARGARET ATWOOD ONCE said to me, "You know, there's a lot of paranoia about the Americans going around. The other day somebody told me that *you're* a CIA agent." It was the mid-1970s, a time when people said that sort of thing more often than they do now. Not long before my conversation with Atwood, an art critic and curator of some eminence, Barry Lord, told me in all seriousness — "Bob, I know you're not going to want to believe this but *listen*" — that the CIA was trying to gain control of the National Gallery in Ottawa, as part of a plan to take over all of Canadian culture.

Given the climate of the moment it wasn't preposterous that someone would identify me as a CIA man and think it worthwhile to report this news to Atwood. Crazy or not, her informant (whoever it was) expressed a view of our respective positions that was not totally different from the opinions held by many cultural activists. In some circles, such as the broadcasting business, I may have been regarded as a wild-eyed Canadian radical who was always complaining about American power over Canadian television and publishing; but among certain people Atwood and I might run into from time to time, people who literally discussed the desirability of redeeming Canadian pride through a shooting war against America, I was seen as a moderate at best and a sellout at worst. After all, I was an admirer of American democracy, not to mention American culture, and those opinions in themselves aroused suspicion. And when I deviated from the official line in Canadian nationalist circles — Canadians Good, Others Bad — my political allegiance was called into question. The purity of Atwood's nationalism, on the other hand, has always been beyond doubt. She fights with enthusaism, wit, and energy for her causes, and if she disapproves of some of those who fight by her side, she keeps it to herself. Which is another way of saying that she's in politics.

Cultural politics has been one of my subjects for thirty-three years. I wrote my first article about the Canada Council (arguing that there should be one) in 1955, when Atwood was a sixteen-year-old high school student. But much of what I've said and written on this subject since the early 1970s has been formulated as an elaboration of Atwood's views, or as a reaction against them. This should hardly be surprising, since a journalist is always looking for the centre of his subject and Atwood has managed to place herself at the centre more often than any other Canadian artist of the century. At the same time, she embodies the astonishing transformation of Canadian artists in the last three decades — from marginal participants in Canadian life to public figures whose work helps set the tone of the country, and from provincial unknowns working mainly for a small home audience to artists who sometimes send their work to a dozen foreign countries. For these reasons, and several others — such as her edgy brilliance, her prickly originality, and her quirky charm — I've edited her, interviewed her, reviewed her, and been attacked by her in my own magazine. I was delighted that an Atwood poem appeared in the second issue of *Saturday Night* that I put out (October, 1968), and pleased that she won a prize for an article published in the centennial issue of the magazine in the last year I worked there. I think *Saturday Night* was the first magazine to carry her picture on the cover (November, 1972). During all this I watched her with a sense of wonder and a firm conviction that if she hadn't existed we would have been forced to invent her.

She would not, of course, be delighted to learn that part of her eminence is due to her ability as a politician. "I'm not a politician," she once said to an interviewer from a literary magazine, in reply to a question about poetry as an agent of change. True, she hasn't run for office or aligned herself with a party. But in a larger sense she is indeed a politician, the emblem and standard bearer for the only persistently interesting political movements in English-speaking Canada during her adult life, feminism and cultural nationalism. She's the heroine of feminists both for what she is and for what she writes, and she's the most articulate and forceful exponent of cultural nationalism.

These movements, of course, have more in common than Atwood. Both were revived in the late 1960s (just as her career was getting under way), both have been far more successful than anyone expected them to be, and both insist on denying — against all evidence — that they have been successful at all. In fact, a distinct feeling of failure, expressed as often as possible in the most alarming terms, is a powerful weapon in their arsenals. Those who praise them for their great accomplishments can expect to be branded instantly as enemies — as I was (in *This Magazine*, which Atwood serves as an editor) when I suggested in *Saturday Night* that the major event of the 1970s was the triumph of feminism. Similarly, in the last two decades Canadian culture has made enormous progress — the work itself is in general even better than I ever hoped it could be, the audience enormously expanded — but it remains an essential article of nationalist faith that our culture is so weak that it's in danger of disappearing altogether if the wrong sort of arrangement (such as a free-trade agreement with the U.S.) is put in place by a careless or ruthless government.

A literal-minded Canadian, given to detailed examination of policies such as affirmative action on the one hand or film development on the other, might imagine that feminism and cultural nationalism are two distinct impulses, each with its own set of problems and solutions. Atwood has always resisted that idea. In her mind the two great movements of her life and her career are so closely identified that in rhetorical terms they sound precisely alike. In 1987, testifying before a parliamentary committee on free trade, she gave her view of the American approach to Canada: "Canada as a separate but dominated country has done about as well under the U.S. as women, worldwide, have done under men; about the only position they've ever adopted toward us, country to country, has been the missionary position, and we were not on the top. I guess that's why the national wisdom *vis-à-vis* Them has so often taken the form of lying still, keeping your mouth shut, and pretending you like it." Toward the end of her talk she added a dash of violence to the sexual imagery, and broadened it to include men, by introducing an ancient myth that I first encountered in *The Tamarack Review* about twenty years ago and later heard in Robertson Davies' 1975 play, *Question Time*. "Our national animal is the beaver," Atwood said, "noted for its industry and its co-operative spirit. In medieval bestiaries it is also noted for its habit, when frightened, of biting off its own testicles and offering them to its pursuer. I hope we are not succumbing to some form of that impulse."

There were those, reading that brutal and hysterical rhetoric in the newspapers, who were enraged. The government, after all, was — like most governments — trying to develop a policy that would produce the greatest number of jobs at the highest wages for its citizens. What did that have to do with the missionary position, or self-emasculation? The Canadian negotiators were trying to keep the influence of certain Americans, such as the auto workers in Michigan, from impinging on the negotiations; the Michigan workers, far from dominating anyone, were convinced that under the Auto Pact their jobs had been lost to Ontario workers by the tens of thousands — and that this had fabulously enriched Atwood's own corner of the world, Southern Ontario, while impoverishing Michigan. Who was the missionary, who the native? But questions of that sort become irrelevant when asked of Atwood. What matters is the unconscious truth of the story she tells: she deals, after all, not in facts and logic but in a commodity much more central to the special intellectual tradition from which she springs: mythology.

SAILORS, lost on the oceans, become experts in spotting signs of land. Residents of the Sahara grow learned in the location of water. And Canadians are authorities on mythology. It is what we spectacularly lack and what we yearn to possess, what we fear may have eluded us and what we dream of finding or reclaiming. Our greatest intellectual, Northrop Frye, spends a lifetime analyzing the power and structure of myth, and our most original thinker, Marshall McLuhan, sees in electronic media the means by which the modern world recreates myth. The speed of news dissemination, McLuhan once wrote, "makes inevitable the handling of vast quantities of information in a highly structured and, indeed, 'mythic' way. Under electronic technology today man lives mythically..."

How natural, then, that a brilliant young student, graduating from Victoria College at the University of Toronto in 1961 (when Frye was not only the greatest teacher and writer in the college, but the principal as well, and McLuhan, a few hundred yards away at St. Michael's, was putting the finishing touches to *Gutenberg Galaxy*), should begin laying the foundations of a career dominated by the same subject? All of Atwood's critical writing has been a search for the mythological underpinning of literature and life — her famous book, *Survival: A Thematic Guide to Canadian Literature*, was an attempt to find in the writing of English-speaking Canada the sort of binding myth that unites cultures elsewhere. But while Frye merely sought to understand mythology, and McLuhan to identify the ways we formulate it, Atwood's project was more daring and more difficult. She would *make* mythology, bake the stuff in her own literary kitchen like Susanna Moodie recreating civilization in the Canadian bush. She would write some of the great stories of her country, rewrite others (such as Moodie's), identify the themes beneath the rest (as in *Survival*), and in the process become, in her own person, one of the commanding myths of our culture. She would also, by drawing easily on literary themes and anecdotes like those in her address to the parliamentary committee, transform the cultural politics of Canada into a long-running national melodrama that no one could resolve or ignore. And if everything in her account of Canadian culture was wildly overstated (particularly the U.S. villains and their compliant Canadian allies), who could be surprised? She did once say that the most influential book of her life was *Grimm's Fairy Tales*.

Until the arrival of Atwood's generation, cultural politics was no more interesting than the Law of the Sea, and we who obsessively wrote about it were often considered tedious eccentrics. True, there were great landmarks to celebrate — the creation of the CBC in the 1930s, the National Film Board in the 1940s, the Canada Council in the 1950s. But the arguments surrounding these institutions — Who should run them? How much money should they have? — were as quiet and dignified as a political science seminar for future deputy ministers at Queen's University. Once in a while some Tory ignoramus would create a little comedy by complaining about sissy ballet dancers on the CBC, and in 1957 I was able to make a two-page feature for *Mayfair* magazine out of the unintentionally funny comments made by MPs about the introduction of the Canada Council bill. But in general these issues were discussed with dignity and without urgency. Then, after the centennial year and the emergence of Atwood's generation, everything changed.

Atwood is only seven years younger than I am, yet I've always thought of her as a member of a later generation. When she graduated from Victoria College I had been working for eleven years and was established as a critic for the *Star*, writing columns she was later to comment on with interesting acerbity. More important, the new literary intellectuals brought a new approach. The busiest, most outspoken members of Atwood's literary generation — such as Dennis Lee and Dave Godfrey, who founded the House of Anansi Press — began with assumptions quite different from mine. Like me, they were deeply interested in Canadian expression in the arts; unlike me, and most people my age, they thought it natural that they should reorganize the culture of the country and, while they were at it, maybe the economy as well. They were "the new nationalists," born of the youth culture of the 1960s, and energized by the arrival of Americans avoiding military service in Vietnam — Anansi's best-selling title was a manual telling draft-age Americans how to move to Canada.

Lee, Godfrey, and the many who followed them brought to cultural issues a fierce passion and a new set of rules. Publishing houses, for instance, should now be Canadian-owned. John Gray, who had been running the Canadian branch of Macmillan since the Second World War and publishing such indubitably Canadian authors as Donald Creighton and Morley Callaghan, now found himself classified as a "foreign" publisher. He was not pleased and, when he retired from the profession, he wondered aloud whether all these young publishers were, as he put it, "serious."

They were and they weren't. They were serious about
cultural politics, but sometimes not quite so serious about
publishing. Not many of them ever learned how to make
handsome-looking books, or indeed even mastered (or hired
others who could master) such basic skills as copy-editing.
But they were quick and avid students of cultural politics,
which — like ordinary politics — consisted of striking moral
poses in public and manipulating power groups and budgets
in private. Just as certain Calgary oilmen were able to find
more money in Ottawa than in the ground, so certain publishers — James Lorimer was a spectacular example — could
understand agencies such as the Canada Council much better than they could divine the needs of potential readers or
find good writers. Some publishers grew so confident in this
role that they imagined their example would serve the whole
country. Once, at a party at Peter C. Newman's house, Dave
Godfrey solemnly explained that most of Canadian industry
could in future become Canadian-owned if the system used
in book publishing were universally applied: just a little
government stimulation would do it. At that time, of course,
Canadian publishing was a long way from being dominated
by Canadian owners (it still is) and the Canadian-owned
part of it required heavy subsidy (it still does). Godfrey was
so giddy with optimism that he refused to let the facts stand
between him and his fantasy.

Atwood came to cultural politics later than the others —
Anansi was several years old when she moved in to spend a
year or two as poetry editor, and it wasn't until 1972, five
years after the press was founded, that it published *Survival*.
That was the key critical book of the period, a work so often
and so lovingly quoted that the drama critic Urjo Kareda
aptly compared it to the *Little Red Book* of Chairman Mao. Its
cleverness made Atwood a public figure that year (she said
in a speech that the media had turned her into a Thing) and
the star performer among cultural politicians. But this role
didn't affect her as it had affected others. For some, cultural

Writing *This Was Expo* in a
Toronto Star office in 1967

A publicity photo issued when
Saturday Night was revived
in May, 1975

Geraldine Sherman and the
author in Jerusalem in 1979

The night in 1981 when
Saturday Night won five golds at
the National Magazine Awards.
From left: Peter Gzowski, the
author (who accepted Christina
McCall's award), Gary Ross,
Derek Ungless, Nigel Dickson

Receiving the Diplome
d'Honneur of the Canadian
Conference of the Arts from
Ed Schreyer in 1981

Jeanne Sauvé appointing the
author an Officer of the Order of
Canada, 1984

The new Doctor of Laws,
Honoris Causa, at McMaster
University in 1986, with
Chancellor Allan Leal

A detail from a drawing by
David H. Cowles for *Toronto*
magazine in December, 1987,
summarizing the year's news
as a dinner party

politics was a personal calamity — their lives turned out to be more politics than culture. Atwood was too nimble for that: she knew when to draw the line between action and art. Of all the artists who played the game, she was the only one who knew how to make her public utterances simple-minded enough to be effective while her real work remained subtle and surprising.

Maintaining the appropriate public persona did involve certain reversals and self-deceptions. In 1974, for instance, she wrote a sour but energetic attack on Mordecai Richler's satiric novel about Canadian nationalism, *The Incomparable Atuk*; under her scrutiny it was made to look almost treasonous. Clearly she believed that satire was a weapon and that Richler had used it on the wrong people. But two years later, in *Lady Oracle*, Atwood herself satirized Canadian nationalists, and to more devastating effect. The ancient argument about facts used in fiction has involved her in even more striking contradictions. Again and again, she has explained that it's an act of colossal ignorance and vulgarity to interpret her books as autobiographical; but in *Life Before Man* she brilliantly reworked the pattern of her own and her friends' recent lives into her most compelling novel. (At least one of her ex-friends was muttering about a libel action months afterward.)

For all her insight, Atwood seems never to have understood her own love of celebrity. "I don't particularly like being a public figure," she told an interviewer in the 1970s. "It's not something I set out to do, it's something I found happening to me. I was quite unprepared, and rather horrified by some of the results." This was nonsense — celebrities are people who set out to be celebrities. Aside from criminals and billionaires, the only people who get sustained public attention are those who want it. Many a good and successful writer lives a private life, but Atwood chose a public one — she chose to chair the Writers' Union, write an article for a weekend supplement about her evolving hair styles, lecture to the Empire Club, become a regular on the poetry-reading circuit, and have her picture taken with her baby for publication. She chose, in other words, to be famous.

But if her statement to the contrary was nonsense, it was interesting nonsense. Why did she feel she had to deny her wishes and needs? Perhaps because she came out of a Methodist college in a Methodist city, where it was a sin to be a show-off, where fading into the woodwork was the recommended course of action and grey the preferred personality colour. While assiduously building her own myth, Atwood has felt required to refute it — as if she were framing some sort of apology to all those other good girls at Vic who may also have wanted fame but failed to achieve it. Arguing that it was all a hideous accident probably convinced no one, but perhaps it calms her own mind.

I FOUND the attitudes of Atwood's generation exciting, unnerving, and challenging. She and her contemporaries possessed, to start with, what now seems the almost unbelievable *chutzpah* of 1960s radicals, part of the counter-cultural aura imported from the United States. The Vietnam war had destroyed the credibility of great American institutions — the government, the universities, the military — and put the weapon of moral righteousness in the hands of the young. In the counter-culture, experience and learning were discredited: actually to know how the world worked was to mark yourself as complicitous with its crimes. So the young people of the 1960s, unlike every previous generation in history, were able to begin with the conviction that they knew better, on almost any subject, than their elders. Whether the problem was founding a university, bringing peace to the world, or publishing a novel, they assumed that they would at the very least do better than those who had come before them. I remember Dennis Lee telling me in a TV interview, not long after the founding of Anansi, that he and his colleagues understood the essentials of publishing bet-

ter than people like Jack McClelland, who had then been
running McClelland and Stewart for a couple of decades.

Even so, the new nationalists' view of American power
over Canada was persuasive and, in general, correct. Canadian culture had always been a kind of resistance movement
against American domination — I think it was Atwood's
mentor, Frye, who said that a Canadian is historically an
American who rejects the revolution. But the new nationalists were now arguing that the resistance hadn't been nearly
powerful enough, and that to work in future — that is, to
maintain an independent Canada — it would need to be
much better organized. I agreed, and in the summer of 1970
I spent a great deal of time thinking about the duties of
Canadian citizenship and my particular duties. Things were
changing for me. In a few months I was to be married for
the second time, and though *Saturday Night* was in financial
chaos I was beginning to think that I had settled in there for
the long haul. Perhaps I was also beginning to feel the
magazine as a weight on my shoulders. It was then eighty-
two years old, a Canadian institution with a grand (though at
times appalling) history. I knew how fragile it was, and that a
strong breeze could blow it away. I was beginning to develop
a peculiar ambition: not to be the *last* editor of *Saturday Night*.

Saturday Night's problems were, in large part, those of the
Canadian market. We had to impress an audience that was
used to first-class publications from New York, but we were
playing to a population that wasn't a tenth the size of the
potential American audience. Even our cover price was set,
indirectly, by the Americans: because their circulations were
so huge, the cost of producing each copy was much smaller
for them. Since we sat beside them on the newsstand we
couldn't sell our magazine at a price reflecting its cost. People who paid one dollar for *Esquire* could hardly be induced
to pay five for *Saturday Night*. The Canadian edition of *Time*
presented a different set of problems. Its costs were extremely
low because most of its material was prepared in New York

for the American edition. It contained a few pages of Canadian news, expertly put together, but its main function was to insert Canadian ads among American articles. Concerns of this sort heightened my sympathy for those who were trying to maintain cultural institutions in this country.

In that summer of change and insecurity I thought back to the time, seventeen years earlier, when I had — it seems absurd now — decided to be a Canadian. In 1953, twenty-one years old, touring western Europe on a three-month leave from the *Globe*, I wrote home to Vernal House, a CPR Morse operator who pounded a brass key in the telegraph room at the *Globe* and contributed poetry to the *Canadian Forum* on the side. The fact that I was in Italy, a country with a sense of identity thousands of years old, may have had something to do with what I wrote: "I'm going to be a Canadian, which may not sound terribly revolutionary but is still, for me, rather important. I had had it in the back of my mind for some time — a year or two — that I would eventually prefer to emigrate to either London or New York, whenever I felt I had enough talent or ability to make a stand. Now, for the first time in years, I feel like a Canadian, I feel, indeed, that there *is* such a thing as a Canadian..."

The letter doesn't give my reasons, but they were as banal as anyone else's. Canada, viewed from a distance, looked more like home than it had when I lived there. Canadians, encountered in Europe, were obviously my compatriots — we could quickly establish the ground of shared interest even if separated by race, class, or language. London, though I could have a lifelong love affair with it, would always be a foreign city. And every time one of the British mistook my accent for an American's I discovered afresh, and viscerally, that an American was not what I wanted to be.

In 1970, after brooding over that experience and many others, I wrote what turned out to be my most quoted piece of the 1970s, "On becoming a Canadian," a Notebook column for the October issue of *Saturday Night*. "My generation of Canadians," it began, "grew up believing that, if we were very good or very smart, or both, we would someday *graduate* from Canada." I noted that the next generation had overcome this demeaning idea, and said that I realized "this country had not been built without sacrifice and that it might indeed take some considerable further sacrifice to keep it alive." I had always regarded reflexive anti-Americanism as the least likeable characteristic of Canadians; in fact, I had been opposed for years to nationalism, as had many people I knew. "What we didn't realize was that if you *weren't* a nationalist, in some sense at least, then somebody else's nationalism would roll right over you." After that painful about-face, I confessed that I was now "taking lessons in a subject everyone has to master eventually, the art of being a citizen of the country in which you live."

I received some interesting responses (Dennis Lee sent me a delightful postcard) and a few sneers from friends who had known me as a sharp critic of the nationalists and couldn't quite see me making common cause with them. The most interesting response came from Atwood, who was then in England. It took the form of an article that began and ended with a discussion of my views, both those in that Notebook and others I'd expressed in *Star* columns long before.

She opened by quoting herself in conversation with a friend: "So Robert Fulford has finally come round. It took him long enough." She then referred to "those early *Star* columns, the ones that assumed everyone knew the Yanks always did it better." What she wanted to talk about, though, was "what I and my so-called generation had been up to when Fulford was grooving on imported jazz." It turned out that they hadn't been much better, and had only slowly realized that Canadians "had let ourselves come under the control of a people who neither knew nor cared to know anything about us," the Americans. As always she included some wonderful detail, imaginatively chosen; as always, she made a strong argument. It was a sharp, timely piece. At the end she said, "those early Fulford columns were not written by a villain but by a symptom. It was our own choices, our own judgments, that were defeating us."

Personally, I didn't feel defeated at all, and I bet Atwood didn't either — but that was just an early version of the defeatism that's necessary to all discussions of culture by Canadian nationalists. In any case, I ran her piece in *Saturday Night* just as she sent it, thus becoming, so far as I know, the only editor ever described in his own magazine as a symptom.

FOR THE LAST two decades, Canadian culture has been obsessed with its own death. The stories that make news are the stories of disasters. If McClelland and Stewart were to publish the greatest novel since *Anna Karenina,* it could expect a nice review on the entertainment pages of *The Globe and Mail* and a ninety-second item on the Friday-night arts section of "The Journal." But if McClelland and Stewart were to declare bankruptcy, or — worse — be bought by an American publisher, the news would run at the top of page one of the *Globe,* lead "The National," and dominate the next day's Question Period in the House of Commons. When the people running the Stratford Festival were fired by their board in 1980 (making the death of the festival at least a possibility), the resulting controversy got more news coverage than thirty years of often astounding productions.

We routinely present our cultural institutions as invalids in need of treatment, and Atwood's description of me as a symptom perfectly fitted the emerging style. This melodramatic approach keeps cultural bureaucrats and politicians alert and for journalists has the further advantage of being easy to report. Editors (perhaps readers, too) may respond with more interest to a piece about the Canada Council's dwindling budget than to an essay explaining the power of Mavis Gallant's new book. The piece on Gallant's stories may not be easy to understand, and in any case will interest only a minority; the Canada Council piece, because it's political,

can presumably be understood by everyone. For these reasons, an outsider with no knowledge of this country might
decide, after scanning our newspapers, magazines, and
television, that we have cultural politics instead of culture.

The pattern was set by an event that stirred all the ambivalence I felt — and still feel — about cultural politics. In
December, 1970, the oldest publishing house in Canada was
sold to an American firm: McGraw-Hill bought out the
Ryerson Press and changed the name of its Canadian
subsidiary to McGraw-Hill-Ryerson. The newspapers made
us aware that we were in the middle of a national tragedy.
They pointed out that the press had been founded in 1829
(as the Methodist Book Room) and had been a power in the
history of Canadian literature. Now its owner, the United
Church, having suffered serious losses, was selling it to the
Americans. Editorial writers thundered, politicians promised action, an Ontario royal commission was wheeled into
place. We were facing a crisis.

What almost no one mentioned was that for a long time
the Ryerson Press had been the source of many of the worst
books in Canada. For all of my time as a book reviewer (by
then more than a decade), it had been considered a joke. It
published an apparently endless series of novels, badly printed
and badly written, whose authors were forbidden to indicate
that their characters enjoyed sex outside marriage. Decades
earlier, Ryerson had been important; in 1970 it meant little
or nothing. Mordecai Richler said it was delightful to hear
that the Americans had taken the damn thing off our hands.
Perhaps, he suggested, the poor fools would like to buy the
RCMP musical ride as well.

Even so — again my ambivalence surfaced — I knew that
book publishing needed some sort of government help.
McClelland and Stewart, for instance, moved anxiously from
crisis to crisis, unable to find the capital that would (Jack
McClelland hoped) put the company firmly on its feet. So I
welcomed the royal commission, even if I knew that the

Ryerson issue was a joke. It was not the first time in cultural politics that we did the right thing for the wrong reason, and it wasn't the last.

MARGARET ATWOOD will make one hell of an old lady. I'd like to be one of the young journalists who gather at her place on November 18, 2019, for her eightieth-birthday interview. I can't imagine what such people will want to ask her, but I can pretty well describe her answers — they'll be tart, aphoristic, defiant, confident. I can hear the reporters talking about her as, the interview over, they pack up their equipment. "What an amazing old broad," one of them is saying. Another is asking, "Did you ever see such a *performance!*" Perhaps they'll understand that it's a performance she's been giving for most of her life.

Her style, when she deals with journalists, is imperious — she seems to believe that she should dictate the terms of her own fame, and often she succeeds. When she's interviewed, her manner conveys her strong feeling that there's a proper way to interview her, and that the interviewer is being judged at every moment on grounds of propriety. After I interviewed her for TVOntario in the early 1970s, the producer said to me, "That little bugger scared you." I hadn't thought so, but he may have seen something that went beyond my everyday nervousness. Certainly her intensity and brilliance have always frightened many of her contemporaries, particularly men; in some, nervousness quickly turns to rage, which then clouds their ability to see the quality of her work. She does not like to hear, of course, that she's intimidating. A woman who interviewed her for CBC radio a dozen years ago used that word, and Atwood — as is her style — quickly interrupted. "May I ask *you* a question? Are you intimidated now?" The interviewer, clearly intimidated, of course said she wasn't, and the interview limped on.

Atwood once wrote a poem, "Speeches for Dr. Frankenstein," in which the doctor looks at his monster and wonders, "Why did I make you?" I've always felt that Atwood identified with Dr. Frankenstein; the monster is her own public personality and its effect on her fellow Canadians. Atwood's career is not a huge surprise to people who read a lot: we recognize her as a sister to the powerful, richly talented and sharply opinionated women who have been major figures in British and American literature in this century — Rebecca West, Virginia Woolf, Mary McCarthy. But to others she seems (or at least seemed, when she first grew famous) some strange monster — a Nietszchean female will and a capacious literary imagination, clothed in an impatient patriotism. To some writers of my age, her talent seemed almost an offence. In the 1970s, after the first great wave of her fame, I mentioned a book of hers to a friend of mine, a good writer. "I'm going to read her," he said. "I'm going to sit down and read her books. Just as soon as I can overcome the blind, raging jealousy I feel whenever I hear her name." For my part, I could no more feel jealousy toward her than envy a Martian: the cultural distance between me and someone who thinks it normal to write a poem about Circe or Persephone is too vast to be bridged by currents of jealousy.

And after a while, most of her fellow authors learned to like her as well as admire her. She became part of that community of reciprocal praise that encompassed writers as disparate as Margaret Laurence, Timothy Findley, and Pierre Berton — the people Laurence liked to call "our tribe." Their attitudes of mutual support turned them into a new force in Canadian cultural history: where writers had previously been isolated individuals, these people bound themselves together in pursuit of their shared goals, the making of a Canadian literature and a Canadian literary community. To this end Atwood dropped any pretence of a critical stance. In 1977 I asked her to review Pierre Berton's new book, *The Dionne Years: A Thirties Melodrama,* because I imagined that the Dionne quintuplets would appeal to her as a Canadian myth. She said she would read it and write a review only if she liked it. This was new to me — someone who on principle wrote *only* favourable reviews — but I realized that I couldn't recall her writing a negative one. I agreed to this curious arrangement, she liked the book, and *Saturday Night* carried her review. Later I read the book and — despite my interest in the subject, based on my father's personal experience with the Dionnes — thought it flat and intellectually underdeveloped. At *Saturday Night* we decided it wasn't a great idea to have Atwood review a lot of books.

That same year she got me involved in the most absurd of my activities in support of Canadian culture: a stage show in which I played myself, or myself rewritten by Atwood. She called me one day in 1977 and said she wanted to take me to lunch and make an offer I couldn't refuse. Somehow I knew she didn't want me to collaborate on her next novel or write the screenplay for *Lady Oracle,* but I went anyway. When I arrived at the restaurant she gave me, even before we ordered, a one-sentence lesson in how to handle interviewers.

"How are you?"

"I'm fine generally, but a bit agitated. I've just been interviewed by a woman from the CBC. Her first question was, 'Mr. Fulford, you write the Notebook column and the Marshall Delaney movie column in *Saturday Night,* you write every weekend in the Toronto *Star* and some other papers, you give reviews on the radio and interview people on television — don't you think that's a bit too much Robert Fulford?' And all I could think of to say was something like 'Well, of course, if you think so, then....' "

"You should have said, 'It's not too much for me. Is it too much for you?' "

Ever since, I've been hoping someone will ask me the same question again, so that I can give Atwood's answer. That's the core of her style: don't let the interviewer dictate the tone of the occasion; throw *her* off guard.

That day Atwood's mission was to recruit me for The All-Star Eclectic Typewriter Revue, an evening at the St. Lawrence

Centre in Toronto to raise money for the Writers' Union. She was one of the organizers and the writer of some of the skits. She wanted me to appear along with William French of *The Globe and Mail* and Douglas Marshall, who was then editor of *Books in Canada*. It would be something about the literary Mafia. Would I take part? She knew I would.

A few weeks later she sent me her script, "The Toronto Literary Mafia," about three characters — Doug the Thug, Frenchie, and The Godfulford. In the program notes she included what purported to be my résumé:

"Editor, *Saturday Night,* and owner of the Marshall Delaney Puppet Show; President, Fulfordburgers Ltd.; Board of Directors, Fulford's Little Living Pills and Condensed Art Capsules; Poor Fulford's Almanac; Fulford Picks the Pics; Director, The Bricklin and Fulfordmobile Co. Ltd. 'As Fulford goes, so goes the Nation' — P. Trudeau."

I was to wear homburg, fur-collared coat, and white scarf. Frenchie was to introduce me: "This is a man whose face you wouldn't notice. He lives in an ordinary house, maybe right near yours. He dresses nice. He's respectable. He even seems to have a legitimate job. But underneath...he's known as...The Godfulford. You want in on the word rackets in this town, you gotta go talk to the Godfulford....You want a reputation, he'll get you one."

French, Marshall, and I were told to show up at a rehearsal studio a few days before the performance. When we did, I saw an entirely new — to me — Atwood. In adolescence she had been a camp counsellor; now she was playing the same role, gleefully and energetically pulling together the camp show for parents' day. The Peer Gynt Suite was playing, and a group to be called the Farley Mowat Dancers — they included Sylvia Fraser, Marian Engel, and June Callwood — were stomping across the floor on snowshoes. Atwood was in the lead, urging them on.

She turned to the three of us. We had some lines and we had to dance a few steps while someone on a sound track sang Atwood's words about us to the tune of the ancient Chiquita Banana commercial. She showed us our dance steps, and we followed her as best we could. French was poor, Marshall was bad, and I was terrible — messages sent from my brain to my legs either are not received or are disobeyed upon arrival. Atwood watched me try to dance, giggled, and suggested I shuffle through it as best I could.

Before the performance, French, Marshall, and I went to a bar around the corner. Calming our nerves with beer, we contemplated our immediate future in horror.

"How did we get into this?" Marshall said, "Atwood has written this satire of us and gotten *us* to perform it."

"I think," I said, "it's part of being a good sport."

But we also knew that only Atwood could have managed it: uniquely, she has the ability to present an unreasonable idea as the only course a sensible human being can take.

Everything went as well as could be expected. Don Harron gave one of his best monologues, Marian Engel (the author of *Bear*) was pursued off the stage by a man in a bear costume, Jack McClelland waltzed around while someone sang "Jack the Knife," and at the end of the evening members of the union — including at least one millionaire, Berton — sang "Solidarity Forever" from the stage. As for our number, the audience applauded and our friends were kind. In the lobby afterward, Nuala FitzGerald, the actress, said, "You've mastered the Abbey Theatre technique of stillness." She was referring to the look of petrified fright that remained on my face from the beginning of the skit to the end. Irving Layton said to me, "You're wasting your time writing," an ambiguous tribute.

For all its terrors, that night stays in my mind as one happy occasion when we writers stopped complaining about society's indifference to us and simply enjoyed entertaining each other — it was an occasion, in other words, when briefly we forgot the national cultural melodrama and turned to a more agreeable art, cabaret.

There was another reason why I found the evening a delightful relief. In the *Saturday Night* offices just a few blocks from the theatre, I was starring in the second act of another long-running melodrama, the one that provided the focus of my professional life from 1968 to 1987.

ELEVEN

*T*urning
the Corner

DURING THE YEARS I was editor, I often met readers whose hazy but pleasant memories of *Saturday Night* went back three or four decades. All of them, at one point or another, had the same piece of personal history to tell me: "When I was growing up, *Saturday Night* was the most respected publication in our house." They seldom told me they had read it, but they remembered its aura of respect. The *Saturday Night* they described was the one B.K. Sandwell edited from 1932 to 1951 and established as the most eloquent liberal voice in English-speaking Canada.

Here it would be fitting to say that from the moment I achieved literacy I read every issue of Sandwell's paper and built my intellectual life around it. In truth I barely knew it existed. In my memory it is seldom lying about our house, and I can't recall my father ever saying anything for or against it. To my embarrassment I've several times been at social gatherings where it seemed the only person who lacked warm memories of the Sandwell *Saturday Night* — of the slick, high-gloss paper, of the Karsh photos of Ottawa mandarins staring up from the front page, of the financial witticisms in "Gold and Dross" repeated over the dinner table by Dad — was the poor wretch charged with following, at a great distance, in Sandwell's wake.

My only connection with Sandwell was through a playmate across the street whose father, P.M. Richards, was the managing editor of *Saturday Night* in the early 1940s. Mr. Richards was a forbidding figure, a no-nonsense Brit who spoke seldom and sharply; the paper he was putting out seemed as distant from my own concerns as he did. I didn't know until much later that for years he was working with one of the legends of Canadian journalism.

A professor from McGill, Sandwell took over *Saturday Night* when it was already forty-five years old and gave it, for the first time, a coherent national identity. He wrote for every issue, turning out editorials, book reviews, and sometimes theatre reviews (under the pseudonym Lucy Van Gogh). He was a civil libertarian in times when it wasn't easy — almost alone, he attacked the federal government's wartime treatment of the Japanese Canadians. His pieces were witty, lucid, and intelligent, but — with one great exception — he wasn't the sort of editor who hires and develops other notable editors or even memorable writers. Most of the people who worked with him left journalism about the time he retired, some (like Richards) for more secure jobs in public relations. The great exception was Robertson Davies, who became literary editor under Sandwell in 1940, when he was twenty-seven, and has been appearing in *Saturday Night*, from time to time, ever since.

Toward the end of Sandwell's career, about the time I was starting to work as a sports writer, I distantly understood that there was trouble at *Saturday Night*. The owners were changing the format, from broadsheet newspaper to magazine; they were kicking Sandwell upstairs and bringing in Robert Farquharson, the managing editor of *The Globe and Mail* (who had only recently allowed the sports editor to give me my first job), as the operating editor. Such changes are always made in response to economic difficulty — no one rede-signs a magazine for the fun of it. But these alterations didn't work, and soon there was a more fundamental change. Jack Kent Cooke, who owned the Maple Leafs baseball team and the noisiest radio station in Toronto, CKEY, bought the magazine and for a while put it out as part of a conglomer-ate that included a women's magazine, a magazine for farm-ers, a motor-sports journal, and a general magazine, *Liberty.* He even owned the press on Richmond Street that had been printing *Saturday Night* for decades. Cooke was brash, pretentious, opinionated, and famously uncouth. Once, it is said, the artist and illustrator Oscar Cahen arrived at Cooke's house to paint a portrait of him. He found Cooke in his study, a copy of the recently published Standard Revised Version of the Bible at his side. Cooke tapped the Book. "You should get this, Oscar," he said solemnly. "It's the best god-damned Bible I've ever read." Ralph Allen's funniest novel, *The Chartered Libertine,* was a satiric account of Cooke's rise to greatness.

When Cooke's purchase of the magazine was announced, Sandwell immediately resigned — according to one story he walked from the board room where he received the news directly to his office, took his lunch in its paper bag from his desk, and went home. (He wrote a column in *The Financial Post* until his death.) Farquharson departed soon after, to run the information services of NATO in Paris. There followed a blindingly fast — by *Saturday Night* standards — succession of editors: four in ten years. For much of that time only the contributions of Davies, whom the great publisher Alfred Knopf called the best reviewer in North America, made *Saturday Night* worth reading.

I believe it was Davies, then the editor of one of his family's papers, the Peterborough *Examiner,* who introduced to *Saturday Night* a former professor who had come to Canada from England to teach at Queen's University and had then edited the *Examiner*'s sister newspaper, the Kingston *Whig-Standard*. This was Arnold Edinborough, the dominant figure at the magazine for the next dozen years. He was the last editor hired by Cooke (in 1958) and he headed the company that took over the magazine when Cooke finally tired of both publishing and Canada and went off to make an enormous fortune in the United States.

Edinborough made it a livelier magazine, but the firm lost money and he was forced out. *Saturday Night* fell into the hands of a promoter who sold stock in the company to adherents of Social Credit, on the promise that this would give them a national outlet for their views. (In fact, so far as I can tell, Social Credit ideas never made more than furtive appearances in the magazine.) Briefly the name was changed to *Canadian Saturday Night,* when the promoter amalgamated another, more obscure magazine with it. This enterprise foundered, the magazine stopped appearing, and *Saturday Night* seemed to be dead.

Edinborough, however, revived it in 1963. He had the encouragement of Maclean-Hunter, which wanted at least one ally in its fight against Canadian editions of *Time* and other American magazines. Maclean-Hunter undertook to print *Saturday Night* and defer payment for the indefinite future. Edinborough was in business once again, and he was to remain editor until 1968 and publisher until 1970.

I STARTED writing regularly for the magazine in 1965, when I was having my second run as a columnist on the *Star.* Harry Bruce, Edinborough's managing editor, suggested that I contribute a movie column. After three or four of my pieces appeared, I was called into the office of my boss, Ralph Allen, the managing editor.

"Someone here has pointed out" — I later understood this

to be a code phrase for Honderich — "that you're writing a column for *Saturday Night.*"

"Yes…"

"Well, we don't mind if you write for them from time to time, but we don't think you should be writing a column. We feel that if we pay your salary, we own your image."

I was pleased, amused, and slightly distressed — pleased to be thought of as someone with an image (that had never occurred to me), amused to hear such a word from the lips of a tough old newspaperman like Ralph, and slightly distressed to realize that my career as a movie critic was over.

"Of course," he said, "if they wanted to let you write it under a pseudonym, that would be all right with us. I don't suppose they would, though."

I didn't suppose they would either, but I asked Harry Bruce about it, and he asked Arnold, and they decided that would be fine. The next column was almost on the press and my pseudonym had to be devised immediately. I chose Marshall as a first name because that's my own and my son's second name and because my father once told me that in every generation of Fulfords there was one Marshall; our branch of the family had been founded in the Ottawa Valley when a lumberman named Henry Marshall Fulford arrived there in 1812 from Woburn, Massachusetts. As a last name I chose Delaney, after Thomas Delaney, my great-uncle by marriage, who was killed in the Frog Lake massacre during the Riel rebellion of 1885, an event described by my great aunt, Theresa Fulford Delaney, in the book she and another woman wrote, *Two Months in the Camp of Big Bear.*

It would never have occurred to me to write under a pseudonym, but there was something peculiarly liberating about it. Sheltered by anonymity, Delaney became a more personal writer than I had been, more open and audacious. Eventually he converted me to his ways, and I found myself shedding at least some of the impersonal quality that dominated my early writing. The Marshall Delaney column also led directly to my new life as an editor. I wrote it under three managing editors — Bruce, Kildare Dobbs, and Jack Batten. Batten lasted only a few months; he didn't like editing, and soon announced he was giving it up. He wondered if I'd be interested in his job. I said I might, and he said he'd mention it to Arnold.

A week or so later — it was the spring of 1968 — Arnold and I met in the bar of the Lord Simcoe, the now-demolished hotel that was built by R. Howard Webster, a fabulously wealthy Montrealer who owned *The Globe and Mail* for some years. Eleven years later Webster's family was to buy *Saturday Night,* with wonderful (and, later, disturbing) consequences for me. In 1968 I didn't know exactly who owned *Saturday Night* and — though I now find this hard to believe — didn't much care. My view of business was exceptionally naive. I believed that editorial work and business were separate and that editors didn't need to think much about what businessmen did. I did not yet understand that in a small business the troubles of the enterprise touch everyone — that the receptionist and the president and all those in between know precisely the nature of the company's failure, and feel its sting. At Maclean-Hunter, when the stock fell, I didn't even hear about it. People who work in small business are denied such luxurious ignorance; the shame of an over-strained line of credit is shared by everyone.

Except for a brief time in the 1950s when *Mayfair* was an independent magazine, a period I regarded as an aberration, I had reached the age of thirty-six without depending for my livelihood on any but the most solid corporations. I'd written for poverty-stricken publications, such as *Canadian Art* and *The Tamarack Review,* but without worrying much about whether they paid me; my real income had been derived from the *Globe,* the *Star,* Maclean-Hunter, and the CBC. Now I was heading, without quite knowing it, toward something much more dangerous.

I understood, of course, that there had been financial

trouble at *Saturday Night,* but I had no idea of its extent. I certainly didn't understand that the magazine hadn't made a profit in at least twenty years. Later on, I used to say that business schools should send task forces to study us. We stayed in the red longer than any other corporation on earth, from the 1940s through all the years I was there, except for one blip around 1977 when we briefly moved into the black by landing a government contract (to design a museum magazine that never appeared). Otherwise, so far as I know, money was lost in every fiscal year from Sandwell's time through the Cooke editors right up to the end of my tenure, in 1987. (My understanding is that 1988 will be another record-breaker.)

Arnold and I did not speak much of losses at the Lord Simcoe. He gave me the impression that things were looking up, and I'm sure he believed it. The company now had two magazines, a teachers' journal called *Monday Morning* having been founded some time before. At our meeting Arnold may actually have said, "We're beginning to turn the corner." If he didn't, he was the only one of several dozen businessmen connected with *Saturday Night* in my time — publishers, ad sales people, directors, chairmen of the board, financial backers — who failed to speak those words. All of them spoke with hope and belief. All were wrong. The magazine turned many corners over the years, but never *the* corner.

After a preliminary chat, Arnold asked me if I would care to replace Batten as managing editor.

I took a deep breath. "I've thought about it," I said, "and I've decided against it. I don't think I would like being managing editor."

Arnold looked at me quizzically.

"However," I went on, "I *would* like to be editor."

Arnold did not seem shocked, but I was. I had never before (and have not since) told anyone I wanted his job.

"What I was thinking," I hurried on, "was that you would move up to be full-time publisher — of *Saturday Night, Mon-*

day Morning, and other magazines that could be developed later. You'd still write for *Saturday Night,* but otherwise I'd look after the content and you'd concentrate on making the business work."

I believed all this as I said it, and perhaps Arnold did too. I didn't know that he had no more taste for business than I.

He nodded thoughtfully, as if people tried to push him out of his office every day of the week.

"That might be a good idea," he said. "Perhaps I could remain as editor-in-chief of all the magazines."

Something told me that wasn't a good idea.

"I don't think so."

He nodded again. We sipped our drinks. We spoke of salary. Arnold said he would call me, and not long after he did. I went to work as editor on July 15, 1968. At that point I had never thought about meeting a payroll and I had never considered the legal issues involved in bankruptcy. I don't believe I knew the deeply ominous meaning of the words "undercapitalized" and "restructure." I had never received a cheque that bounced, and never written one.

A MONTH OR SO before I was to turn up for work, I ran into David Fry on the street. He was a stockbroker and a major investor in *Saturday Night.* David shook my hand. "I'm delighted you're coming to edit the magazine," he said. "This may be the thing that will save us."

I thanked him, smiled, and walked away, the word "save" echoing in my head. Until then I hadn't understood that saving something was part of the job description. It turned out that David had more in mind than the survival of the magazine. A substantial part of his fortune was at stake, money he had lent the company in recent years. In a sense, he — not Edinborough or the general manager, William Nobleman, both shareholders — was now the real owner. This is the sort of thing I learned in the next few months: when you lend a company more than it's worth, you own it.

On the other hand, Maclean-Hunter's unpaid printing bill was probably as great as Fry's unpaid loan, so Maclean-Hunter could also claim to be the owner. Neither Fry nor Maclean-Hunter, of course, was interested in claiming this prize. Each hoped that with a little more help and guidance the magazine would sail on to success and eventually repay them both. In the end it repaid neither.

Over the years, as revenues declined, *Saturday Night* had steadily cut back — from a weekly to a fortnightly to a monthly; from a large broadsheet to a magazine the size of *Time*. Then the number of pages were reduced: at one point, early in my time there, we brought out an issue with thirty-two pages. "This isn't a magazine," I said to one of our faithful contributors, Doug Fetherling, "it's a god-damned pamphlet." Nor did we spend lavishly on staff. In my first year I was the editorial department, though I shared a secretary (Sara Waxman, the actor Al Waxman's wife) with Edinborough. There was also a designer, who did *Saturday Night* and *Monday Morning*, and after some months I acquired a full-time assistant editor: Anastasia Erland, a woman of great imagination and infinite patience. In the early 1970s I also took on a full-time secretary. Until the end of 1974, that was the staff.

The budget for writers, photographers and illustrators was similarly meagre. But no matter how low we made our expenses, we still didn't bring in enough money to pay them. Living like paupers, we were living beyond our means. My life at *Saturday Night* was an illustration of the line from *David Copperfield* — "Annual income twenty pounds, annual expenditure nineteen nineteen six, result happiness. Annual income twenty pounds, annual expenditure twenty pounds ought and six, result misery." Between the time I arrived in 1968 and the time I left in 1987, much happened and much — I think — was accomplished. But someone glancing over nothing but the balance sheets would see only one really striking change — the number of zeroes at the end of the loss. From the mid-1970s on, we were a growing company —

staff grew, revenues grew, costs grew, and losses grew. At one point, around 1970, someone said that all we really needed to get us over the hump — or, perhaps, turn the corner — was $20,000. At another time, possibly in 1978, someone said that what was needed, to put us on our feet, was a fresh investment of $200,000. And in my last two months at *Saturday Night* the marketing director came up with a plan that would increase our circulation and finally put us in the black. It would require a fresh investment of about $2,000,000.

For many years the ugliest problem at *Saturday Night* was our inability to pay writers on time. Most of the publishers and managers I worked with over the years saw writers' fees the way they saw the bills of other suppliers — as obligations to be postponed. I argued that we should pay the writers, photographers and illustrators as promptly as we paid the staff, for the humane reason that they needed the money and for the practical reason that they wouldn't work for us again if we didn't. Eventually, in the 1980s, the executive editor, Dianne de Fenoyl, created a category — "Like Payroll" — into which we directed the cheques of contributors; finally they began to receive their money on time. But over the years we usually paid late as well as little, and often lost writers on that account. Members of the board seldom understood. Once, when I handed around a list of unpaid contributors, a board member said, "I don't see why you're making a fuss about this." He pointed to Ron Haggart's name on the list. "I happen to know Ron Haggart has a good job. He doesn't need the money." But we needed Ron Haggart, and couldn't have him if we didn't pay him.

Worse, our cheques sometimes bounced. Occasionally my own payroll cheque was returned, but that shame could be contained within the office. It became more public when Morley Callaghan called to say we had sent him a bad cheque for $200. That day, in a hysterical fit, I announced that we would sent out only certified cheques — which of course spread the bad news even further. In the early 1970s Harry

Malcolmson, a lawyer and part-time art critic, came to the office to deliver an article. I handed him a cheque, $125, for a piece he'd written months before.

"And Harry, do me a favour? That's drawn on the bank downstairs. Cash it before you leave the building."

"Why?"

"Don't ask questions. Just get your money on the way out. It's there now. It might not be there tomorrow."

"You're kidding."

"Harry, take my advice."

I think he got his money — in fact, all the people who wrote for *Saturday Night* got their money, eventually. But along the way I discovered a certain truth. When you pay writers late — assuming they normally work for the CBC, Maclean-Hunter, or other quick-paying markets — it's almost as if you haven't paid them at all. The money may come as a pleasant surprise, but the exchange has lost the feeling of a commercial transaction. The writing becomes a kind of favour, and whatever indebtedness may be involved is charged against the editor. In those years I ended up in debt to many writers.

MONTHS AFTER I arrived at *Saturday Night* I still had no idea what sort of magazine I wanted to make it. The ideas I'd formed before starting now seemed silly or impossible — most of them would require staff writers or at least a corps of well-paid freelancers, like those I'd worked with four years earlier at *Maclean's*, and I now saw I wasn't likely to acquire such people. But in the office there were even more distressing problems. I wasn't getting along with Edinborough, and he wasn't getting along with Nobleman, the former Maclean-Hunter ad salesman he had recruited as general manager. Since there were only three of us running the place, this made almost everything uncomfortable.

Arnold liked to read his work aloud to a colleague. He would dictate something to his secretary, edit it, then come to my cubicle holding it in his hand. I would be editing something or, more likely, pretending to edit something while I worried about the magazine's (and my) future.

"Look, I don't want to interrupt you," Arnold would say, "but just listen to this..."

Bruce, Dobbs, and Batten had told me they found this impossible to deal with. Apparently they had simply listened in sullen silence. I decided on blatant rudeness. About the third time Arnold did it, I picked up the phone as he spoke and began dialing.

That was a minor irritant. The larger problem was that anything I liked, Edinborough didn't; anything he liked, I didn't. Oh, if pressed we might have been able to agree that Shakespeare was a hell of a poet and that it was a good thing the Germans lost the Second World War. Beyond that, we had little in common. I thought it a great coup, for instance, when I acquired Mordecai Richler as a monthly columnist; Edinborough found something wrong with almost every column Richler produced. I was pleased by an article Peter Gzowski wrote for us on the growing prevalence — in movies, books, and conversation — of the word *fuck*. Edinborough was appalled.

"Look, I don't like this," he said, fingering the proofs with distaste. "I don't think it's funny, and readers will be upset."

"Well, Arnold, you know, you're the publisher and I'm the editor. I mean, you're not *supposed* to approve of the whole magazine."

"I should approve of *every word*."

I never learned why Edinborough hired me in the first place, and I never understood what turned Nobleman against him. Certainly they were enemies before I got there. In my first month on the job I realized that Nobleman saw Edinborough as the main barrier to the prosperity of the company; Edinborough saw Nobleman as, at best, a bore and a nuisance. Neither appeared to respect the other as a businessman. In 1970 Edinborough left, and Nobleman became publisher.

The next four years were in some ways the most difficult
of my working life. I was trying to learn how to edit a journal
of a peculiar kind while living with the threat of bankruptcy.
At some point in the early 1970s it was impressed on me that
I was responsible for the survival of the magazine. If I left,
Nobleman said, there wouldn't be much point in going on
with it. Obviously, I couldn't quit this job, as I had quit
others — the consequences were rather more serious. And
day after day, as the bills accumulated, the end of *Saturday
Night* was always a lively possibility. Around 1972, when we
failed to pay some crucial bill, word spread that we were
closing. Norman DePoe of the CBC phoned to say that he
had a film crew on the way to cover the final day in the life
of the magazine. I told him we weren't shutting down, but
the incident wasn't surprising; it was almost routine.

IN EDINBOROUGH'S time, the subject matter of *Saturday
Night* was never defined — the magazine was intended to be
serious journalism, and sometimes achieved that goal. But
you never knew what it might be serious *about*. Edinborough
would publish an analysis of American policy in Vietnam in
one issue, then not mention the subject again for six months.
African development, British socialism, the Japanese economy — they would all appear from time to time in the
magazine, then vanish. It seemed to me the magazine was
everything and nothing. It needed a focus, and the focus
was obvious. *Saturday Night* would be a magazine about Canada. We'd stop pretending that Canadian readers wanted us
to explain the American presidency to them; we couldn't do
that with authority anyway. But we could probably do a
reasonably good job of writing about Canada.

That was one of the assumptions on which I edited the
magazine from 1970, and it was crucial to whatever success
we had. A magazine has to be a combination of the predict-
able and the surprising; it must define its sphere and then
develop original ideas within that sphere. Our sphere was

Canada — its society, politics, culture, business — and our emphasis was on the emerging question of Canadian survival.

I'm not at all pleased when I glance at some of the issues I edited in those years; but there are more than a few that seem reasonably good. In November, 1970, for instance, Peter Gzowski wrote a piece about the use of drugs in his own life, his children's, and the life of a friend who had died after taking LSD; Harry Bruce contributed a devastating review of Pierre Berton's CPR book; Peter Desbarats wrote about a sex-film producer in Quebec; and Allan Fotheringham (who I think was making his first appearance in a national magazine) satirized the mayor of Vancouver. There was a lovely travel article on Spain by Myrna Kostash, a funny piece by Anastasia Erland, an art column by Harry Malcolmson, and one of the brilliant cartoons that Martin Vaughn-James was producing for us that year. John Ayre wrote a fine report on a right-wing fringe group, the Edmund Burke Society, and I briefly reviewed new novels by Hugh Hood and Brian Moore.

The least impressive contribution was my Notebook column, mainly about the federal finance department's recent White Paper on taxation. In those years, and for a long time after, Notebook was written in great haste, usually cobbled together at the last moment in between proof-reading and meetings with potential backers. It wasn't until 1980, when the magazine was finally on a secure footing, that I found the time to make Notebook any more than ordinarily interesting.

Recently I came across a letter written in 1974 that captures, better than my memory, the tone of those years. David Lewis Stein, a journalist and novelist, had remarked in a letter that he thought *Saturday Night* was now just about the only place he could practice honest journalism. My reply to him was uncharacteristically bitter. I seem to have wanted to get a few things on the record.

"Well, *Saturday Night* may be honest," I wrote, "but that's all you can really say for it. It ain't brilliant, it ain't innovative, it ain't influential, and it ain't popular. The problem is money. There's not much money to pay the writers, and this means that most of the writing is on a doing-us-a-favour basis, which means that the writers write what they want, when they want. This is fine when they are good, which they sometimes are, but it is bad when they are self-indulgent or silly or thin in their research or thoughtless.

"There is no way to balance the magazine — no way, for instance to keep from running far too much Maritimes stuff (I happen to have pretty talented friends there) as opposed to B.C. stuff (I have friends there, too, but they don't write as much). I'm not producing the kind of magazine I'm capable of producing. But the lack of money affects more than that. There's no money to finance circulation promotion, which every magazine needs. All magazines suffer from circulation attrition. People die, move, get sick of the magazine, decide not to give it to their aunts this Christmas, etc. The subscription list naturally shrinks, and the only way to keep it steady is continual direct-mail selling. *Saturday Night* has no money to spend on this, so the circulation continues to shrink — it's a miracle we've kept it as high as it is, 75,000 or 80,000. And money also affects timing. We have no real schedule for *Saturday Night*, because we don't know when we will have the money to print it. I can't time an article to appear just before an election, or some such. The newsstand people never know when they're going to get *Saturday Night*, so they don't put any effort into pushing it, for which one can easily forgive them. The newsstand-buyers (not to mention the subscribers) are continually getting last month's copy — even, sometimes, the copy of the month before last. Right now it is May 9 but the April issue just recently got on the newsstands and the April copies to subscribers went out only yesterday, May 8. As for the May issue, I've been finished with that for a long time and it's not such a bad issue, but right now it's sitting, unprinted, at the printers. When the printers get some money they'll print it.

"So if all these problems are caused by a lack of money,

why don't we get some more money? There are four sources: government, readers, backers, and advertisers. Government (in the form of Canada Council, etc.) gives us some and may give us a little more but, as with all cultural agencies, they will never give us enough. The readers, too, give us some money, in the form of subscriptions — but, again, not much. Backers — well, we have a board of directors who have been generous, but they do not see it as their function to provide endless sums of money for a losing operation. That, finally, leaves advertisers. We get some ads, but we need about twice as many as we get. The reason we don't get them is that the magazine, in its present form, does not seem attractive to ad people — unlike, say, *Toronto Life* or *Toronto Calendar* or *Quest* or one of those other magazines they admire. They think *Saturday Night* is 'dull' or 'highbrow' or something like that. It doesn't have zing. Demographic surveys (we can prove our readers love Scotch, airplane travel and everything else expensive) don't matter at all if the agency people don't like the magazine itself.

"All this leaves me in an unbelievably difficult position. We now owe the writers just a bit over $15,000.

"Well, I'm not giving up. Yet. Right now there's a new plan afoot: a new design, new editorial style, new content, etc. Meanwhile, I enclose, deplorably late, your cheque for $200."

NOBLEMAN and his helpers in the advertising department — at one point there were two salesmen plus Nobleman, as against a single editor — were unable to sell enough ads to keep us afloat. We had one salesman who came to work for us, spent a year in the office, and — I believe — sold not a single ad, though he was full of useless ideas for editorial features. Nobleman was endlessly coming up with schemes to "restructure" (how I learned to hate that word) the company and provide working capital. From the beginning it was agreed that if only sufficient capital could be injected, we would sail happily into the future. Quite early in my time, David Fry's capital was exhausted, and we began looking for other investors. This involved me in many tense meetings; the subject of bankruptcy was often invoked and the directors (I became a director of the company in the early stages) were informed of our fiscal responsibilities to the staff in the event of the company's going under. Once Nobleman and I visited a lawyer who, we had been told, might be interested in making a small investment. He looked at our financial statements, sighed, and delivered his verdict: "You can sell it for the tax loss." Nobleman and I must have appeared downcast. "Don't worry," the man said. "It's nothing to be ashamed of. With some companies, their losses are their main asset." I stared at him. "Their tax-loss carry-forward," he explained. "Someone — it has to be someone in your business — buys you out and uses your losses against his taxes for five years." He paused. "You might be able to get a fair bit of money for this one."

Hardship was slowly teaching me patience. I am still not regarded as notably patient, and as an editor I was much less patient than certain of my colleagues, such as Gary Ross, Bernadette Sulgit, and Tecca Crosby; each of them, and others too, showed at *Saturday Night* that they could deal with a writer's long-term problems better than I. Nevertheless, I was learning that, whatever might be accomplished at *Saturday Night*, it wouldn't be accomplished in a hurry.

Raising money, I discovered, requires not only patience but the ability to eat a toad for breakfast and smile at the same time. Often I found myself dealing with ignorant condescension and self-satisfaction. Once Walter Curtin, a photographer who did some work for us, offered to take me out to lunch with a famous advertising executive he knew. This man, he said, would tell me how we could sell ads. I went, and the ad man told me how to edit *Saturday Night*.

"What you need is more entertaining articles," he said.

"I see."

"For instance, I saw an article the other day, How to Make

the Perfect Martini. That's the sort of article people want to read."

"I see."

"You need articles that will help people enjoy their daily lives."

"I see."

After coffee we all shook hands and I went back to the office. This is small business, I said to myself, and you are a small businessman. Nobody drafted you. You asked for it.

But I liked that idiot better than the people who said to me, "I think the magazine has improved," always implying that last year (whichever year was last year) it had been terrible. I also liked him better than people who, at parties, would say, "How are things at *Saturday Night?*" The honest answer, given only to intimate friends, was: "Unbelievably terrible, and if I weren't such a stubborn ox I'd walk away from this shameful mess and beg Honderich to take me back." The answer I gave was usually along the lines of: "Not bad, really, thanks. We're not making any *money*, of course, but we're not losing a lot either."

Nobleman, meanwhile, was scurrying around, trying to interest investors. He attracted Arthur Gelber, who had inherited a large amount of money and had spent much of his time organizing institutions such as the National Ballet and the Ontario Arts Council. At a cocktail party Gelber asked June Callwood, "Is *Saturday Night* worth saving?" I think she said it was; in any case he joined the board, invested in the magazine, and for a couple of years provided short-term loans at no interest to carry us past crises. William Neville, later a major figure in the federal Conservative Party, was with us for several years. Recently he said to me, "It was the only board I ever served on where the first order of business at each meeting was which director would pay the postage bill." James Gillies, a York University professor and an MP in the 1970s, was on the board for a couple of years. His main task was also to provide small short-term loans: he kept about $1,500 in his bank account for this purpose, sending it over to *Saturday Night* when needed, then putting it back when Nobleman was able to return it. Ephraim Diamond, the head of the Cadillac Fairview development company, also became a director. Our board sometimes met in the executive offices of his company, in the northern suburbs of Toronto.

Nobleman and I went to Vancouver one day to talk to John Nichol, a rich businessman and former senator who had expressed some slight interest in investing. I asked Nobleman what we could tell Nichol that he couldn't learn from reading the magazine and the balance sheets. "I think he just wants to find out whether he likes us," Nobleman said. I liked Nichol. Aside from his money, he was famous mainly for being the only Canadian voluntarily to resign from the senate. "My wife said I had to get out of Ottawa because I was turning into a prick," he explained. Apparently he didn't like us: he didn't invest.

Over the years we attracted a couple of dozen people to our board — some because they had been talked into it, some because their business interests got them entwined with the magazine, some because they vaguely favoured good causes, and a few because they liked the magazine and wished it well. I had one director who informed me that he not only didn't read *Saturday Night*, he didn't read any other magazines either; I think five or six others could have made the same statement. This experience made me sensitive to the lives of people who run museums and find themselves more or less under the control of trustees who come to the museum only to attend meetings and parties.

Gelber suggested that since *Saturday Night* hadn't made a profit in a long time it should officially become a non-profit organization. That would qualify us for Canada Council grants and other government money. I didn't like that idea, and I told Nobleman so. In fact, hearing my voice across the years, I'm astonished by my arrogance. "I don't *get* Canada

Council grants," I said to him, "I *give* Canada Council grants." (I'd served on a couple of committees handing out funds.) But gradually I was persuaded that public money could help us without influencing us, and in the next seven years we asked for and accepted grants from the Canada Council, the Ontario Arts Council, and the federal secretary of state.

But by the spring of 1974 our non-profit company, Second Century Canada Publications, was also in trouble: grants, revenues, and help from the directors didn't cover our costs. It was also obvious that we needed a new publisher. Nobleman had decided to run for the Conservatives in the federal election (in the end he didn't get a nomination).

I think it was Gelber who suggested we talk to Edgar Cowan, a public relations man whom I'd known slightly for some years. Cowan was leaving MacLaren, where he had run the public-relations arm. He came with an interesting background — former owner of a folk-song club, former associate producer of a TV show, founding partner of a local TV station, fairly ardent Liberal — and sounded promising. He thought he knew what would make the magazine work, though he didn't seem to be a great magazine reader. At one point he mentioned a British magazine he admired, *Nova*. I liked it too, for the design, but I recalled that it carried only short text-pieces, mainly to explain the photographs. I wondered whether he cared much about writing and reporting; I don't think I ever learned the answer.

Cowan was, at least from time to time, supremely confident. He was an effusive fellow, the sort of enthusiast who interrupts a meeting to say: "I got it, I got it, *I got it!*" He loved his new image as a publisher. He had stepped up in the world. "Speaking as a publisher," he would say.

Cowan saw himself as an idea man. As he often explained, he had his best ideas in the shower, and when one of them came he could hardly wait to get to the office and share it. One morning he said to me, "How do you like this for a headline? SATURDAY NIGHT PUBLISHER INTERVIEWS U.S.

PRESIDENT." He explained that he would go to Washington for an exclusive interview with the president and that this would publicize *Saturday Night*. He wasn't concerned about the fact that he had never interviewed anyone for a magazine before, and he didn't think it would be difficult to set up an appointment. I asked what he and the president would talk about. "Well, about Canada and... Canadian-American relations." The president was Gerald Ford, a man of unremarkable views, and there seemed no reason to think he would have anything more to say on these subjects than on others. Finally Ed gave up that notion, having consumed no more than forty-five minutes of my time discussing it. But I believe that — as on other occasions — he resented my failure to find his ideas as inspiring as he did.

I sensed that I might not be the perfect editor for him.

"If you think you can make it work better with someone else, Ed, don't worry about me — I'll be glad to step back."

"Nope. You're part of the package."

We talked as *Saturday Night* managers always did — we spoke of restructuring the ownership of the company and of how well it would run if properly capitalized. We discussed a redesign, because on such occasions magazines must always be redesigned. We hired a consulting art director, Ralph Tibbles, with whom I'd worked at *Maclean's* in the early 1960s. We talked about which wealthy capitalists would back us.

Meanwhile, I was still putting out what we now called "the old *Saturday Night*," and Nobleman was still the publisher. There was always trouble with the printing bill — we were allowed to pay sixty days late, no later; until we came up with the money, the printer didn't print.

Then, in the fall of 1974, our directors' patience ran out and Nobleman couldn't make a payment to the printer. September came and went, with no September issue. It was prepared (I have the only copy, a proof) but never printed. What had been obvious to those inside the magazine for a long time was now clear to everyone else: *Saturday Night* was pretty well bankrupt. The directors met on a Sunday at our office and issued a statement: we were suspending publication. We said we hoped to re-start the magazine in the near future, but the newspapers ran our obituaries anyway. Nobody expected to see us appear again. Certainly I didn't.

NOBLEMAN HAD always said that if *Saturday Night* went out of business, it would create a national sensation. I had argued that we'd vanish with barely a trace. Nobleman was right and I was wrong. When we suspended publication the news appeared on front pages and TV broadcasts across the country. As I wrote later, "Nothing in its life was ever as celebrated as *Saturday Night*'s apparent death." People who had never before said a word about us now discovered that our magazine was a vital national institution. A Committee to Save Saturday Night issued an open letter to the federal secretary of state: "We the undersigned strongly urge you to provide *Saturday Night* magazine with the funds it requires to continue publication...We must not let *Saturday Night* die." Like most such statements, it was organized by people whose own careers were involved — I think Morris Wolfe, our TV critic in that era, drafted it. But of course I was delighted that it attracted 207 signatures, including those of Davies, Atwood, Richler, and McLuhan. A great many others were also moved — as if (in William French's words in the *Globe*), with the magazine's death "part of what it means to be Canadian died, too." Tom Symons, the founding president of Trent University and a major figure in the development of Canadian studies, later told me that when he and his wife heard the news they sat down and tried to figure out how they could back the magazine by putting another mortgage on their house.

We asked two directors of the old company to continue paying the office rent and phone bill for a couple of months, so that we could work out a way to breathe life back into the magazine. The rest of the staff was dismissed, and of course Cowan and I weren't getting paid. Linda Sandler, a poet who

had written for the magazine, came in and handled the telephone while we plotted our next move. We had Tibbles' handsome redesign for the magazine and a business plan full of
the usual hopeful numbers (including a "worst case scenario"
that turned out to be not nearly pessimistic enough). We
believed $400,000 would be a secure foundation, and we
would raise all of it before spending any of it — an investor
might put in (or promise) a unit of $25,000, but the money
wouldn't be used until $400,000 was raised.

In the summer of 1974, Cowan picked up about $150,000
in promises of investment for the new company, but that left
us a long way from our goal. On the day after we shut down,
one of the many calls I received was from my dear friend Jim
Knight, who in 1954 had suggested that *Canadian Homes and
Gardens* hire me. Now he was working in the public affairs
department at Imperial Oil, down the hall from the man who
handed out corporate donations.

"Bob, it's old Jim." He never announced himself any other
way, even when he was young.

"Lovely to hear from you. How are you?"

"I'm fine, but listen, I have an idea. What would you think
if Imperial Oil were to give you a hundred thousand dollars."

"Well, I don't think, no, uh…"

"Think about it."

I thought about it. I see, that in my Notebook column for
May, 1975, I claimed I "never hesitated"; in fact, I did. Imperial Oil was of course the Canadian branch of an American
multi-national. Would we destroy our credibility if we
accepted its money? I consulted Abraham Rotstein of the
University of Toronto, then as now the most interesting of
the economic nationalists and a good friend to the magazine.

"Take it," Abe said. "Those multi-nationals should be doing
something for this country."

We went to Imperial Oil with our business plan, and we
were promised a grant of $100,000 provided we raised all
the other money elsewhere.

Now we had $250,000, in theory. But investors were still hard to find — until I got another phone call, this one from Murray Frum, a land developer. I had met him in 1966 when his wife, Barbara, was writing a column for the *Star*; by 1974 the Frums and my wife and I had been close friends for years.

Murray offered to invest in the magazine and help us find other investors. I resisted at first, because business can destroy friendships and I was anxious not to lose this one. Murray said not to worry, everything would be okay. (He was right — he left our board in 1979 and our friendship continues to flourish.) Soon after, with everyone's agreement, he became chairman of the board; through the rest of the 1970s he was the main reason we stayed alive.

Even with Frum, and a couple of other investors he brought in, we were still short. We decided — I think it was Murray's idea — to ask our subscribers to provide the balance, about $50,000. We sent them each a brochure outlining our plans and asked them to buy subscriptions at ten dollars each, twice our former price. We would cash their cheques only if the magazine were revived. Grants from the Canada Council and the Ontario Arts Council paid for the mailing.

This made me nervous. If the response were lukewarm, there wouldn't be any reason to go ahead; we could look silly. As Morris Wolfe said, the mailing was a referendum on the future of the magazine: the readers would make the final decision.

At about that time I experienced the only psychosomatic illness of my life. While Cowan and I hurried from office to office, looking for money, my stomach began hurting. After a few days, thoughts of an ulcer passed through my mind, followed immediately by thoughts of cancer. I consulted an internist, who found nothing. "In your head," he said, tapping his skull. Sure enough, when the crisis at *Saturday Night* passed, the stomach pain vanished.

Perhaps it began to disappear the day I crossed St. Clair Avenue from *Saturday Night* to the post office in the Meighen building and found an enormous, bulging mail bag waiting for me. In any direct-mail campaign, three per cent is a good response, five per cent remarkable; we drew more than ten per cent. We had stated our goal as $50,000 but privately decided that we'd be satisfied with $40,000. We received more than $64,000 in subscriptions and another $1,274 in outright donations. Before the last mail bag came across the street I felt confident enough to hire Bernadette Sulgit from *Toronto Life* as the managing editor. In May, 1975, the first issue of the newest version of our magazine appeared. "Say Good Morning to *Saturday Night*," said the advertising.

If my time with Nobleman and Edinborough from 1968 to 1974 was Phase I of my life at *Saturday Night*, then the time with Cowan (1975 to 1979) was Phase II and the final period, ending with my resignation, was Phase III. They were all difficult and all enriching, but the middle period was the least satisfying. I no longer had the moral independence of my first years — after all, I'd committed myself to fund-raising, and I was partly responsible for all that investment. Nor did I have the large-scale financial backing that came my way in the 1980s. Worse, I was more a businessman than I had ever wanted to be. I was almost co-publisher. I not only sat on the board, I sat on the internal finance committee — "the cabinet," Cowan called it — that met every Monday morning to run the magazine. I was involved in hiring the advertising sales people and the circulation managers. When a sales manager had a nervous breakdown shortly after joining us, I visited him in the Clarke Institute and tried to figure out how his work might be covered. I knew when we wouldn't be able to meet our payroll or our printing bill, and I knew when General Motors cancelled its ads. It began to seem that the financial problems were just as depressing as in the Nobleman years, but more complicated. There were months when I was forced to take the business problems of the magazine more seriously than I took the content. Often, it showed.

Even so, there were triumphs. Sandra Gwyn, who had been writing for us since 1970, now came into her own as a reporter and a stylist — her beautifully made articles, on Newfoundland culture and on the people of Labrador, were openings onto new territory; her profile of Ed Broadbent remains, I think, the best piece ever written about him. In 1977, she wrote an article for our ninetieth anniversary issue that became the seed for *The Private Capital*, the book that won her a governor-general's award. Christina McCall, who had written for us from Ottawa in the 1960s, came on the staff as executive editor and brought her high literacy and political shrewdness to the magazine. When she left it was to work on *Grits*, the wonderful book that consolidated her reputation and provided us with two of our best cover stories of the 1980s.

But I was seldom as happy with the magazine as I wanted to be, and early in 1979 I confessed to Peter Herrndorf, then a CBC vice-president, that I thought it was time for *Saturday Night* to renew itself editorially — again. Herrndorf asked me if the members of our tiny staff would work this through by themselves or bring in outsiders to help. I said that I thought there should be some outsiders involved, though I had no idea who they might be. It didn't occur to me for a moment that these outsiders would lead *Saturday Night*, and its editor, to their best years by far.

TWELVE

*M*eeting
Citizen Black

DURING MY FIRST twelve years at *Saturday Night*, I lived, editorially, a hand-to-mouth existence. In the first half of the 1970s I had one editor working with me; in the second half I usually had two. If we managed to produce the current edition on time and have a few stories lined up for the next two or three issues, we were doing well. But long before I left *Saturday Night*, in 1987, that was changed. We still suffered through deadline crises, but usually we knew in rough outline the shape of the next ten or twelve issues and sometimes we had stories planned well beyond that. Nine months after I said goodbye to *Saturday Night*, my successor was still publishing pieces I'd discussed or assigned.

This transformation was the direct result of two failures. One was the closing of *Weekend* magazine, a supplement that ran in daily papers across the country. During its last two years, the editor of *Weekend*, John Macfarlane, raised it to a level of quality approached by few magazines in this country. Given a generous budget, he attracted the most talented people in the country and imported two superb designers from England. The result was excellent; I can still recall my acute feeling of envy when I opened it every Saturday morning. The owners apparently didn't share my enthusiasm, however. In 1979 they killed the magazine, which put Macfarlane on the market.

The other failure was *Saturday Night*'s: five years after Cowan and I had gone cap-in-hand to potential investors, it was clear that we couldn't make a go of it. We had exhausted not only the original $400,000 but also more money provided by the board and invested by several members of the staff (I among them). We were broke.

That autumn Cowan anounced that he hoped to start a pay-TV network and wanted to leave the magazine. (He founded C Channel, which quickly died.) Bernadette Sulgit and I thought of Macfarlane as a possible publisher, and took him to lunch. He seemed no more than mildly interested. "I wouldn't like to be *only* a publisher," he said. He seemed to have an idea that he should influence the editorial side of the magazine. That sounded ominous, but a day or two later I decided it was a good sign. I'd known John since the 1960s — he was assistant entertainment editor of the *Star* when I left — and found him both intelligent and, in the best sense, ambitious. In the early 1970s, when he was briefly working in advertising, I'd asked him to serve as a consulting editor of *Saturday Night*, an offer he'd declined. Now it occurred to me that if he were publisher we could also exploit his talents as an editor.

But it didn't seem likely we'd get him — until, suddenly, we got not only him but a new set of owners as well. In 1975 Norman Webster, then a *Globe and Mail* reporter and now the editor, had invested $25,000 in *Saturday Night* through Dascon, the company he owns with his sister, Margaret Gallagher, and his brother, Will. Later the Websters had put in more money, until they were the largest shareholders. Now Norman decided that Dascon would buy out the other

owners, which meant it could use the tax loss against the
profits of other enterprises. He also decided to make Macfarlane, with whom he had worked on the *Globe*, publisher.

John and I first had lunch together, as publisher and
editor, at an Italian restaurant in the mall at Yonge and
Charles streets. I remember the place because it took my
assistant an hour on the phone to get a reservation. It was a
day or two before Christmas, and most restaurants were
filled with office parties.

John turned out to be the best Christmas present I ever
received. When we met, we knew that our friends and our
enemies were predicting tension between us — two editors,
neither of them a shrinking violet, each with a reputation to
protect, working in the same office, the older one working
for the younger. How could we not clash? "The gossip mills
assume bloody warfare," reported *Quill & Quire*, the publishing trade journal.

Perhaps we had grown old enough to see each other's
virtues, or perhaps we were both so shell-shocked — he
from *Weekend*'s collapse, I from *Saturday Night*'s endless
troubles — that we were more interested in comforting than
controlling each other. In any case he said at one point, "I
don't see why we can't get along," and I said I didn't see why
either. I also said that, if the Websters wished, I'd stay on the
board of directors, but I wanted to be relieved of all other
work on the business side. Macfarlane agreed; I don't think
he wanted me looking over his shoulder anyway. So my
career as a businessman ended, and I stopped thinking about
ad sales and circulation campaigns and the bank line. I was
now able to work full time as a journalist.

It turned out that Macfarlane and I had the same sort of
magazine in mind, but our ways of working toward it were
entirely different. As anyone who deals with him soon learns,
Macfarlane is (to use two words he applies to himself) "com-
pulsive" and "obsessive" about issues that seldom bother
journalists. He dresses with more care than anyone else in

the magazine business, he worries about how the office should be decorated, and he is capable of issuing a memo instructing an editorial staff to keep the workplace tidier. If he were a schoolteacher, he would give marks for neatness. For nineteen years my desk at *Saturday Night* was chaotic, the despair of my assistant and the other editors — they grew so used to seeing their memos disappear on my desk that they began leaving anything of importance on my chair. Macfarlane, on the other hand, never left behind a messy desk.

That same obsessiveness served him well when he dealt with editorial matters. And, in our new *Saturday Night* environment, he had a lot to do with the content of the magazine. It was Macfarlane who suggested we hire Derek Ungless and Gary Ross, both of whom had worked on *Weekend*, as art director and senior editor. I liked them from the start, and liked them even better when I discovered their ambitions for the magazine. Their ideas of how we might work, and Macfarlane's too, were sometimes grander than my own — Gary, for instance, wanted to commission projects that might take a year or two to prepare. Having lived with uncertainty for so long, I'd never let myself think that way. Gary and John helped change me. Soon I was sharing the direction of the magazine with them, and enjoying it.

From the spring of 1980 to the summer of 1987, the number of people planning *Saturday Night* grew steadily. At the beginning it was Macfarlane, Bernadette Sulgit, Ross, and me; then others proved themselves valuable to the magazine and also helped run it. If *Saturday Night* had been a one-man magazine when I started there, it was now the work of a varied, competitive, and steadily changing group. Ron Graham and David Macfarlane, two gifted writers who developed with the magazine of the 1980s, became part-time editors as well. And from the late 1970s on, we used the job of assistant to the editor as a way of (to quote an old Ralph Allen phrase) growing our own editors. Each assistant I hired would spend a year or so sitting outside my office, typing my letters and being secretary to the whole editorial department. Eventually she would do some part-time work as a fact-checker and finally, if things worked out, become an editor or writer. In this way we developed Dianne de Fenoyl, who is now executive editor; Tecca Crosby, who became an associate editor and then left for the Ontario Film Development Corporation; Dianna Symonds, who is now an associate editor; and Eileen Whitfield, who now writes for *Saturday Night*. Each of them joined us in a mainly secretarial job and ended up a member of the editorial group. The extent of their influence was decided not by their titles but by the ideas and energy they could bring to our weekly planning meetings. As they grew used to the process, they learned to come up with an idea, get it approved, and then guide it into print. Sometimes my own role in even a major article was no more than that of cheerleader.

This process — admittedly complex and constantly shifting — was never understood outside the magazine. To my embarrassment, I was almost always credited or blamed for everything we published, as if all the other people on the masthead were humbly doing my bidding. The more that power at *Saturday Night* was diffused in reality, the more it was centralized in myth. People like to see magazines in this way, and can't be persuaded otherwise. When journalists came to interview me, I would carefully explain our system of shared responsibility; they would go back to their newspapers or magazines and write pieces about "Fulford's *Saturday Night*." When I resigned, an affectionate piece by Linda Matchan in the Boston *Globe* included this passage: "If, as Ralph Waldo Emerson wrote, an institution is the lengthened shadow of one man, then for the last 19 years *Saturday Night* has been the lengthened shadow of Fulford."

Flattering and well-meant, but a long way from the truth. At its best *Saturday Night* was the mingled shadows of at least a dozen talented men and women. Once Tecca said to me, "One of the problems of working here is that everybody thinks Bob Fulford does everything at *Saturday Night*," and I sympathized with her. The fact that I was a celebrity in a small way — on TV once or twice a week, in the *Star* every Saturday — made me something of a brand name, and encouraged people to attach the brand to everything in *Saturday Night*. But in fact other editors brought in Peter Foster, Elspeth Cameron, Michael Bliss, Barry Callaghan, and Urjo Kareda, writers who produced superb material for us. I made the first contact with Ron Graham, who started with us in 1980 and has steadily built his reputation ever since, but it was Gary Ross who worked closely with him for several years. Curiously, Graham's first proposal to the magazine — he wanted to write an article about working on the TV version of Peter C. Newman's *The Canadian Establishment* — seemed only mildly promising to me. My rule has always been that good articles don't come out of television shows, and I almost told Graham to forget it. (I should have remembered that Sandra Gwyn's first *Saturday Night* piece, a decade earlier, had resulted from a radio documentary about Ottawa.) But I gave him a little encouragement, and his first draft, full of charm and energy, surprised all of us; the article ran in October, 1980, with a painting of Conrad Black as the cover illustration. Ron turned out to be our best discovery of the 1980s, what Gwyn had been to the 1970s. And, having become an associate editor, Ron in turn discovered Robert Mason Lee, a young Alberta newspaperman whose article on the Keegstra case was one of the best pieces we published.

I was another writer who developed at *Saturday Night* in the 1980s. During my first dozen years as an editor, my writing hadn't improved much, if at all. More pressing matters had so filled my time that I seldom managed to spend even one whole day at the typewriter. Nor did I have time for more than cursory research. But now the Websters had provided financial security, Macfarlane had taken over the business affairs, and Gary Ross was handling a large share of the commissioning and editing. There really wasn't anything to keep me from writing.

To begin with, I spent much more time on my Notebook column; my brief and often hasty commentaries of the 1970s were replaced by longer and more carefully researched essays. Some of them were planned over several months and many were on subjects suggested by my fellow editors — Barbara Moon, for instance, suggested a piece on the Charter of Rights that produced more response than anything I'd written in years. Now I was getting serious editing, for the first time since the mass quitting at *Maclean's* in 1964. My draft always went around the office and never failed to benefit from the criticism of my colleagues. "I don't know if you're paying me to tell you this sort of thing," Ross said about one Notebook I sent around, "but I don't really think this works at all." That was exactly what he was paid for. I rewrote the piece until we agreed that it worked.

I also wanted to write occasional features for the core of the magazine, but I wasn't sure what form they should take. Except for a couple of travel pieces, I hadn't written a real magazine article since the 1960s, though I'd edited hundreds of them. If I were to write articles, what would they be like? That spring and summer I happened to read three pieces of journalism that pushed me in a new direction.

One was Gzowski's book about cannibalism, *The Sacrament;* another was *The Powers That Be*, David Halberstam's account of media empires in the United States; the third was the Jim Coutts chapter from Christina McCall's *Grits*, which I edited for the September, 1980 issue (in which we unveiled Derek Ungless's brilliant new design). Those three items had one quality in common: they were clear and compelling narratives that were made to carry more ideas and theory than we routinely expect in journalism. Much good journalism works that way, but Gzowski, Halberstam and McCall had (or so it seemed to me) made this technique work uncommonly well. I began to wonder, should I be doing something like that?

Pretty soon I was writing my first full-length piece for *Saturday Night*, "The Rise and Fall of Modern Architecture," in which a profile of Eberhard Zeidler served as the armature for an overview of recent changes in his profession. Later I took a similar approach to profiles of the Canadian ambassador to the UN, a psychiatrist, an opinion pollster, two newspaper editors, the head of the CBC — and, in my last year at the magazine, Mila Mulroney. The best of these pieces were better received than any previous writing of mine.

In fact, as we developed and refined the whole magazine, it attracted far more praise than anything else I've been associated with. We won all the National Magazine Awards it was possible to win, we were now quoted more than any other magazine, the letters to the editor were warmly enthusiastic, the best writers in the country were willing to write for us, and — even though we kept pushing up the price of a subscription — our circulation was steadily climbing. After a while we were selling more than 135,000 copies, which meant that several hundred thousand people were looking at *Saturday Night* every month.

There was only one problem. We were losing a fortune.

THE IDEA BEHIND the funding of *Saturday Night* in the early 1980s was simple: if you produce a superb magazine, possibly the best magazine anyone in Canada ever produced, it will attract advertising. Norman Webster believed this, John Macfarlane believed it, and I didn't argue with them. After a couple of years, Norman was satisfied that this process was well under way. He was proud that John and the editorial staff, using the Webster money, had been able to make enormous improvements in our magazine. "The problem before," he said in an interview, "was a lack of consistency. Sometimes it was getting great articles, but it was unusual to get a number of them in a row. The problem was a lack of resources and the lack of ability to plan. Now it has been put on a firm footing, and Fulford is doing his best work."

Norman expected that eventually the people in the advertising agencies, and their clients, would share his enthusiasm.
We couldn't hope that they would buy our space on a strict
cost-per-thousand basis — we weren't a mass-circulation
magazine, after all, and reaching one of our readers was
bound to cost more than reaching a reader of *Chatelaine* or
Maclean's. What we hoped instead was that we would become
so vital a part of national life that advertisers couldn't stay
out of our pages. But in 1983, when *Marketing* magazine
published a four-page analysis of *Saturday Night*, nothing
like that had happened. "Here is a magazine," wrote Rob
Wilson, "that…reaches an audience that exhibits an extremely
high demographic profile. Conventional wisdom says this is
ideal for the advertiser…Yet, it is plain to see that *Saturday
Night* is not benefitting by those presumed advantages."

Wilson asked some people in advertising why this was so,
but none of them knew for sure. Ann Boden, the media
director at McKim advertising, came up with the oddest
answer: "Its demographics are very high — the chairmen of
boards, the presidents, politicians…In fact, its demographics
may be too high. A lot of clients don't have a clear handle
on who their buyers are, so they tend to go a bit broad." She
seemed to be saying that the editorial approach that had
consumed so much Webster money was working against our
advertising sales.

My guess is that it was simpler than that — advertising
people just didn't like the magazine. They thought it boring.
All those articles on politicians, artists, and business people
didn't impress them, no matter how many prizes we won.
We might publish the best article anyone had ever written
or ever would write on, say, John Turner or Michael Pitfield;
but many advertising people regarded Turner and Pitfield
as inherently boring, like most Canadian subjects. If Ron
Graham and Christina McCall and all the other writers had
somehow been twice as good as they in fact were, it still
wouldn't have been noticed in the agencies. In my nineteen

years at *Saturday Night* I almost never met an advertising executive who gave any sign of having read the magazine. Ad people pretend that they work according to quasi-scientific statistical systems, but my observation is that they back what they like — and they didn't like us. In the end, I think we were defeated more by personal taste than anything else.

We weren't betting everything on the advertisers, however. Before Macfarlane joined us, in the days when Cowan was publisher, we had developed the beginnings of a sideline in contract publishing. We helped to set up a magazine called *Policy Options* and an architectural journal, *Trace*. Macfarlane decided to expand this work into a division called Publishing Services, which eventually designed and edited magazines for the Royal Bank, the CBC, and many other institutions. If *Saturday Night* persisted in losing money, the theory went, then Publishing Services would make it back.

The trouble was, Publishing Services also lost money. Contract publishing was a competitive business, we needed to pay first-class staff, we had trouble figuring out how much to charge. It was not an easy money-maker, and apparently would, like the magazine itself, require patience. I remember the meeting of the board — April 29, 1985 — when Norman grasped the full horror of the situation. In the fiscal year just completed, the company had lost $1,043,700, several hundred thousand dollars of it attributable to Publishing Services. I wrote in the minutes: "Norman Webster said that Publishing Services' results were a great shock. The purpose of Publishing Services is to make profits and support the enterprise as a whole. But its present course — if extended — would be to impoverish us and eventually kill the magazine." I think that was the day when Norman lost the last of his faith in the future of the company. From that point until twenty-five months later, when the Websters sold the magazine, we rarely saw a smile on his face. After a while, I realized that he was in over his head. He was losing not only his own money but his brother's and his sister's as well — and losing it at a rate he had never anticipated. The Websters were the best owners I ever knew; their money made it possible for everyone who worked for *Saturday Night*, the publisher and editor above all, to look like first-class professionals. But neither their patience nor their fortune was inexhaustible.

IN THE SPRING of 1987, with the losses still mounting, the three-man management of the company — the head of finance, the marketing director, and Macfarlane — worked out a marketing plan. It involved spending a great deal of new money, perhaps $2-million, on expanding circulation. They suggested three possible courses for the Websters: invest this new money, close down the magazine, or sell it. Norman took about eight hours to decide that he wanted to sell it.

After that, things moved both quickly and haphazardly. Norman did not mention to me that the magazine was for sale, but others were told. His brother Will, I understand, informed a neighbour, the financial man at the Cineplex Corporation, so somebody from Cineplex came down to look at our books and decided not to buy. There were other approaches, equally casual, as I discovered later. No broker was hired to survey the market and work out an appropriate price.

Then, just about quitting time on June 17, Norman came into my office and told me he had sold the magazine to Conrad Black's company, Hollinger. A few minutes earlier he had delivered the same message to John Macfarlane, with something else added. Black, who had never met Macfarlane, had decided that he didn't want him to stay on. "But you still have a job, John," Norman had said. Black wanted only the magazine, not Publishing Services; it would stay with the Webster family, and Macfarlane could continue to run it. This idea didn't please him. He had been pushed out of his main job, publisher, and he eventually sued the Websters for constructive dismissal. In effect, Black and Webster fired Macfarlane on the front page of the *Globe* two days later.

"Publisher John Macfarlane was not invited to retain his job," said the news story.

What could have caused them to act so ungraciously? Such matters are usually arranged far more discreetly — almost always, the rejected employee is allowed to retain his dignity by resigning. Certainly there can't have been any personal animus on Black's part. In any case, this was the first aspect of the change of ownership that I found disquieting. There were to be others.

"They're going to announce it tomorrow morning on the wire at ten," Norman went on. "So I'd appreciate it if you'd call in your staff at nine-thirty and tell them."

"Norman, I'm sorry, but tomorrow is about the one morning this year when I can't possibly be here. I'm due at York University to get an honorary degree and give the commencement address. Maybe I could call my staff tonight."

Norman didn't like that idea — he knew it would spread the news immediately. So we agreed the staff would be informed by someone else. Norman said he was sorry things hadn't worked out better, but added that he thought Conrad Black admired the magazine and wanted to keep me on as editor. I thanked him for all his help over the years and said that I wished we had found a way to provide him with dividends rather than problems. We shook hands.

Geraldine and I were to go out for dinner an hour later to celebrate her birthday with Marjorie Harris and her husband, Jack Batten. There was a pleasing symmetry in that event: Jack had escorted me into *Saturday Night* nineteen years earlier; now he and Marjorie were the first people, aside from Geraldine, to hear of the event that seemed likely to lead to my resignation.

The next morning, in the brilliant sunshine at York University, I stood before the chancellor, wearing academic robes, while the University Orator read an encomium which of course mentioned my years at *Saturday Night*. Among the hundreds of people there, only half a dozen of us understood the irony of the moment. I wasn't thinking about that, though: as always on such occasions, I was desperately worried about my speech. My subject was the literary imagination, and I'd been working on it for weeks. It seemed to go off all right. Then I sat back for an hour or so, watching the students as they came forward to accept their degrees. Perhaps my own situation was touching me more deeply than I cared to acknowledge, but somehow that morning became stirring and almost mystical — the beautiful young people, the delighted parents, the joy in achievement. As I said afterward to someone, "It was so *un*cynical."

There was a luncheon for the chancellor's party and our families and friends. Just as it got going, someone came in to say that the news about Conrad Black was on the radio.

BEFORE I went over to Black's headquarters at 10 Toronto Street to talk about *Saturday Night*'s future and mine, I knew a good deal about him. I knew he was an expert deal-maker who had started out with a few million dollars from his father and multiplied it by fifty or so. I knew he was set apart from other Canadian businessmen by his intellectual ambition — he's the only multi-millionaire who has written a thick biography (of Maurice Duplessis), has produced a regular newspaper column on public affairs, and likes to refer to money by the archaic term "specie."

Oddly, I had less reason to be suspicious of Black than the majority of my fellow journalists. Most journalists I know instinctively dislike capitalists and capitalism; I, on the other hand, often argue that freedom is impossible without private ownership and a healthy economy is impossible without private business. I actually believe in free enterprise and free markets. Nor am I as critical of Black's views on world affairs as most journalists: I'm neither Reaganite nor Thatcherite, but my view of the Soviet Union and of communism in general probably doesn't differ in any significant way from

Black's. For at least a decade I've been a close student of the neoconservative movement, and found in the work of its best writers a great deal to admire.

Sometimes I even enjoyed the column Black wrote in *The Globe and Mail*, though I never met anyone else who did. I did not, however, enjoy the sour and arrogant column he wrote just before our meeting. That month he turned it into a report on his own amazing accomplishments as head of Hollinger and included a dismissal of his former colleagues at Dominion stores as "an inbred, furtive, over confident and, in some cases, disingenuous management." I also knew about Black's feud with his biographer, Peter C. Newman. A day after Black's purchase was announced, Peter dropped in at my office to give me a copy of *The Establishment Man: A Portrait of Power*. He signed it, "Bob — Do not go tiger hunting with this man, Peter."

When I arrived at Toronto Street I was inspected by a secretary and a security guard and then taken upstairs to a sitting room. A woman in a maid's costume came in, said we were having steak for lunch, and asked how mine should be cooked. I said "medium," a serious mistake — it was close to inedible when it arrived. Indeed, the cuisine at Hollinger was in all ways a disappointment. Truman Capote once said, "The real difference between rich people and regular people is that the rich people serve such marvellous vegetables. Delicious little tiny vegetables..." By Capote's standards, Black is not a rich person.

I was on time, but I waited for twenty minutes, leafing through old magazines. Finally Peter White came in. He is Black's aide in many things, and later became publisher of *Saturday Night* (a job he left in the summer of 1988 to become principal secretary to Brian Mulroney). He strongly reminded me of Robert Vaughn in the movies: condescending, cool, stiffly alert, a man one would never get close to. Before Black joined us, White suggested that *Saturday Night* should do a story on the deteriorating quality of the public service in

Ottawa. A long-time backer of Mulroney, he had worked on appointments in the early stages of the Tory government. I said that as it happened we had Charlotte Gray preparing a piece on that subject. White said, "I'd like to see that before…"

Perhaps he saw a look on my face. He didn't finish his sentence. But I understood immediately that things would quickly change at *Saturday Night*. In eight years, so far as I know, Norman Webster never asked to see an advance proof of an article, even when people he knew well were the subjects.

Finally Black joined us. In the conversation that followed he seemed particularly interested in telling me about his friend Andrew Knight, the former editor of *The Economist*, who was now running Black's *Daily Telegraph* and *Sunday Telegraph* in London. I mentioned that I'd never met him.

"The amazing thing about Andrew," Black said, "is that he knows *everyone*."

"It's true," White said. "I do believe Andrew Knight knows every important person in the whole world." Suddenly it occurred to him — his face is like that electric sign on Broadway that gives the news in giant capital letters — that he might have insulted me, a wretched fellow who had reached the age of fifty-five without once shaking the hand of Andrew Knight. "Sorry, Bob, I didn't mean that…"

Black went on, "Everyone asks about him. When I saw Katharine Graham the first thing she said was, 'How's Andrew?' And when I was speaking to George Shultz he asked me, right away, 'How is Andrew?' And so did the Aga Khan. And Henry Kissinger, when I saw him, he said [here Black went into a German accent], 'Howss Undrew?'"

He sat back, well satisfied. He had dropped the names of Katharine Graham, George Shultz, the Aga Khan, and Henry Kissinger, all in one paragraph. It occurred to me that I might never see this feat equalled in my lifetime.

Black turned out to be an extremely uncommon million-aire, not so much in the content of his conversation as in his

manner. He was more theatrical than any other businessman of my acquaintance. His personality had a staged,
directed feel to it. It was also oddly familiar. Where had I
seen it before, a large, handsome man with a supercilious and
condescending manner and a baroque vocabulary? Of course:
Orson Welles in *Citizen Kane*. I was talking to Citizen Black.

Eventually I raised the question of editorial independence. White said that in his understanding the owners of a
newspaper controlled, to some significant extent, the policy
of the newspaper. I said that was usually so, but a newspaper
had an editorial page where corporate opinion was expressed.
Most magazines have no such page. White said *Maclean's*
had one, a "publisher's page." I said no, they had an editor's
page, or column. "Kevin Doyle — isn't he the publisher?" he
asked. "No," I said, "the editor." In any case, at *Saturday Night*
we had no editorials. I wrote a column, Notebook, with my
name on it. Because it is written by the editor it may have
more force than a column written by someone else, I said,
and yet views appearing in it are *my* views, not the publisher's or the owners'.

The question of independence reminded Black that he
had been called at eight-thirty on Saturday morning by John
Bassett, whose work in private broadcasting I'd discussed in
the current issue. Bassett told Black (who had been announced
as our owner a day before) that he was angry about my piece
and felt mistreated. Black said he had read the article and
found it basically fair. But, he said, he would have asked me
not to focus so exclusively on Bassett — I had let off the
others involved in commercial television. Bassett had been
the only person dealt with at length. Perhaps, he said, that
wasn't quite fair.

I interrupted him to say that this — the owner's views, the
owner's friends — is exactly what a writer or an editor should
not be thinking about. A journalist should analyze the situation
(this happens to be one I have written on for about twenty-
five years) and write the best possible article. Peter White

interrupted to say that perhaps the thing to do, if such an article came up, would be to call Black before it appeared and warn him that he might have a hostile phone call from Bassett. I imagined how this would work. Would we be given a list of Black's friends? Would we then call him every time one of them was mentioned?

Black went on to say that he does not try to control the content of the *Telegraph* newspapers, but makes his views known. Often, he said, he calls the Washington correspondent of the *Telegraph* and "harangues" (Black's word) him about how the United States should be interpreted to Britain. Black seemed to have no notion of what a nightmare this must be for the Washington correspondent's editor in London — or for the correspondent himself. The more Black tried to reassure me, the less I was reassured.

I raised the question of John Macfarlane, and said he was an essential part of the magazine, editorially as much as in any other way. I suggested that they consider changing their mind. This evoked more condescension from White.

"You're very loyal, Bob," White said, as if loyalty were the issue. Black said that the Macfarlane idea was a "non-starter." Case dismissed.

I raised the issue of job security. Would staff members be credited with their time spent on the magazine after it moved to new ownership — someone who had been there for seven years, for instance, would now be wondering whether he or she would still have this seniority (for purposes, above all, of severance pay). They said yes, those who came to the new management would retain their seniority, but not all employees of the magazine would be hired by the new management. This was news. I had thought, after conversations with the Websters ("They're taking your whole masthead," Will Webster had said to me) that the only employees in jeopardy were those who worked partly for *Saturday Night* and the rest of the time for Publishing Services.

Now it became clear that Black and White wanted, with my help, to cut the *Saturday Night* staff. White drew out of his pocket a payroll list, and Black brought out his copy. They asked me to go over the list and grade employees as Excellent, Good, or Fair. I said I was not prepared to do that. They asked me whether I would care to name certain employees who were particularly valuable. I mentioned a couple, but realized this wasn't a good idea and stopped. The point of this exchange was that they did not at that moment accept responsibility for *Saturday Night* employees they didn't want. (Later, after I mentioned this back at the *Saturday Night* office, Norman Webster spoke to White and word came back that I had "misunderstood" Black and White. In the end, no one was dismissed.)

They asked me about the marketing analysis prepared by management. I said I thought it defined the problems of *Saturday Night* but I had no idea whether the business plan would work.

Our discussion was for the most part amiable. Toward the end I said I wasn't sure I wanted to be part of the new arrangement. It would require a great deal of effort from me — effort of a non-editorial kind, on the business side, and I wasn't at all sure this was right for me now. In the end my strongest feeling was that Black's and my ideas about editorial freedom were incompatible. I also thought that the magazine was understaffed — and since almost all members of the staff were people I had chosen and developed, I would have had great difficulty deciding which of them were dispensable.

"Bob," said White abruptly, "what do you make from your TV show?"

I told him. He asked if I had another source of income. I said I wrote a column for the *Star* on Saturday. He wanted to know what this brought me. I told him.

Black said, "But Peter, this is none of our business."

I said I didn't mind answering. I knew White would eventually explain. Finally he said, "Well, Bob, if you did quit, we wouldn't want you to be on your uppers." His concern was my welfare.

I said he shouldn't worry.

Later, walking back to the office to discuss this meeting with my colleagues, I thought about my choices. Staying would be uncomfortable, but leaving would be difficult too. What made up my mind was an image that suddenly came to me: a thick pile of phone messages waiting on my desk. These were requests for interviews from "The Journal," "As It Happens," *Maclean's*, and four or five newspapers. If I decided to stay on at *Saturday Night* I'd have to respond to every one of those calls: the editor of a magazine can't avoid answering questions. And every interviewer would ask a variant of the same question, "How do you like working for Conrad Black?" An honest answer would have been, "Not much so far, but I'm going to see how it works out." That would hardly inspire the staff, the contributors, the advertising people, or my new employer. Several friends of mine suggested that I hang on and, in six months or so, make the new owner fire me; that way, I'd be eligible for whatever severance pay goes to someone who has spent nineteen years in a job. But I decided I could do without severance pay. To stay for even a week I would have had to lie copiously, and I didn't have that many lies in me.

THE NEXT MORNING I sent my resignation over to Hollinger, and within an hour Peter White called me. Apparently Black and White were not devastated. In fact, White told me, they already had my replacement in mind: John Fraser, the London correspondent of *The Globe and Mail*. What did I think of that idea? I thought it a pretty good idea. Fraser had gone to Upper Canada College with Black and was probably the best journalist who enjoyed Black's confidence. He had never worked on a magazine, but he was a quick study. Later that day Fraser phoned and we talked about whether he should take the job. Do it, I said, but get an ironbound contract. He first said he didn't want the job; it would bring too much turmoil to his life. But soon he came around.

A few minutes after White's call, the news having been released, phone calls began pouring in. But I, no longer editor of *Saturday Night*, was not required to field them. I decided not to discuss my meeting with Black and White. My view was that an orderly transition would be best served by discreet silence. My fellow journalists could figure things out for themselves.

The response in the newspapers reminded me of the time the magazine shut down in 1974. Once again I was able to read my obituaries without the inconvenience of dying, a pleasure denied those whose careers are uniformly successful. Most of the public comment on my resignation was kind ("tragic," said Atwood), but the past tense produced a chilling effect — "Fulford was a great editor and a great Canadian," said a columnist in the Vancouver *Sun*. There were also a few razor blades hidden among the roses, some of them not immediately recognizable as such. In the Toronto *Sun* Douglas Fisher speculated on some future federal appointment for me (CBC? CRTC? UNESCO?) and ended, "I think he'd make the perfect editor-in-chief for the Toronto *Star*." I'm not sure Fisher's readers understood him, but I did. He dislikes me almost as much as he dislikes the *Star*.

All this made interesting if rather melancholy reading. Then something happened that turned our corporate melodrama into a farce. The Webster-Black deal had been expected to close on June 30, but for some reason the principals refused to sign the final papers. On July 2 word seeped through the *Saturday Night* office that there was a misunderstanding between them, though its nature wasn't explained. At five p.m. John Macfarlane issued a memo saying that the sale had not yet taken place. "Therefore, until further notice it's business as usual." Macfarlane had expected to close his office that day, but he discovered that, technically at least, he was still publisher. He got on the phone to Maclean Hunter and Southam, both of which expressed interest in buying *Saturday Night*.

In the *Star* the next morning, an article written by Richard Gwyn from London provided the details. Black and Webster, when they originally made the deal, had apparently signed a piece of paper before Webster's lawyers saw it. Black believed that, in return for promising to continue publishing *Saturday Night*, he would receive the magazine plus $250,000 cash from Webster, to cover certain unpaid bills. Webster, for his part, thought that the paper entitled *him* to get $250,000 from Black. When closing day came, they were separated by half a million. This seemed impossible: how could two such experienced people make a mistake of that size? Neither of them explained the problem in public, then or later — Webster wouldn't even discuss it with one of his own staff who wrote the story for the *Globe*.

The appalling aspect of the dispute was what it said about *Saturday Night* as a business: one of the richest men in Canada not only wouldn't pay money for the magazine, he expected a bonus to take it off Webster's hands. Fortunately, this was obscured by the laughter that surrounded the mix-up. In the *Star* Joey Slinger wrote, "Two of our outstanding tycoons have made a deal in which, to coin a phrase, neither knows who is to do what or with which or to whom." They came out sounding "like gold medalists in the Dumb-dumb Olympics." In a letter to the editor of the *Star*, Pierre Berton said the misunderstanding sounded like a Second City skit. George Bain, in *Maclean's*, called it a boffo performance. In our office gloom was briefly replaced by merriment.

John Fraser was on the phone instantly. "I trust you savour life's little ironies as much as I do," he said. He was torn — on the one hand, this unlikely turn of events made wonderful gossip; on the other, if the deal failed to go through he'd look ridiculous. He had told the *Globe* he was leaving and just about everyone in the business knew he was to edit *Saturday Night*. "Now, this new possibility — I'll be the bride left at the back of the church." He also said his agent was having trouble making a deal with Black. "It may turn out I'm too expensive for Conrad Black. I can dine out on that forever." But the Webster-Black deal finally closed, six days late, and Fraser's agent settled with Black, at a salary about fifty per cent higher than mine, with a five-year contract providing for handsome severance pay. So far as I know, it was the first contract ever signed by an editorial employee at *Saturday Night*.

I wrote Fraser a note of congratulation: "I hope you stay nineteen years and have as much fun as I did." I encouraged the staff and contributors to stay with him — after all, *they* wouldn't have to deal with Black. "*Saturday Night* will endure," I said in my speech at John Macfarlane's farewell party. "Any magazine that can survive Jack Kent Cooke can survive Conrad Black." I think it will. Perhaps it will improve. Many subscribers wrote to tell me they were cancelling their subscriptions, but I couldn't join them. Aside from my affection for the writers and editors, curiosity will force me to pick up every issue.

Fraser couldn't come to *Saturday Night* until the autumn, so I told Peter White I'd stay till Labour Day. Predictably, the summer was unsettling. For one thing, John Macfarlane was no longer there, and after nearly eight years it seemed strange not even to discuss Notebook with him. I'd always known he was important to the magazine, but I truly understood it only after he left. And there was also something eerie in discussions about articles I'd never see in manuscript and issues I wouldn't edit.

My colleagues became affectionately protective. They sensed that I was depressed, and I was — because we had never made *Saturday Night* work financially, despite all our brave hopes; because we had become a source of hideous embarrassment rather than pride to our benefactors, the

Websters; because the magazine I'd once nurtured like a sick child was now in the hands of an owner I didn't admire; because I'd probably never again edit writers as talented as those who worked for *Saturday Night*; because I was giving up Notebook, the best pulpit in Canada, which I'd carved for myself; and because I'd soon be saying goodbye to people I greatly prized, our staff and our writers. In the first week of July, when a Toronto *Star* reporter interviewed me, I said, "I haven't faced up to leaving my colleagues. I don't believe I have dealt with that emotionally."

Even so, in my last weeks at the office I began to feel not only relieved but buoyant. For one thing, I had achieved an ambition that at moments had seemed nearly impossible — I was not to be, after all, the last editor of *Saturday Night*. A small triumph, but I was glad to have it. I also realized that just up ahead there was a time when I'd be responsible for no one's writing but my own. After nineteen years, that seemed breathtakingly attractive. *Saturday Night* was a burden. I sought it, I fought to keep it, and I was proud to shoulder it; but it was a burden. As it lifted, I decided to avoid taking another job for at least a year, maybe two or three. I'd write and make television programs. I'd do whatever else seemed interesting, such as accepting a part-time appointment at University College in the winter of 1987-88.

I made one more decision before I said goodbye to my friends at the office. I love reading the memoirs of people whose work engages me, and I'm sorry that many of the interesting Canadians of my time, including several of those prominently mentioned in this book, died without leaving an account of their lives. I admire the three volumes of memoirs written by Hector Charlesworth, one of my predecessors in the editor's office at *Saturday Night*, and I decided to emulate him — though not necessarily in three volumes. I began thinking about my own story and what it might mean, and sat down to write this book.

ACKNOWLEDGEMENTS

Geraldine Sherman suggested the title and provided a valuable criticism of the text; those are two of several thousand reasons why her name appears on the dedication page. Gary Ross was my editor, and — as he has so often — earned my intense gratitude by greatly improving my work. Beverley Slopen, my agent, was helpful and infectiously optimistic at every stage. David Kent and Janice Whitford at Collins were enthusiastic and supportive publishers. Nigel Dickson, one of the great stars at *Saturday Night,* took the photograph that appears on the jacket. Diane Gee, my sister and my researcher, was, as on many previous occasions during the last two decades, enormously helpful. Joanne O'Brien of Satellite PC Services transformed my barely coherent manuscript into immaculately processed pages. Joan Murray of the McLaughlin Gallery in Oshawa was kind enough to comment on Chapter Six and John Macfarlane of *The Financial Times* provided some useful suggestions for Chapter Eight. Barbara Moon of *Saturday Night* helped me outline this book in the summer of 1987. Peter Richardson and his colleagues at University College provided the welcoming atmosphere in which I did much of my work. Many others influenced all of my writing, including eventually this book; their help is acknowledged in the text.

INDEX